CONTEMPORARY ISSUES IN APPLIED AND PROFESSIONAL ETHICS

RESEARCH IN ETHICAL ISSUES IN ORGANIZATIONS

Series Editors: Michael Schwartz, Howard Harris and Debra Comer

Recent Volumes:

Volume 6:   Crisis and Opportunity in the Professions — Edited by Moses L. Pava and Patrick Primeaux — 2005

Volume 7:   Insurance Ethics for a More Ethical World — Guest Edited by Patrick Flanagan, Patrick Primeaux and William Ferguson — 2007

Volume 8:   Applied Ethics: Remembering Patrick Primeaux — Edited by Michael Schwartz and Howard Harris — 2012

Volume 9:   Ethics, Values and Civil Society — Edited by Michael Schwartz, Howard Harris and Stephen Cohen — 2013

Volume 10: Moral Saints and Moral Exemplars — Edited by Michael Schwartz and Howard Harris — 2013

Volume 11: The Contribution of Fiction to Organizational Ethics — Edited by Michael Schwartz and Howard Harris — 2014

Volume 12: Achieving Ethical Excellence — Edited by Michael Schwartz and Howard Harris with Guest Editor Alan Tapper — 2014

Volume 13: Conscience, Leadership and the Problem of 'Dirty Hands' — Edited by Matthew Beard and Sandra Lynch — 2015

Volume 14: The Ethical Contribution of Organizations to Society — Edited by Michael Schwartz, Howard Harris and Debra Comer — 2015

RESEARCH IN ETHICAL ISSUES IN ORGANIZATIONS
VOLUME 15

CONTEMPORARY ISSUES IN APPLIED AND PROFESSIONAL ETHICS

EDITED BY

MARCO GRIX

University of Auckland, Auckland, New Zealand

TIM DARE

University of Auckland, Auckland, New Zealand

United Kingdom − North America − Japan
India − Malaysia − China

Emerald Group Publishing Limited
Howard House, Wagon Lane, Bingley BD16 1WA, UK

First edition 2016

Copyright © 2016 Emerald Group Publishing Limited

Reprints and permissions service
Contact: permissions@emeraldinsight.com

British Library Cataloguing in Publication Data
A catalogue record for this book is available from the British Library

ISBN: 978-1-78635-444-0
ISSN: 1529-2096 (Series)

Printed and bound by CPI Group (UK) Ltd, Croydon, CR0 4YY

ISOQAR certified
Management System,
awarded to Emerald
for adherence to
Environmental
standard
ISO 14001:2004.

Certificate Number 1985
ISO 14001

INVESTOR IN PEOPLE

CONTENTS

LIST OF CONTRIBUTORS   *vii*

EDITORIAL BOARD   *ix*

INTRODUCTION   *xi*

SUPPLY AND DEMAND IN THE DEVELOPMENT OF
PROFESSIONAL ETHICS
   Hugh Breakey   *1*

HOW SHOULD THE CONCEPT OF A PROFESSION BE
UNDERSTOOD, AND IS THE NOTION OF A
PRACTICE HELPFUL IN UNDERSTANDING IT?
   Stephan Millett   *29*

TRANSFORMATION: AN EXAMINATION OF THE
VIRTUOUS CHARACTER FROM THE PERSPECTIVE
OF PROCESS PHILOSOPHY
   Giuseppe Naimo   *41*

MODEL LITIGANT GUIDELINES – CURRENT AND
EMERGING ISSUES
   Ian H. Gibson   *61*

LOCAL ACTION, GLOBAL SHAME
   Nicholas Munn   *85*

POSTHUMOUS DONATION AND CONSENT
   Frederick Kroon   *103*

ALTRUISM AND GENEROSITY IN
SURROGATE MOTHERHOOD
    Ruth Walker and Liezl van Zyl   *121*

CONTEMPORARY ISSUES IN THE
PROFESSIONALISATION OF CHILD CARE
IN AUSTRALIA
    Stephen Kemp   *135*

MEASURING ETHICAL AND EMPIRICAL
CONSEQUENCES OF DE-INSTITUTIONALISATION
    Paul Jewell, Matthew Dent and Ruth Crocker   *149*

RISKY BUSINESS – THE ETHICS OF JUDGING
INDIVIDUALS BASED ON GROUP STATISTICS
    Vanessa Scholes   *169*

ABOUT THE AUTHORS   *189*

LIST OF CONTRIBUTORS

Hugh Breakey   Institute for Ethics, Governance and Law,
                         Law Futures Centre, Griffith University,
                         Nathan, Australia

Ruth Crocker   Disability & Community Inclusion, School
                         of Health Sciences, Flinders University,
                         Adelaide, Australia

Tim Dare   School of Humanities: Philosophy,
                         University of Auckland, Auckland,
                         New Zealand

Matthew Dent   Advocacy Tasmania, Hobart, Australia

Ian H. Gibson   Australian Association of Professional and
                         Applied Ethics, Melbourne, Australia

Marco Grix   School of Humanities: Philosophy,
                         University of Auckland, Auckland,
                         New Zealand

Paul Jewell   Disability & Community Inclusion, School
                         of Health Sciences, Flinders University,
                         Adelaide, Australia

Stephen Kemp   School of Historical and Philosophical
                         Inquiry, University of Queensland,
                         Brisbane, Australia

Frederick Kroon   School of Humanities: Philosophy,
                         University of Auckland, Auckland,
                         New Zealand

Stephan Millett   School of Occupational Therapy and Social
                         Work, Curtin University, Perth, Australia

Nicholas Munn   Faculty of Arts and Social Sciences,
                          University of Waikato, Hamilton,
                          New Zealand

Giuseppe Naimo   School of Philosophy and Theology,
                          University of Notre Dame Australia,
                          Fremantle, Australia

Vanessa Scholes   School of Business and Enterprise, Open
                          Polytechnic of New Zealand/Kuratini
                          Tuwhera, Lower Hutt, New Zealand

Liezl van Zyl   Faculty of Arts and Social Sciences,
                          University of Waikato, Hamilton,
                          New Zealand

Ruth Walker   Faculty of Arts and Social Sciences,
                          University of Waikato, Hamilton,
                          New Zealand

EDITORIAL BOARD

INTRODUCTION

This volume consists of selected proceedings from the 22nd Annual Australian Association of Professional and Applied Ethics (AAPAE) Conference. The event was hosted by Philosophy at the University of Auckland's School of Humanities, 9–12 July 2015. It was the first time that the AAPAE Conference was held outside of Australia. The event officially commenced with Tim Mulgan's keynote address, *How Should Utilitarians Think About the Future?* Tim is Professor of Philosophy at the University of Auckland and Professor of Moral and Political Philosophy at the University of St Andrews. The second keynote speech, *Doublethink in Global Prioritisation*, was given by Hilary Greaves. Hilary is a Fellow and Tutor in Philosophy at Somerville College and a Philosophy Lecturer at the University of Oxford.

The conference theme – *Contemporary Issues in...* – was intentionally kept open-ended and inclusive. Any topic in the field of professional and applied ethics from A (like abortion, advertising, affirmative action, ageism and animal rights) to the other end of the alphabet (like veterinary ethics, workplace ethics and xenotransplantation) was welcome. The issue of *Research in Ethical Issues in Organizations* that you are currently holding in your hands (or perhaps reading on your screen) contains a selection of the large range of issues currently being researched by professional and applied ethicists in Australasia.

The issues addressed in the chapters in the volume revolve around, roughly:

- the development of professional ethics norms;
- links between *profession* and *practice*;
- the dynamic nature of virtue ethical agency;
- model litigant guidelines;
- tensions between local and global norms;
- posthumous body part donation and consent;
- surrogate motherhood, altruism and generosity;
- the professionalisation of child care;
- consequences of closing facilities for people with disabilities; and
- discrimination resulting from organisational use of group risk statistics.

Hugh Breakey offers a supply and demand account of the development of
norms of professional ethics, describing the factors which motivate actors
to *demand* the creation of a norm, and the myriad push-factors (including
moral springs such as status, identity, role, narrative, tradition and excellence) that *supply* the elements out of which a norm, and the accompanying
motivations to act upon it, can be fashioned. He also explores the
significance of 'spoilers', who stand to benefit from the non-existence of
professional ethical norms. By understanding the demander-groups, the
supply-factors and the spoilers at work, he argues, we can come to an
improved understanding of why professional ethics emerge in any given
case and – because both demand- and supply-factors differ in each case –
why we require them in the professions yet not in non-professional business contexts.

Stephan Millett explores the concept of *profession* by drawing on the
idea of *practice*, particularly as laid out by MacIntyre, who provides a rich
set of connections to other notions, including *internal* and *external goods*,
virtue, and *institutions*. In order to sharpen the distinction between professions and other practices, Millet further considers that professionals characteristically serve the public good (beyond ordinary moral requirements),
and that professions monitor and manage the use of dangerous knowledge
(on the basis of a tacit social contract).

Based on the notion that character virtues do not simply materialise
fully formed but are the results of transformative processes, Giuseppe
Naimo discusses an account of virtue ethics from the perspective of process
philosophy. Character states never emerge in a contextual vacuum, but
rather develop against the backdrop of a social environment. Accordingly,
in a professional setting virtues are shaped by interactions and exchanges
that embody industry practices and professional codes. If the latter necessarily shape an individual's character development, perhaps the common
criticism that virtue ethics lacks the kind of prescriptive rules for decision-
making and action usually expressed in terms of codes and practical guidelines loses some of its bite.

Ian H. Gibson chronicles the emergence of 'model litigant' rules in
Australia since the mid-1990s, rules specifying how government agencies
should behave when participating in litigation. Gibson is sceptical about
the rules. They are, he argues, poorly worded and it is unclear whether and
how courts should enforce them. In addition, he maintains, the courts had
already developed high standards for government litigants before the rules,
standards they continue to apply. The recent introduction of overarching
obligations in many Australian states, along with the development of case

management by the courts, provides further reason to consider the rules redundant. If they are to be regarded as important, he concludes, both they and their rationale should be made clearer.

Due to modern communication technology, especially the internet, the global community has access to information about local actions of particular agents, and, insofar as these actions are perceived as wrong, the latter are exposed to the accumulated wrath of the former, often with disastrous consequences. In his chapter, Nicholas Munn considers criteria for the legitimacy of online criticism. Not only should we take into account the relative power of the target, the proportionality between original offence/harm and that (likely) caused by global criticism, and whether the target could have reasonably expected for information about local actions to become content that 'goes viral', but we should also consider whether the target acted as a private individual or in some public role, and especially whether the target's behaviour constitutes a violation of moral norms or rather a breach of mere etiquette.

Frederick Kroon points out that many countries have responded to low posthumous organ donation rates by accepting presumed consent. While demand for posthumous sperm procurement (PSP) is currently low, it has been suggested that moving to presumed consent regimes might increase demand and supply in that case too. Having set out the debate about the various notions of consent as they have been applied to the two cases, Kroon provides a critique of the notions of implied and presumed consent and of one way in which the notion of presumed consent has been applied PSP by Kelton Tremellen and Julian Savulescu. Kroon argues that though couched in terms of consent, Tremellen and Savulescu's argument actually relies upon conceiving of organs as what Kroon calls a 'pure resource', something in which we cannot sensibly be said to have interests after death. In the case of sperm, but not organs, he argues that a 'relationship-centred model', which gives weight to concern for future offspring because of their relationship to the donor, is more plausible than the pure resource alternative.

In their chapter, Ruth Walker and Liezl van Zyl object to the altruistic approach to surrogacy because the presumption of self-sacrifice renders it exploitative as surrogates are prevented from properly regarding their own interests and meeting legitimate needs for self-care. Revolving around the value of generosity instead, gift-surrogacy fares better because gift-givers can legitimately expect acknowledgement and reciprocation, but it too leaves surrogates vulnerable to exploitation. Therefore, the authors argue in favour of a professional model for surrogacy that requires not just reciprocation but also compensation. Unlike commercial surrogacy, the professional approach avoids the creation of undue financial incentives whilst offsetting the enormous cost that unpaid surrogacy currently imposes on surrogates, thereby enabling women to do the generous thing which they are already disposed to do.

Stephen Kemp examines the evolution of child care commodification in Australia. At this relatively early stage in the professionalisation process, he argues, the practice of child care meets some of the necessary criteria for profession-hood to a reasonable degree (e.g., existence of systematic knowledge in the performance of occupational tasks, often acquired through tertiary study and training) while rather failing to meet others (e.g., existence of role-specific norms and peer-group regulation). What is more, professional child care may be especially prone to a tension between the requirement of professional emotional detachment and the fact that a substantial degree of emotional attachment between carer and child is implicitly part of the service. However, professionalisation has undeniable benefits for child care stakeholders, including society at large because it relies on well-developed future citizens.

There is common scepticism about the institutionalisation of people with disabilities: we are inclined to think people will have better lives in supported residences. Paul Jewell, Matthew Dent and Ruth Crocker ran an empirical study to examine this common view, seeking to find out whether community living in supported residences produced more fulfilling lives and better outcomes than the institutions they replaced. The study produced disturbing results, suggesting that people living in supported residences were no better off than those in institutions. The study showed that those in supported residences were often isolated, without telephone and friends outside the residence, and with little or no family contact, no disposable money and no job. However the impact of the change to supported residences is difficult to determine, since no quality of life research had been conducted before de-institutionalisation. The authors conclude that (a) positive measures (e.g., opportunities for work, education and play) need to be added to de-institutionalisation to achieve satisfactory outcomes and (b) policy would be better informed and more effective if data were collected before and after significant changes.

Organisations often deal with applications – for employment, insurance, parole, for instance – on the basis of group risk statistics. When they do so, they may seem to fail to respect the applicants as individuals. Vanessa Scholes accepts that organisations have reason to statistically assess applicants, but argues – against Ferdinand Schoeman (1987) and Fred Schauer

(2003) — that there are legitimate ethical concerns about that approach. She suggests ways of 'increasing applicant agency' in the process, including an increased focus on whether the factors used to assess applicants are static or dynamic, a greater transparency of the process to applicants, and the use of statistics specific to individuals.

The 10 chapters in this issue of *Research in Ethical Issues in Organizations* are merely examples of the almost 30 papers read at the 22nd Annual AAPAE Conference, but they are a fair representation of the variety of topics addressed during the event. Once again, we would like to thank all presenters and other guests for their contributions, and for making the conference such an enjoyable and successful event.

Marco Grix
Tim Dare
Editors

SUPPLY AND DEMAND IN THE DEVELOPMENT OF PROFESSIONAL ETHICS

Hugh Breakey

ABSTRACT

How can we explain the development — or equally the non-development — of professional ethics norms in a particular case? And how can we enhance compliance with existing professional ethical norms? In this chapter, I develop a supply/demand theory of professional ethics. That is, I consider the demand-forces and pull-factors that call for the construction, reform or continuance of a professional ethos. These demands may come from various stakeholders, including individual service-providers, the professional community, actual and prospective clients and the general public collectively as interested third parties. The supply-side, on the other hand, constitutes the ethical materiel out of which norms emerge: these are the felt-motivations of individual professionals at the coalface of action that drive them to recognize, acknowledge and act upon a professional norm. This material includes traditions and stories, the conscious application of common-sense ethics, explicit endorsement of public moral codes, internal excellences within the activity, a discrete community capable of cultivating attractive role-identities and so on. As well as considering such

Contemporary Issues in Applied and Professional Ethics
Research in Ethical Issues in Organizations, Volume 15, 1–28
ISSN: 1529-2096/doi:10.1108/S1529-209620160000015001

ethical-materiel, I canvas the institutional and cultural supports that facili-
tate the production of these motives.

Keywords: Professional ethics; professionalization; moral motivation;
common morality; business ethics

INTRODUCTION AND ASSUMPTIONS

This chapter develops a supply and demand explanation of professional
ethics. It describes the various pull-factors impelling various actors to
demand the creation of a norm, and the myriad push-factors (including
moral springs such as status, identity, role, narrative, tradition and excellence) that *supply* the elements out of which a norm, and the accompanying
motivations to act upon it, can be fashioned.

What I aim to help explain, in particular, is why we do not see strong
community-constructed codes arising in other sectors that may have similar
sorts of demanders. Why don't we see professional collective codes of conduct arising for car mechanics, naturopaths and product salespersons? Is
that the demanders in this case possess less urgent needs? Or is it that we
lack the supply-side materiel, and the cultural and institutional facilitators
of that materiel?

In focusing on explaining the emergence of strong professional ethical
codes, this project differs from myriad sociological explanations of how
professional *organizations* and *communities* emerge. These inquiries share
much in common, and I will draw on some sociological literature in what
follows. In particular, many of the demand-side features will be similar, at
least for those sociological theories that allow for a multiplicity of causal
factors and — with Weber rather than Marx — emphasize individual agents'
deliberate projects to construct a profession (Macdonald, 1999, pp. 1–7,
27–29). Yet the inquiries remain separate: it is possible to construct a
powerful professional organization where the 'ethic' remains mere rhetorical gloss or slick public relations spiel. In contrast, I focus exclusively on
the construction of genuine ethical norms.

Looking at professional ethics this way involves making a few major
assumptions.

First, I assume that genuine recognizably ethical drives to act against
one's narrow self-interest exist, and that enhancing these drives constitutes

one important method of improving compliance with professional standards. Naturally, I do not suggest that ethical culture and mindset compromise the *only* mechanisms for improving compliance. Instead, they make up one part of a larger portfolio of mechanisms. We can see this, for example, in Charles Sampford's 'integrity systems' approach, where moral motives sit alongside legal instruments, economic incentives, governance mechanisms and more (1994). Similarly, moral norms constitute just one part of Justin O'Brien's CEDAR approach, where (E)thics takes its place amongst factors including Compliance, Deterrence, Accountability and Risk (O'Brien & Dixon, 2013 – see similarly the three-level governance approach of Macaulay & Arjoon, 2013). Thus, while I focus here exclusively on improving the motivational push of professional norms, this must be understood as one part of a larger toolbox of potential levers of reform, including economic, political and governance mechanisms. Of course, attending to ethics can respond to the 'enemy outside' by fixing the 'enemy inside' (Macaulay & Arjoon, 2013, p. 521).

My second assumption is that merely wanting a norm to exist (say for the collective benefit of one's group) does not wish that norm into existence – even if the community that wants the norm is the very community that would shoulder its obligations. A norm exists when individuals at the coalface, voluntarily and with little thought for who is watching, comply with the norm on the conviction that the norm warrants respect.[1] Crucially, that a norm would be in a group's collective interest does not at all show that the norm exists and that it regulates each member of the group. As the well-known phenomenon of the 'tragedy of the commons' illustrates (Hardin, 1968), a group can unanimously recognize they would all be better off with a norm motivating a shared course of action, and at the same time bemoan that they do not possess such a norm. What this means is that as well as having demanders *outside* a service-providing-sector calling for the construction of a norm, we can equally well have demanders *inside* that sector who desire the norm and yet lament its non-existence. This is why in what follows, I will include professionals themselves as 'demanders' for the norm, and consider the supply-side question of normative motivation separately. Professionals themselves are not norm-suppliers (instead, they constitute a special case of demanders).

My third assumption is that merely because a norm is justified – even consciously accepted as justified by the agent in question – does not guarantee that agent's compliance. Plainly, working out the ultimate justification for, and articulation of, professional norms remains a matter of no small moral and philosophical significance. But my question here lies elsewhere. Here our interest concerns how to motivate widespread compliance with (and hence to establish the social reality of) a professional ethic. Compliance is not (only) a question of whether the norm can be morally and philosophically justified from an objective standpoint. The question of compliance amounts to a question of *motivation*. In any given case, for any given agent, that agent can have diverse motives to comply, myriad temptations to excuse herself, unhelpful habits or cognitive lapses that stymie compliance, or pressures to defect from the norm. As Heath (2008) stresses, in the context of business ethics, non-compliance typically derives less from a disagreement about values, but more from the availability and self-interested employment of excuses and rationalizations. Equally, an ultimate justification can sometimes seem far off and removed – perhaps because the 'norm-demanders' are not present, appreciative or vocal. Furthermore, a well-known and widely accepted principle may, in some situations, impose especially onerous duties, and hence require greater motivational force than usual to secure the same level of compliance.

As a result of these several factors, having a single objective justification for a professional norm (though no doubt important) does not exhaust our interest in other supply-side ethical materiel that may bolster widespread respect for the norm, and drive compliance with its obligations even in the face of substantial temptations and pressures. Thus, while the following supply factors draw on moral justifications for professional ethics, I focus on felt-motivation rather than objective justification. When I draw on a particular justificatory story for a professional norm, the question in each case is how far that particular justification taps into the emotions, relations, habits and thought-processes of the decision-making professional. How does the situation and context of the professional conspire to make a particular justification vivid and salient, and so capable of driving compliance?

As a final assumption, I limit the following analysis to contemporary liberal democracies. In structurally different political, economic and social conditions, a very different demand-supply formula may appear.

THE PROFESSIONAL ETHIC

What is the professional ethic that is being demanded and supplied in each case? Naturally, and importantly, differences can arise between the content that is demanded even by different constituents of a single professional organization – and even stronger differences in desired content can emerge when we consider the demands of clients, individual third-party stake-holders, and the community at large. And even if there was univocal agreement by all these disparate demanders, the supply-side materiel might drive the performance of a norm with quite different content again.

Yet, in each case, there remains a single designated object that the contest revolves around: that is, the professional ethic that aims to regulate the conduct of the professional in her professional activities.

Moreover, I will take it that the ethic in question, to count as a professional ethic on any ordinary construal, will contain the following staple features.

First, the professional ethic is collectively created by the profession itself, and is articulated in the profession's self-understanding and usually delineated in concrete codes of conduct. That is, the professional community or organization constitutes the final arbiter and decision-maker on the substance of the ethic, though of course that collective may well select that content in response to pressures or opportunities created by community or client expectations. The profession also makes some effort at policing compliance with the ethic, and possesses an array of sanctions it can draw upon in cases of serious breaches.

Second, in terms of substance, I take it that the professional ethic will always require competent standards of service, backed up by (at least quasi-)fiduciary duties to clients, namely, to act in their interest, heed their choices, and respect their confidentiality.[2] The professional ethic, in other words, centres on the service to the client, and scrupulously avoids tainting that service with any ulterior motives. Despite this client-centred focus, there will usually be some obligations to the society more generally (or to its institutions, such as lawyers' duties to 'the court'). There may also be certain duties owed to the profession itself, and largely for its collective benefit.

DEMANDERS

'Demanders' include all stakeholders who call for the construction, continuance or reform of the professional ethic. We can characterize them as saying, 'We want all those providing this service to be bound by an ethic because ...' Demanders include those calling for a profession to be created in a service-sector where no profession currently exists. (This is why I will speak throughout of 'service-providers' rather than of professionals, unless the context makes it clear that a profession has already been created.)

Demanders fall into three main groups: individual service-providers; clients and prospective clients; and the society at large.

Individual Service-Providers

Individual service-providers can benefit from professional norms on several different bases, and so desire the norm's construction, reform, continuance and enforcement. Cultivating the norm in these ways requires coming together as a collective, so although these are reasons that will appeal to individual service-providers, they impel action as a collective.

One of the major benefits to individual service-providers from a professional norm's existence is the creation of a climate of trust between prospective clients and service-providers.[3] Even setting aside the desirable social status that this trust nourishes, such trust carries an array of material and other benefits. It enhances widespread use of the service, allowing prospective clients to trust professionals implicitly and employ their services without hesitation. The trust also helps to gain or sustain the service-sector's social and legal license to operate. This is especially relevant if any specific legal exceptions are required to facilitate the smooth running of the professional service, such as confidentiality duties allowing professionals to avoid legal reporting duties (McGraw, 2004) and special exceptions required by the medical profession in dealing with drugs and human bodies (Rhodes, 2001). Trust in the specific service-sector also prevents potential clients attempting to fulfil their needs by taking their business to a cognate service-provider (such as going to an accountant or an estate-planner instead of a financial planner). In this way, the professional ethic can favourably impact upon inter-sector competition.[4] Generic trust in the profession also removes the need for an individual to establish their own trusted brand, which helps restrain costly intra-sectoral competition (constraints on individual advertising help here too (McGraw, 2004)).

The creation of a professional ethic requires competency standards, which usually mandate various educational or knowledge-based standards (such as entrance exams) that professionals must meet. For the self-interested professional, these standards tend to create the happy result of barriers against other practitioner's easy entry into the market, creating a quasi-monopoly that inflates service-costs. (For this reason, presumably, many professions make the educational requirements greater than ordinary competence would require (McGraw, 2004)).

Additionally, the self-regulation offered by a professional organization may be viewed by the professional as preferable to regulation by the government. Laws created by legislators and regulators remote from professional realities and priorities can prove clumsy and ham-fisted.

So far, these demanders have been quite self-interested. The creation of the professional ethic, and its articulation and enforcement through the professional community, promise substantial financial and legal benefits. But the professional committed to high standards of service and moral rigour also benefits from the development of a profession-wide ethic. In particular, possessing a standardized ethic prevents each individual professional being faced with market or occupational pressures to lower their standards (as Davis, 1991 relates in his exploration of the pressures placed on engineers' ethics that ultimately led to the *Challenger* space-shuttle disaster).

Summing up, for reasons based on improved social status, legal exemptions, expected financial rewards and improved support for individual's own moral standards, individual professionals constitute key demanders for the development of a professional ethic. To rehearse a point made earlier, however, the presence of this demand does not itself magically create the desired professional norm. The ethic itself must be constructed out of available materiel and supported by the requisite institutions.

Individual Clients and Prospective Clients

Clients and prospective clients help drive the development of professional ethics, for it is they who are usually the norm's most direct beneficiaries.

Why do clients demand professional norms? Or, more specifically, why do clients of *certain types of* services (such as medicine and law) demand norms protecting them *in ways that normal purchasers of market services and products do not*? After all, most purchasers of services in the market could be expected to desire increased care and attention for their wishes, confidentiality and decision-making autonomy. Why is the demand for the norm different for the particular services we tend to recognize as professions?

As the literature shows, clients of these services suffer several distinct types of special vulnerabilities, which together give greater urgency to their demands for fiduciary treatment.

First, many such services provide for very basic, and even inescapable, human needs in modern society. Medical needs (including doctors, nurses and pharmacists) and legal needs furnish obvious examples. Sometimes the need for such services can be urgent indeed − so urgent the client cannot select amongst service-providers. The emergency room presents a striking example here, but many serious illnesses require diligence and high standards from myriad service-providers the patient may never meet (such as pathologists). For other services, even if they do not cater to people's fundamental or urgent needs, such services constitute unavoidable parts of other important endeavors: endeavors required at the societal level. Engineers, architects and accountants provide examples here. These services are at least somewhat inelastic;[5] if service provision in these sectors is sub-quality, a prospective client cannot simply engage a different sector to answer to her needs.[6]

Second, prospective clients suffer from knowledge (epistemological) vulnerabilities. Clients lack information about the specific area of expertise wielded by the service-provider. Moreover, because that expertize often involves years of study and the capacity to judge subtly amid conflicting signals and pressures, ordinary clients are ill-equipped to become informed. Worse still, the level of their knowledge deficit rises to such an extent that they are not only unable to prospectively judge high-quality service, they usually cannot *retrospectively* do so. That is, having been given legal, medical, engineering or pharmacological advice, clients rarely find themselves in a position to accurately judge the quality of that advice. (Compare this to the services offered by a car mechanic. Even if we know little about how cars work, or what was wrong with our car in this instance, we can usually at least tell if the mechanic has succeeded in fixing the car.) Even if the advice fails to achieve its desired effect, the client may not know whether this misfortune resulted from poor advice or other factors. This means that poor service cannot educate any given client; as well as not being capable of self-education to learn prospectively about service quality, the client cannot even learn for themselves (except fitfully, unreliably and occasionally) about the quality of the service they have received. In turn, this means that normal reasons we have for trusting to people's personal responsibility for informed decision-making and self-education (Attas, 1999; Breakey, 2012) cannot apply in this case. Furthermore, the inability to make accurate retrospective judgements means that ordinary market pressures fail to act in productive ways. That is, market pressures that might otherwise respond to poor service provision when previous consumers vote with their wallets, and by this means send signals to other market players, will not function well in this context. As Davis (1988, p. 353) puts it, the market can prove deaf to the 'invisible quality' we demand of professionals like lawyers and doctors.

Third, the service itself involves the client making herself vulnerable. Certain services require of the client that she exposes, warts and all, her personal history, future plans and even physical body to the service-provider. This process of exposure, and the resulting knowledge and documents in the hands of the professional, create new vulnerabilities.

A fourth vulnerability emerges because if the provided service is very poor, the result may be catastrophic for the client. Even if clients were able to accurately judge the quality of service after they have put the advice into practice, the potentially exorbitant costs of faulty (accounting, legal, engineering, medical − one might add financial) advice render trial-and-error 'shopping around' for a high-quality service-provider fraught with peril.

These four factors combine to create a perfect storm of vulnerability. As a result, clients and prospective clients demand high-quality services with host of a quasi-fiduciary obligations on the part of the service-provider.[7] Moreover, the clients require these *as standard* across the service-sector, because they cannot (even with appropriate and judicious self-education) select high-quality services for themselves. They thus demand the ethos because they need professionals, as a rule, to be trustworthy in confidence, competence and intention.

While important, these vulnerabilities do not *ipso facto* create the reality of a professional ethic (as Rhodes (2001) can sometimes seem to imply in the context of professional medical ethics). Service-providers can simply *exploit* these vulnerabilities, secure in the knowledge that clients will in any case have to engage with them. After all, in other market sectors, profiting because of a buyer's need or ignorance is often seen as morally excusable, if not outright good business.

Wider Community/Third Parties

Clients are not the only non-professionals who possess a stake in the services offered by professionals.[8] Specific third parties, and sometimes the community at large, can suffer from professional malfeasance.

Third parties can suffer from discrete ethical failures, such as when a negligently engineered bridge collapses on top of them − or the spacecraft they are piloting explodes (Davis, 1991). These victims are not the paying clients of the professional − yet they suffer directly from failures of ethics and competence. Equally, the entire society can suffer from large-scale and widespread ethical failures. The clear example here is the Global Financial Crisis, created in no small part by failures in ethics on the part of accountants, bankers and financial advisers (Curtis, 2008). The Global Financial Crisis savaged investor trust, slowed economies and drove up unemployment, creating countless victims who bore no relation to the initial ethical failures.

Complicatedly though, third parties can also be threatened by professionals' faithful *allegiance* to their professional ethic. Professional codes primarily benefit the client and/or the profession itself – and these priorities can impact on those in the wider community. Such victims (and those concerned for them) still count as 'demanders', because they rarely wish to purge the entire professional ethic. Rather, they constitute reformers, who want the ethic to remain, but to be more responsive to third parties' needs. Common examples of this type of third-party demander include those persons at risk because of legal or medical confidentiality duties that prevent alarms being raised or prevent information (such as their legal innocence) being brought to light.

Another demander/reformer group includes those prospective clients who would benefit from increased advertising and knowledge of fee structures, as many professional norms constrain various forms of direct advertising. In such cases, the community's demands can be represented through courts, which may strike down as illegal these barriers to the ordinary flow of market information.

How do each of these types of demanders make their demands felt?

Not all demanders are equal when it comes to forcing and facilitating the development of professional ethical norms. Each wields different tools, with varying effectiveness.

Clients and prospective clients can vote with their feet and with their wallets, especially in cases where a visible and reliable portion of the service-sector display appropriate standards. In such a situation, if the overwhelming majority of clients flood to service-providers able to demonstrate high-quality standards (such as through membership in a bona fide professional organization), then market pressures work to drive the ethic and the institutions that support it. Clients can also try to hold out for improved contracts and established expectations between professionals and clients. Sometimes, they will be able to pursue serious breaches of ethics through civil (or even criminal) law.

Third parties and the general community enjoy less direct control over service-providers. This demander-group can determine the service-sector's social status – retracting its standing in the face of breaches of trust (as has occurred, to some extent at least, with bankers and accountants in the face of the Global Financial Crisis). The community also wields another tool; their capacity to vote for changes in legislation and regulation. Each of these levers amount to clumsy fixes for breaches in standards and ethics, but they can change the structural environment in ways conducive to future improvements. For instance, a legislative change in who can use the term 'financial adviser' can empower professional organizations by requiring membership in return for use of the sought-after term. This can in turn elicit larger improvements in standards.

Through the mechanism of government, the community can also offer a 'carrot' approach to improving supply. For example, in Australia, the *Professional Standards Councils* provides an example of a government institution designed to improve and invigorate professional organizations. In return for demonstrating professional standards, and education and enforcement mechanisms, organization-members can enjoy limited liabilities, as well as official state recognition of their professional status.[9]

Service-providers themselves possess different means at their disposal – most obviously by deliberately cultivating any of the following supply-side factors that can improve their own compliance. They can also play a crucial role in progressing their fellow service-providers' ethical standards, such as by esteeming colleagues who fulfil their professional role-identity, or who demonstrate excellence in their standards of service. Service-providers can also facilitate ethical development by joining and supporting professional organizations with high standards – and being on guard for those organizations succumbing to the ever-present temptation to focus more on increasing member benefits than on moral standard-setting.

SUPPLY FACTORS

Unlike demanders, supply factors are not persons or groups, but sets of motivations that drive intrinsic respect for the norm and ensure compliance occurs in the field, in the face of the inevitable temptations and pressures to defect. Supply factors provide a completion to the sentence: 'As an individual service-provider, I obey this norm because I think/feel that ...'

As well as listing the major supply factors driving compliance with a professional norm, this section also notes, where relevant, any institutional or cultural prerequisites (or facilitators) for a given supply-factor. For instance, a society that provides little social status or material reward for a professional group can expect no professional compliance on the basis of a fair *quid pro quo* with the local community, as the social benefits that trigger such a norm do not exist. This means that other supply factors must be brought to bear to secure widespread compliance in such an environment (a subject Iseda (2008) explores in the context of engineering in Japan).

In what follows, I gesture towards the general institutional facilitators of the norm in question; but a finer-grained analysis (honing in on a specific service-sector in a specific country) would reveal more granular institutional requirements. For example, while many of the following supply factors require a vibrant and well-resourced professional organization, this requirement equivocates between a professional organization that holds a legal monopoly on service-delivery, an organization that is purely voluntary and holds no regulatory recognition, and the many cases in between — such as where ordinary practice does not require professional membership, but membership tends to be recognized with greater remuneration and responsibility (McGraw, 2004). In some cases, a voluntary organization might be enough to develop the supply-factor, but other contexts will require the reliability and standardization of an organization possessing legal clout.

A Byword: Self-Interest as Norm Motivation

The above definition for a professional norm requires that self-interest cannot itself count as a supply-factor, as supply requires some type of intrinsic respect for the norm per se (and not merely complying in those instances where compliance will redound to the agent's personal advantage). However, self-interest still bears mention in this context. As Williams (2002, p. 94) observed in his work on the norm of truthfulness: 'it is vital that on many occasions there are obvious reasons of self- or group-interest ... constant injections of reasons for action which are obviously self-interested help to warm the tubes of the normative circulatory system'. In this spirit of 'warming the tubes', it is worth enumerating the self-interested reasons that professionals may have for obeying the established norm.

First, in cases where there are social, legal or financial benefits to the members arising from the existence of the professional norm, each professional contributes to the continuance of those benefits from her current compliance. The actual benefit she herself derives from her own actions is mediated and indirect, to be sure, but nonetheless furnishes one reason to comply. This motive usually requires institutional facilitation by an established professional organization that receives manifest social, legal or financial benefits from the community and clients.

Second, while professionals can rely somewhat on their branding as a member of a professional community in good standing, personal branding still matters. Professionals providing high standards of quality service can create a proven track record, and enjoy at least word-of-mouth advertising and referral on its basis.

Finally, professionals have a self-interested reason to avoid legal, social, financial or employment-based sanctions for non-compliance. This motive requires an effective self-regulating professional organization, or at least pro-active regulatory and legal governance, capable of assigning blame and sanction for wrong-doing.

Turning from self-interested motives for compliance to genuine ethical support-factors, I list six distinct types of motives: 'desirable role-identity', 'excellence', 'common morality', 'covenants', 'constructed virtues' and 'true glory'.

Desirable Role-Identity

Distinct role-identities can be inspiring and admirable, both from the outside (as ordinary community-members appraise the professional) and from the inside (the felt experience of a practitioner living up to her role). The admiration accruing to such identities provides a reason to live up to them. In an insight going back to Aristotle (350BC/2002) and playing a central role in the ethics of Hume (1739/1969), people like to take pride in themselves by becoming people they admire. Provided that those role-identities include compliance with the key professional norms and virtues — which is usually one part of what makes the role-identities so admirable in the first place — this self-admiration can constitute a major factor in propelling compliance.

The desirability of certain role-identities can be almost irremovable from the particular service provided. For example, the very nature of the medical professional involves healing, which is at once an exercise of power and inherently beneficial to those receiving it. One might doubt whether any society throughout history failed to revere its healers in some way.

Often though, role-identities need to be brought to life in various ways. They may be vivified in narratives and myths — such as stories celebrating lawyers defending the wrongly-accused innocent. Traditions, too, may burnish the role-identity with the lustre of ancient lineage; contemporary medical professionals can draw a line in their current virtues all the way back to the Hippocratic Oath, and feel themselves following in the footsteps of a steeped tradition. Professional roles can partake of previous traditions infused with attractive notions of honour, such as gentility and noblesse oblige (Macdonald, 1999, p. 10). Alternatively, the allures of the role might be hammered home by famous leaders or historical personalities whose feats become front-page news — such as investigative journalists who uncovered major political scandals. When studies of professional ethics and education touch upon the high ideals of aspirants to the profession (Kelly, 1998; Luban, 2003), it will often be such stories that drive the aspirant's wish to belong.

While important, it may not be easy to construct these supply-side factors. All these facilitators of supply-side admiration for role-identities require an existing canon of historical or fictional figures and steeped traditions.

Another reason for wanting to live up to a role-identity emerges when one feels *invested* in the identity. Whether or not the general community admires the role-identity, the professional may nevertheless *identify* with it (Hall, 1982; Newton, 1982). The identity forms part of their self-concept, and they aim to live up to it simply because it reflects how they see themselves. A key here lies in the creation of a sense of ownership over the distinctive role-identity. The fact that the profession itself develops the professional ethic, and that its members can see the ethic as reflecting their own thinking, work, practice and commitments, enhances this sense of personal and collective investment. So too, substantial barriers to entry into the community (through educational and other requirements) can nourish this sense of collective ownership over the role-identity and its moral components.

The sense of ownership and identification thus requires the existence of a professional organization constructing the code of conduct, especially if the organization encourages widespread debate and participation amongst the professional community whenever the code is constructed, reformed or considered. Similarly, institutional barriers preventing easy entry to the community encourage a sense of distinctive identity.

Other factors may help. Many codes have restrictions on advertising — constraints that can cultivate the profession's *dignity*, raising it above the rough-and-tumble of ordinary market players, and augmenting its attractions and aura of honour.

Excellence

As MacIntyre (1981) argued in *After Virtue*, practices can create their own standards of excellence, and traditions can help hone and encourage those standards. In turn, these standards give rise to virtues, understood as emotional and intellectual traits that empower excellence in the practice. Many

people find the pursuit and achievement of excellence intrinsically reward-
ing; MacIntyre (1981, pp. 175–177) refers to these emotional rewards, and
the desirable way of life accompanying them, as the 'internal goods' of a
practice. As such, excellence, and pride in one's excellence, provides a distinct drive towards professional virtue (see Iseda, 2008).

Of course, the excellences of a given practice may not turn out to result
in recognizable *moral* virtues (though MacIntyre (1981) argues that some
staple virtues will emerge across all practices). The excellence of salesman-
ship, for example, might revolve around rhetorical manipulation, by hook
or by crook, in teasing open a buyer's purse-strings. But for many professions, ethical constraints draw the borders within which the pursuit of
excellence may take place. The doctor who excels at healing, and the lawyer
who expertly wields the law in defense of her client, are required to perform
excellently *within the bounds* set by their professional moral obligations.
Breach of the norms amounts to cheating, and the cheat fails to
achieve – the cheat no longer even attempts to achieve – the activity's
excellence. As such, while the pursuit of excellence may not explicitly focus
on other-regarding ethical imperatives, it can nevertheless provide a strong
drive to comply with ethical norms.

This supply-factor, often simply characterized as 'doing the job well',
can be facilitated by various institutional means, including practices of
apprenticeship and education (MacIntyre & Dunne, 2002), the significance
of mentors and noted figures of excellence, and of community communication of standards and recognition of exemplars. Generally speaking, the
more networked and closely knit the community, the more we might expect
commonly held standards of competence and excellence to emerge and to
attain strong motivational force. Team-environments will be a paradigm
case of such close-knit groups.

Common Morality

Several notable theories of professional ethics (e.g. Beauchamp &
Childress, 2009) see professional ethics as the direct application of common
moral principles onto the fact-situations presented by the professional's
expertise and the client's various vulnerabilities.

Along with several other authors on professional ethics (Freedman,
1978; Rhodes, 2001; Tapper & Millett, 2014; Veatch, 1979), I find this avenue leaves several major features of professional ethics unexplained; in
particular, the nature of its substantial differences from ordinary business

ethics.[10] Even so, I can hardly deny that, for the greater part, professional ethics parallels, specifies or elaborates on common-sense moral principles, such as beneficence, honesty and respect for others' autonomy. To the extent, then, that the professional harbours a respectable moral character, their ordinary commitments to these everyday moral principles will serve as a supply-side driver to their professional ethical conduct.

Even though this supply-factor rests upon moral inclinations that are (*ex hypothesi*) widespread across the population, institutional facilitation can still be helpful. Codes of conduct delineated and publicized by professional organizations draw attention to how ordinary moral principles apply in complex situations, and highlight morally relevant issues that might otherwise lie unnoticed. Community interaction that creates avenues for peer advice and mentoring can similarly facilitate the activation of ordinary moral fillips. Even academic studies and official reports on ethical issues can help by clarifying how ordinary morality applies to professional contexts.

As well, we can think of the teaching of professional activity constrained by ethical norms, as developing 'scripts' (habitual and set cognitive processes for handling complex problems) that themselves fit within moral bounds. Because scripts developed without conscious ethical reflection can lay the groundwork for moral catastrophes (Gioia, 1992), the development of morally constrained scripts can prove a vital mechanism for rendering complex work morally justifiable as well as intellectually manageable.

A commitment to ordinary moral principles can also drive the need for standardized codes consistent across the profession. If moral standards cannot secure consistency among professionals − either for reasons of some members' immorality, genuine and legitimate moral diversity, or the latitude allowed by 'imperfect' duties (Igneski, 2006) − then a professional's high moral standards can prove an impediment to their employment prospects. As noted earlier, a professional organization enforcing standardized codes of conduct can be a necessary institutional requisite empowering individual professionals to resist race-to-the-bottom market or occupational pressures to lower their standards (Davis, 1991).

For all these reasons, even when professional obligations rest upon the relatively secure foundations of ordinary morality, institutional commitments to specific obligations can still enhance awareness and compliance.

Covenants, Fairness and Tacit Contracts

'Common morality' approaches to professional ethics apply ordinary moral principles *directly* to the fact-situations emerging in professional activities.

By saying it applies 'directly', I mean this application is not mediated through other contingent acts and circumstances, such as the existence of contracts or conventions. (Tapper and Millett (2014) stress this important difference.)

A further approach takes key principles of common morality – such as good faith, trustworthiness, respect for fair *quid pro quos*, and principles of fair contribution to collective goods – and then applies them to the existence of various social arrangements, conventions and expectations that arise in professional activities. On this footing, the ultimate justification for the professional ethic lies in common morality – but the existence of these mediated social and institutional structures shapes the ethic's substance, and triggers the motive to comply.

Three supply-side factors warrant note under this contractual-fairness banner (Veatch, 1979).

The first supply-side factor emerges as a sense of fairness or loyalty towards *one's professional peers*. This arises when the profession gains in some clear way from the existence of the professional norm. The most obvious benefits will take the form of high social status, increased financial remuneration, and/or legal exceptions for professionals engaged in their work activities. The institutional requisite here is a functioning professional community that secures social, legal or economic benefits for its members (Iseda, 2008). But even without such tangible benefits, the collective profession may enjoy increased trust from its clients and prospective clients. Over time, individual professionals' compliance to the ethic builds a climate of trust that all future professionals inherit. As Rhodes (2001, p. 496) observes in the medical context, patients implicitly trust their doctors, 'because a history of doctors (for the most part) acting for their patients' good has made medicine trustworthy. Physicians today are the heirs of trust …' For this reason, a professional who betrays that trust betrays the community of professionals. The defecting professional takes advantage of the benefits created by others in her group without similarly contributing to the collective good – and indeed undermines that good by risking the malfeasance coming to light, and potentially eroding that trust. Eschewing such unfair exploitation, the professional who adheres to the moral standard does the fair thing by their fellow professionals, who similarly constrain their self-interest in pursuit of the wider collective goal. As Davis (1988, p. 347) describes this motive: the principle of fairness demands, 'each person voluntarily receiving the benefits of a morally permissible practice to do her prescribed part of maintaining the practice'. The practice must be real, of course; if few other professionals actually performed their role, then the principle would not create collective benefits, and so not compel compliance based on group loyalty.

A second supply-side motive draws on the drive towards reciprocating the benefits the larger community bestows upon the profession and its members.[11] A professional might feel obliged to reciprocate towards the community by performing special obligations either (a) because she feels that an implicit contract has been constructed between her profession and the society for special privileges and she wishes to respect the substance of that tacit contract or (b) because she feels that the tacit bargain struck between community and profession represents a fair exchange, and as the beneficiary of the community's privileges, she thinks she should uphold her end of the *quid pro quo*. (These two ethical drives interweave, but they can be teased apart. The first looks to whether a tacit contract can be surmised to have taken place. As an ethical driver, this motivation presumably will be stronger in those professions, such as law and medicine, where an explicit oath takes place. The second motive attends to the fairness of the current arrangement in terms of relative costs and benefits, irrespective of whether a tacit contract could be imputed.) These two ethical drives require the existence of genuine benefits for the profession (social status, legal exceptions or improved remuneration), the visibility of these payoffs to ordinary professionals in their day-to-day work, and the implicit understanding that these rewards follow from the profession shouldering special obligations.

The third supply-side motive emerges through a professional's respect for the implicit contract (or for the spirit of explicit contracts) she undertakes with individual clients. Ordinary morality, we might say, requires not only adhering to the letter of one's explicit promises and undertakings, but a more demanding requirement of trustworthiness, which includes living up to the spirit of any agreements or arrangements, and not allowing others to labour under a misconception of one's character or intensions. This requirement acknowledges that a person deserves another's trust only if she has their interests at heart and cares about what happens to them. This broad virtue of trustworthiness can itself be one component of the moral virtue of 'integrity' (Breakey, 2016; Graham, 2001, pp. 246–247) – a virtue specifically earmarked by Dolovich (2010) in her description of the character required to live up to a lawyer's professional responsibilities. These virtues of trustworthiness and integrity then attach to the agreement forged with the client, or the client's expectations about the service. (Alternatively, if the client's expectations turn out to be unrealistic or misplaced, then the trustworthy professional must be clear about the substance of the service she intends to provide – she cannot allow the interaction to proceed under a misconception.)

This motive does not require iron-clad, black-letter contracts, as it presses the virtue-holder to live up to the spirit of reasonable agreements. Even so, such motives can still benefit from social and institutional facilitators, such as clear, established and reasonable expectations of service held by clients and promulgated by the professional body. Clear statements by the professional about her obligations, both as general commitments and towards individual clients, can help trigger her sense of honesty and integrity, and attach them to her professional ethic.

Summing up, trustworthiness, integrity and a sense of fairness can drive respect for covenants, *quid pro quos* and tacit contracts, providing important supply-side materiel for a professional ethic.

Constructed Virtues

If professional ethics require special obligations, reflect Rhodes and Smith (2006) in the context of medical ethics and Dolovich (2010) in the context of legal ethics, then wouldn't it require special virtues in professionals? Virtues can be defined here as enduring character traits governing emotional and cognitive responses to situations, that drive the responder to behave in appropriate and productive ways (Hursthouse, 1999). For example, the virtuous agent feels the appropriate amount of fear (or anger, sadness, happiness) at the right times, in the right way and directed towards the right objects. 'Right' in all these cases refers to a larger standard, such as actions, relationships and work capable of consolidating into a full and complete (excellent) human life, or of psychological health more broadly (Macaulay & Arjoon, 2013, p. 514).

This way of thinking about ethics dates back to Aristotle (350bc/ 2002) – and so does the hypothesis for how such character traits are acquired: namely, through repetition and habit, and immersion in a culture teaching and exemplifying the appropriate human excellences. Teaching the explicit rationale for the virtues helps, of course, but cannot supplant the need for emotional and cognitive habit-forming over an extended period of time. An example would be medical personnel working in a team for a lengthy period, where professional aspirants can witness, emulate and practice the ways that experienced professionals handle challenges. At this early stage, the newcomer's conscious motive for acquiring these virtues may be merely to fit into the team and function within it (Rhodes & Smith, 2006).

But after habit and cultural immersion have done their work, the professional medical practitioner has inculcated a new emotional and cognitive
perspective with which to approach their work. True, the process might, in
some cases, create work habits that are less than conducive to professional
virtues (Kelly, 1998). But often, the practitioner will find themselves cultivating emotional responses that tend to elicit morally proper actions in
future professional work situations (Rhodes & Smith, 2006). They will
have learned to 'think like' a doctor, engineer or lawyer — and part of that
'thinking like' will guide their moral deliberation and action in constructive
ways (Davis, 1991).

These supply-factor's institutional facilitators have less to do with professional organizations and codes of conduct, and more to do with lived
practices and work-experience, on-the-job training, internships and appren-
ticeships. Teamwork, mentoring and leadership can all be key drivers in the
development of professional character.

True Glory

Ethicists tend not to rank the pursuit of social approval and admiration,
on its own, as a proper moral driver. They have strong reasons for not
crediting such a motive; not all good acts will enjoy social approval, and
not all approval-eliciting acts will be good, meaning that the naked pursuit
of status will only contingently track actual good behaviour (and will, in
any event, be done for the wrong reasons). Often, we conclude from this
that only duty *for its own sake* — irrespective of social acclaim — constitutes
the proper motive for moral action. But as Smith (1790/2006) observed, a
middle position lies between these two poles. A person can be driven to
receive social admiration for personal virtue, but only on condition that
they actually possess such virtue. This motive of 'true glory' (as Smith
termed it) finds no happiness in undeserved admiration, but revels in social
approbation when based in fact.

Individual professionals can receive social admiration for their own
work, and commonly enjoy a general social status deriving from respect for
the profession generally. A professional who yearns after true glory will
enjoy basking in this status — but only to the extent that she herself, and
the profession more generally, actually warrants it. This approbation then
serves as another supply factor motivating the professional to high standards, and driving her to encourage her fellow professionals to the same
heights. The cultural requisite for activating true glory is the existence of

social respect, trust and status for the profession (Iseda, 2008), or at least for individual professionals who are known to perform well. Peer respect within the professional group itself may prove even more motivating.

SUPPLY AND DEMAND INTERACTION

Supply-side ethical materiel interacts with demander's needs in a variety of ways. This section sketches some of the standard and not-so-standard relationships between the two.

Supply-Side Factors May Not Match Demanders' Wants

We can perhaps all-too-easily conceive of a situation where supply does not meet with demand, in the sense of clients and communities calling for improved norms and better compliance, and a service-sector deaf to their entreaties − or a sector continually rebuffing the community with syrupy rhetoric about change and reform, without undertaking any meaningful action (the contemporary banking sector may furnish an apt example here − see O'Brien & Dixon, 2013, p. 964). After all, service-providers might reap a considerable profit by engaging in practices that a professional ethic would prohibit.

Supply can fail to match demand in other ways. In particular, the profession might enjoy strong supply-side drivers, but this ethical materiel might not match up to the specific content demanded by the community. Supply factors possess their own internal laws and constraints; it is not simply that *any* of the above supply factors can be shaped to motivate compliance with *any* given other-regarding ethical obligation.[12] For example, the pursuit of excellence or a desirable role-identity might clash with a community's wishes, such as if the profession holds that its 'dignity' proscribes direct advertising, while the public demands the greater information and competition that advertising can generate (McGraw, 2004). Alternatively, the ethic might rely primarily on the direct application of common morality − but in a case where the community demands obligations in excess of everyday moral burdens, then these will go beyond what the supply-side factor can supply. Professionals might find that their everyday moral character fails to motivate these additional burdens.

A different situation can arise where an ethic emerges without major input from demanders: where supply exists without demand. The internal goods of an activity, a desirable role-identity, and constructed virtues can all arise through the natural collaborations of a close-knit community of peers; communities can spontaneously discuss and construct norms for their practices (Hall, 1982; Newton, 1982). External demand for the services rendered by this ethical community may ensure the profession and its ethic continue to flourish, but the ethic was not itself driven by, nor created in response to, such demanders.

Supply Can Create Demand

While stressing the distinction between the two, and noting that we can have demanders without supply, and supply factors present without these resulting from demanders, supply factors can form a part of demanders' reasoning. Potentially, a service-provider envisaging a future profession might, reflecting upon the internal goods and felt-pleasures of each of the supply-side factors noted above, come to *demand* the creation of the professional ethic. The desire for social status presents a clear example of this. A service-provider might wish she was part of a sector that enjoyed social respect (and true glory), and therefore demand the development of a professional organization with high standards. In this way, the goods furnished by supply-side motives can form part of the portfolio of reasons some professionals might become demanders.

The Dangers of In-Group Ethical Constructions

Some of the supply factors noted above can be constructed entirely 'in house' – that is, purely by the service-sector and through its own activities and deliberations. The service-sector might allow scant participation or even observation by third parties and the general community in constructing these ethical supports. Such internally constructed supply factors can include excellence, virtue-construction, and desirable role-identity.

Some theorists (McGraw, 2004; Veatch, 1979) harbour suspicions about the moral legitimacy of these internally constructed professional norms, at least when those constructs impact upon non-members. Certainly, it is true that, detached from client or community input, such norms may be more focused on ensuring and improving member benefits (even if just the internal goods of the activity), rather than on fiduciary duties to clients or wider duties to the community. Even if such norms do attend to the public interest, it may be the public interest as paternalistically interpreted and articulated by the profession (Veatch, 1979).

Yet, such in-house ethical supports should not be dismissed too quickly. Internally constructed professional norms can be powerful motivators for action by providing ownership and a distinctive role-identity. The professional can think of such norms as powerful expressions of her identity, and feel a strong identification with and ownership of them for this reason. As such, these norms may well be worth encouraging, so long as the good they motivate outweighs the bad they countenance. Freedman (1978, p. 14) suggests this line of argument when he pictures professional doctors as 'zealots for health': their exaggerated emphasis on the ideal of health may cause them to falter with respect to some ordinary moral requirements, but society gains far more than it loses from allowing this extreme commitment in its healers.

BLOCKERS/SPOILERS

Whether a professional ethic is developed and nurtured is not only a question of supply and demand. It also depends on the existence and power of 'spoilers', who stand to benefit from the non-existence of the professional ethic and its ensuing obligations and enforcement regimes. We can think of spoilers as saying, 'We resist the imposition of this norm because ...'

One important spoiler group comprises service-providers (and prospective service-providers) who benefit from weak barriers to market entry. These include would-be service-providers who do not possess the educational credentials required for professional accreditation (Frumento & Korenman, 2013). Some service-providers might also benefit from avoiding high compliance costs, especially if their preferred market strategies involve practices that clash with the demands of a professional ethic. Such spoilers can have much to lose from the imposition of new professional standards — such standards may see them forced out of a potentially lucrative market or forced to act in ways that threaten their profit-margins within that market.

Along with this group of service-providers, we might also note their prospective clientele (though these rarely have any political voice). It may seem strange to think of clients benefiting from the *removal of* professional status, but the standards and processes required by the professional ethic and its regulatory machinery can carry significant costs and require significant personal investments (such as in time-consuming education). These factors often conspire to inflate the cost of the service, and impact upon its easy and timely availability. To budget-conscious consumers, or in cases with lower stakes, professional standards may present as a barrier to their preferred way of engaging the service. They would prefer to try their luck in an unregulated market rather than to bear the inflated service-costs of a professional.

Another important spoiler comes in the form of product creators that stand to increase sales through unregulated, unprofessional sales strategies and marketing. Creators of financial products and pharmaceutical companies — consider 'natural' therapies — can fall into this bracket. Many pharmaceutical companies, for example, would prefer to advertise (e.g. as occurs in the United States and New Zealand) and even market directly to consumers, rather than having their products sitting behind the mediating layer of professional medical providers. For this reason, such providers can possess strong reasons for marshalling resistance to, or otherwise corrupting, professional ethical norms.

CONCLUSION

By understanding the demander-groups, the supply factors, and the spoilers at work, we can come to an improved understanding of why professional ethics emerge in any given case. We can also begin to see why we require these norms of the classic professions (such as medicine, law, engineering), while we do not require them of ordinary business actors. Simply, the presence of both demanders and supply factors differs in each case. Businesses do not normally deal with clientele who suffer sweeping and multifaceted vulnerabilities, ensuring these businesses face less demand for stronger and more standardized ethical conduct. As well, without a specialized field of knowledge requiring lengthy study, fewer natural barriers stand in the way of market entry. This renders the formation of a closely knit and recognizable community of peers less likely, in turn removing many of the institutional supports for the creation of supply factors. As well, a specific service, with standards distinct from mere monetary outcomes, naturally acquires its own notions of excellence. Business management, on the other hand, involves shifting between many different activities, making attributions of excellence murkier.

The above analysis also provides resources for reformers aiming to improve compliance with professional norms. Reformers can consider which groups of demanders to empower, and what levers of power those demanders might be able to wield that can impact upon compliance. Equally, reformers can look to the supply-side and assess what resources and institutions could be strengthened to enhance the norms' internal allure to its duty-bearers. To be sure, the foregoing analysis implies that aspiring reformers cannot simply 'build' an ethic from scratch; ethical drivers rely either on intrinsic human sensibilities (such as for common morality), entrenched cultural values (such as for true glory and the bargain for social status) or virtues constructed over lengthy periods and through long traditions of practice (role-identities, excellence and constructed virtues). But the reformer can, nevertheless, consider what cultural or institutional requisites and facilitators exist − or could exist − within the profession that could provide a fertile ground for the future growth of such ethics.

In such ways as these, the foregoing analysis aims to aid not only our understanding of professional ethics, but our practical reform efforts.[13]

NOTES

1. This definition constitutes a mix of how social scientists and philosophers typically view norms. Philosophers tend to stress that norm compliance only counts when the norm is obeyed for the right reasons − but for our purposes here I count any motive that drives respect for the norm as such, rather than just the philosophically 'right' reason (which of course would be much debated by different schools of thought). Social scientists (such as from international relations studies) will recognize a norm only when they see widespread compliance, and expectations of compliance, regardless of whether the motive for obeying the norm involved respect for the norm as such. My definition thus straddles the two approaches.

2. These are well-known features; for example Tuch (2014, p. 111).

3. See Rhodes (2001). Naturally, further trust often must still be built, over time and individually with each client. Even here however, the larger collective ethic helps; it helps frame client expectations and fit a model of 'professionalism' that each individual can employ to demonstrate their trustworthiness.

4. Some sociologists see this inter-profession competition as a key driver in professionalization (Macdonald, 1999, p. 15, 33).

5. Though note that there can in some cases be rival service-providers able to be drawn in from cognate areas. See note 4.

6. One special case of this inelasticity arises when the service, through its very nature, can only be performed with state authority. In such cases, market competition cannot improve standards of service. This unavoidable-state-monopoly, applying to politicians, public servants, judges, police and armed forces, need not create

recognizably *professional* ethics (though state prosecutors are professional lawyers) – but it does drive the formation of other ethical codes, and attendant enforcement measures.

7. Deen Sanders employs an analogous supply-demand line of thought in his formula for determining the need for regulation or professionalization, outlined in Sanders and Roberts (2015). On the formula's numerator, Sanders places the vulnerabilities created by complexity, necessity for engagement and the risk of using non-experts, with trust in existing sources of expertise placed in the denominator.

8. The community takes an increased role as demander in contemporary democratic contexts (sometimes referred to as Mode 2 societies) where the collective searches and creates knowledge, and then articulates informed political demands. See Sanders and Roberts (2015, p. 19).

9. See http://www.psc.gov.au/

10. Even if the reader thinks common morality fully explains all professional moral obligations and their binding status, this chapter's argument can still be seen as a study in how to use various ancillary motivational devices to augment compliance with (what the reader in question will see as) ordinary moral duties as applied to special situations.

11. Sociologists refer to this community-profession bargain as the 'function/ functionalist' theory of professionalism (Newton, 1982), and its contractual mechanism as a 'regulative bargain' between profession and state (Macdonald, 1999, p. 11).

12. Montesquieu once made this point with respect to the monarch's use of honour as the principle to motivate nobles' compliance with their obligations of state. The monarch may at times wish to demand actions that deviate from honour's requirements, but he cannot do so without undermining the very ethos that holds his country together: "Honor has its laws and rules and is incapable of yielding, as it depends on its own caprice and not on that of another" (Montesquieu, 1748/ 1989, p. 27). In other words, the supply-factor proves incapable of answering the demander's desires. For discussion of Montesquieu's point in a professional ethics context, see Breakey (2014, p. 76).

13. This chapter benefited from helpful comments from Deen Sanders and Charles Sampford, as well as from participants at the *22nd Annual Conference of the Australian Association of Professional and Applied Ethics*, July 9–12, 2015, and from an anonymous reviewer for *Research in Ethical Issues in Organizations*.

REFERENCES

Aristotle (350BC/2002). Nicomachean ethics *(J. Sachs, Trans.)*. Newbury, MA: Focus Publishing/R. Pullins.

Attas, D. (1999). What's wrong with "deceptive" advertising? *Journal of Business Ethics*, *21*(1), 49–59.

Beauchamp, T. L., & Childress, J. (2009). *Principles of biomedical ethics* (6th ed.). New York, NY: Oxford University Press.

Breakey, H. (2012). *Intellectual liberty: Natural rights and intellectual property*. Farnham: Ashgate.

Breakey, H. (2014). Wired to fail: Virtue and dysfunction in Baltimore's narrative. *Research in Ethical Issues in Organizations, 11*, 51–80.

Breakey, H. (2016). Compromise despite conviction: Curbing integrity's moral dangers. *Journal of Value Inquiry*, 1–16. doi:10.1007/s10790-016-9541-1

Curtis, G. (2008). *The financial crisis and the collapse of ethical behavior: greycourt.* Greycourt White Paper No. 44

Davis, M. (1988). Professionalism means putting your profession first. *Georgetown Journal of Legal Ethics, 2*(34), 340–357.

Davis, M. (1991). Thinking like an engineer: The place of a code of ethics in the practice of a profession. *Philosophy & Public Affairs, 20*(2), 150–167.

Dolovich, S. (2010). Ethical lawyering and the possibility of integrity. In T. Dare & W. B. Wendel (Eds.), *Professional ethics and personal integrity* (pp. 125–185). Newcastle upon Tyne: Cambridge Scholars Publishing.

Freedman, B. (1978). A meta-ethics for professional morality. *Ethics, 89*(1), 1–19.

Frumento, A. J., & Korenman, S. (2013). Professionalism and investment advisers. *Journal of Investment Compliance, 14*(1), 32–41.

Gioia, D. A. (1992). Pinto fires and personal ethics: A script analysis of missed opportunities. *Journal of Business Ethics, 11*(5/6), 379–389.

Graham, J. L. (2001). Does integrity require moral goodness? *Ratio, 14*, 234–251.

Hall, R. T. (1982). Emile Durkheim on business and professional ethics. *Business & Professional Ethics Journal, 2*(1), 51–60.

Hardin, G. (1968). The tragedy of the commons. *Science, 162*, 1243–1248.

Heath, J. (2008). Business ethics and moral motivation: A criminological perspective. *Journal of Business Ethics, 83*, 595–614.

Hume, D. (1739/1969). *A treatise of human nature.* Baltimore, MD: Penguin Books.

Hursthouse, R. (1999). *On virtue ethics.* New York, NY: Oxford University Press.

Igneski, V. (2006). Perfect and imperfect duties to aid. *Social Theory and Practice, 32*(3), 439–466.

Iseda, T. (2008). How should we foster the professional integrity of engineers in Japan? A pride-based approach. *Science and Engineering Ethics, 14*, 165–176.

Kelly, B. (1998). Preserving moral integrity: A follow-up study with new graduate nurses. *Journal of Advanced Nursing, 28*(5), 1134–1145.

Luban, D. (2003). Integrity: Its causes and cures. *Fordham Law Review, 72*(2), 279–310.

Macaulay, M., & Arjoon, S. (2013). An Aristotelian-Thomistic approach to professional ethics. *Journal of Markets & Morality, 16*(2), 507–524.

Macdonald, K. M. (1999). *The sociology of the professions.* London: Sage.

MacIntyre, A. (1981). *After virtue: A study in moral theory.* London: Duckworth.

MacIntyre, A., & Dunne, J. (2002). Alasdair MacIntyre on education: In dialogue with Joseph Dunne. *Journal of Philosophy of Education, 36*(1), 1–19.

McGraw, D. K. (2004). A social contract theory critique of professional codes of ethics. *Information, Communication and Ethics in Society, 2*, 235–243.

Montesquieu. (1748/1989). *The spirit of the laws.* New York, NY: Cambridge University Press.

Newton, L. (1982). The origin of professionalism: Sociological conclusions and ethical implications. *Business & Professional Ethics Journal, 1*(4), 33–43.

O'Brien, J., & Dixon, O. (2013). The common link in failures and scandals at the world's leading banks. *Seattle University Law Review, 36*, 941–972.

Rhodes, R. (2001). Understanding the trusted doctor and constructing a theory of bioethics. *Theoretical Medicine, 22*, 493–504.

Rhodes, R., & Smith, L. G. (2006). Molding professional character. In N. Kenny & W. Shelton (Eds.), *Lost virtue*. Bingley, UK: Emerald Group Publishing Limited.

Sampford, C. (1994). Law, ethics and institutional reform: Finding philosophy, displacing ideology. *Griffith Law Review, 1*(1), 1–38.

Sanders, D., & Roberts, A. (2015). *White paper: Professionalisation of financial services*. Parramatta: Professional Standards Councils (PSC).

Smith, A. (1790/2006). *The theory of moral sentiments* (6th ed.). New York, NY: Dover Publications.

Tapper, A., & Millett, S. (2014). Is professional ethics grounded in general ethical principles? *Theoretical and Applied Ethics, 3*(1), 61–80.

Tuch, A. F. (2014). The self-regulation of investment bankers. *George Washington Law Review, 83*, 101–175.

Veatch, R. M. (1979). Professional medical ethics: The grounding of its principles. *The Journal of Medicine and Philosophy, 4*, 1–19.

Williams, B. (2002). *Truth & truthfulness: An essay in genealogy*. Princeton, NJ: Princeton University Press.

HOW SHOULD THE CONCEPT OF A PROFESSION BE UNDERSTOOD, AND IS THE NOTION OF A PRACTICE HELPFUL IN UNDERSTANDING IT? [*]

Stephan Millett

ABSTRACT

This chapter asks whether it is helpful to consider a profession to be a practice and to what extent this meshes with the idea that 'profession' is a moral concept. It examines MacIntyre's concept of a practice as an activity that pursues internal goods, finds that MacIntyre's articulation of the concept by itself is not enough to describe what it is to be a profession and seeks to supplement this with ideas from others, primarily Miller and

[*] A version of this chapter was presented at the Australian Association for Professional & Applied Ethics (AAPAE) Annual Conference 9–12 July, 2015, The University of Auckland. The present version has benefitted from discussions with, and editing advice from, Alan Tapper and constructive criticism from an anonymous reviewer.

Contemporary Issues in Applied and Professional Ethics
Research in Ethical Issues in Organizations, Volume 15, 29–40
Copyright © 2016 by Emerald Group Publishing Limited
ISSN: 1529-2096/doi:10.1108/S1529-209620160000015002

Davis. This supplementation, however, still leaves open the question of the origin of a profession's authority (or licence) to use what can be called the 'dangerous knowledge' that differentiates the work of professions from other occupations. For this, Veatch provides useful ideas.

Keywords: Professions; practices; institutions; dangerous knowledge

INTRODUCTION

Given the prominent place professions, and the concept of being a professional, have in contemporary society, developing an understanding of what makes something a profession rather than some other form of occupation is an important undertaking. However, the question of what makes something a profession is not easily answered. Dictionary-type definitions are not all that helpful in addressing this question (Tapper & Millett, 2015), however, two concepts from MacIntyre's (2007) social theory – the related notions of social practices and institutions – present themselves as suitable candidates to explore with a view to understanding what a profession is.

To begin, it seems important to distinguish in what sense the term 'practice' is being used. Schatzki (2001) provides a useful starting point in understanding practices, noting a distinction between the 'philosophical practice thinkers' such as Ludwig Wittgenstein, Hubert Dreyfus and Charles Taylor, social theorists such as Pierre Bourdieu, Anthony Giddens and a number of ethnomethodologists, cultural theorists such as Michel Foucault and Jean-Francois Lyotard and the positions of those (e.g. Joseph Rouse and Andrew Pickering) who present the concepts of science and technology as forms of 'activity' rather than as forms of representation.

One factor common to most theorists, particularly in philosophy and the traditional social sciences, Schatzki notes, is that they agree that practices are enacted by persons. They are 'embodied, materially mediated arrays of human activity centrally organized around shared practical understanding' (Schatzki, 2001, p. 11).

PRACTICE AS A REGULARITY OR
NORMATIVE ACTIVITY

Rouse (2001) usefully distinguishes between two ways of viewing practices, practice as a regularity and practice as a normative activity.

Perhaps the best-known version of practice as a regularity is from Bourdieu (1977), who positions his theory of practice firmly within his idea of *habitus*. For him,

> the habitus, the durably installed generative principle of *regulated* improvisations, produces practices which tend to reproduce the *regularities* immanent in the objective conditions of the production of their generative principle. (p. 78 emphasis added)

Or, to repeat Bourdieu's epigrammatic summary, habitus is 'history turned into nature' (p. 78).

Viewing practices as regularities in the social world, however, does not assist much in understanding the concept of a profession. It does nothing, for example, to address the normative role implicit in Michael Davis's assertion that 'the claim of professionalism is primarily a moral claim' (1988, p. 343). So, what of a normative conception of practice?

Perhaps the most influential conception of practice as a form of normative activity is from MacIntyre (2007) for whom a practice is not a simple regularity, but is normative as it has necessary connections to virtue. This conception offers a promising avenue for exploring practice and the professions.

MacIntyre uses the word 'practice' in a very particular way:

> By a 'practice' I am going to mean any coherent and complex form of socially established cooperative human activity through which goods internal to that form of activity are realized in the course of trying to achieve those standards of excellence which are appropriate to, and partially definitive of, that form of activity, with the result that human powers to achieve excellence, and human conceptions of the ends and goods involved, are systematically extended. (p. 187)

There are two kinds of goods possible to be obtained from a practice in MacIntyre's conception: 'goods externally and contingently attached' (p. 188) to the practice and 'goods internal to the practice' (p. 188). Of goods internal to a practice there are at least two different kinds: the excellence of the products of the practice and the good of the practitioner living out a greater or lesser part of his or life as *a practitioner*. External goods, when achieved, are always some individual's property and possession and are 'characteristically objects of competition in which there must be losers as well as winners' (p. 190). The more any one person has of these goods, the less others have. Internal goods, by contrast, are 'the outcome of the competition to excel, but it is characteristic of them that their achievement is a good for the whole community who participate in the practice' (pp. 190–191).

MacIntyre counts a wide variety of activities as practices, in his carefully defined sense of the word: 'arts, sciences, games, politics in the Aristotelian sense, the making and sustaining of family life all fall under the concept' (p. 188). He mentions only farming and architecture as practices that are also occupations, but he doesn't discuss the relation between practices, professions and occupation. He does distinguish between virtues and professional skills. 'Someone who genuinely possesses a virtue can be expected to manifest it in very different types of situation, many of them situations where the practice of a virtue cannot be expected to be effective in the way that we expect a professional skill to be' (p. 205). However, he is here using a surprisingly loose sense of 'professional', in which 'the virtues of a good committee man ... a good administrator ... a gambler or a pool hustler are professional skills professionally deployed' (p. 205).

For the purposes of this chapter, the first question that arises here is: must professions be seen as practices in MacIntyre's sense? It seems clear that professions generate both internal goods (health, justice, education, personal care, etc.) and external goods (money, honours, power, prestige). In addition, professional practitioners typically live a greater part of their lives as professionals engaged in professional practice and are thus positioned to exhibit the virtues of the profession.

Although these elements of MacIntyre's social theory do not describe only professional practices, it is possible to establish a stronger connection between professions and practices through MacIntyre's assertion that 'every practice requires a certain kind of relationship between those who participate in it' (p. 191) — such as might be observed in the various activities in which members of this or that profession mutually engage. But for this assertion to be useful for understanding the relationship between professions and practices, there needs also to be a story that explains *why* people enacting certain practices come together into a group and then, as a group, require certain practices to be undertaken as a condition of continued membership of the group. Some part of that story might include the possession of certain virtues, which MacIntyre describes as 'those goods by reference to which, whether we like it or not, we define our relationships to those other people with whom we share the kind of purposes and standards which inform practices' (p. 191). It may be that MacIntyre's focus on the role of virtue is helpful in developing a theory to explain what a profession is.

For MacIntyre (2007, pp. 186–195), 'virtue' is a concept necessarily connected with practices and is always secondary to acceptance of a prior account of social and moral life — that is, virtue needs always to be seen in the context of a pre-existing understanding of social life. It is a concept developed in three sequential stages: (i) a background account of a 'practice', (ii) an account of the narrative order of a single human life and

(iii) an account of what constitutes a moral tradition. He adds that 'each later stage presupposes the earlier, but not *vice versa*' (p. 187). A virtue for MacIntyre is

> an acquired human quality the possession and exercise of which tends to enable us to achieve those goods which are internal to practices and the lack of which effectively prevents us from achieving any such goods. (p. 191)

The role of virtues and their connection to practices makes them valuable in understanding what a profession is in that members of a particular profession will require certain virtues of those who are admitted to the profession. However, virtues can also be exhibited outside the contexts of professional practice — and practices themselves are not confined to professional contexts, so even with the addition of virtues, the concept of a practice is not enough to describe a profession. If the concept of a practice is to contribute to a suitable account of what a profession is, it stands in need of supplementation.

INSTITUTIONS

One candidate for supplementation is the concept of an institution, again referred to by MacIntyre for whom institutions are distinct from, but necessary to, practices in that no practice can survive in the absence of something like an institutional structure (2007, p. 194). But, just as with practices where 'without the virtues there could be a recognition only of ... external goods and not at all of internal goods' (p. 196), MacIntyre's notion of an institution involves the virtues. For him institutions are distinct from practices in that institutions are necessarily concerned with external goods, but

> institutions and practices characteristically form a single causal order in which the ideals and the creativity of the practice are always vulnerable to the acquisitiveness of the institution, in which the cooperative care for common goods of the practice is always vulnerable to the competitiveness of the institution. In this context the essential function of the virtues is clear. Without them, without justice, courage and truthfulness, practices could not resist the corrupting power of institutions. (2007, p. 194)

For example, without the virtues medical professionals might be more swayed by a hospital's institutional administrative imperatives than by the medical needs of their patients. But what are the characteristics of an institution? Beyond giving examples of institutions (e.g. marriage, war, families, cities, Benedictine monastic life, law, a university, a farm, a hospital, the modern individual), and urging that they not be confused with practices (p. 194), MacIntyre does not create a clear description of what an institution is. Perhaps Seumas Miller can add something.

Miller (2009) sets out an 'individualist, teleological (normative) account' (p. 179) of the professions, in which the members of professions are 'institutional role occupants' defined in terms of what they do together and by the 'collective ends' of what they do. The ends are, specifically, collective or jointly-produced goods that should be 'made available to the whole community because they are desirable and the members of the community have a joint right to them, for example, health, shelter, and justice' (p. 179).

Members of a society have what Miller calls an 'institutionally prior needs-based right' to some of the collective goods that professionals produce (such as health, shelter and justice). Other goods produced by professions, such as lawyers' collective end to administer justice, presuppose an existing institution or framework and as such are '*institutional* moral rights' (p. 180). Miller distinguishes the professions from other occupations, noting that professions: pursue collective goods; do not have a primarily economic relationship to their clients or community (and have special fiduciary duties to their clients); possess expert knowledge; have professional autonomy to make discretionary judgments and occupy an institutional role.

In terms of this last distinguishing characteristic of a profession Miller notes that to be strictly accurate a profession is a set of 'institutional role occupants' and that 'members of the professions are members of a professional body that is itself an institution' (p. 183). Professionals thus described enter into a professional role morality in which the institutional rights and duties they accept are also moral rights and duties, but rights and duties are reserved only for members of the profession. These institutional rights and duties are impersonal but partial: the professional owes a duty to clients only because they are clients. The duty does not extend beyond that. Institutional rights, such as professional autonomy, are possessed *because* a person is a professional, not because they are person or citizen.

Miller's account of the institutional nature of the professions does help in understanding what a profession is, but it does not explain what is meant by an institution. On this, Searle is helpful.

For Searle (2005) '... if you presuppose language, you have already presupposed institutions'. And in setting out what an institution is, rather than asking the question 'What is an institution?' Searle suggests we ask 'What is an institutional fact?' To put this in terms of professions, rather than ask 'What is a profession?' we would be better served by asking 'Under what conditions might we say of something, it is a profession?'

He then proposes (pp. 6–7) three elements that he says are necessary to explain social and institutional reality: *collective intentionality, the assignment of function* (e.g. using a found object as a tool) and *status functions*. Intentionality is 'that feature of the mind by which it is directed at, or about ... objects and states of affairs in the world' (p. 6). For there to be collective intentionality a group of people need knowingly to direct their minds to the same objects or states of affairs in the world. It is 'the basis of all society, human or animal' (p. 6). When this is combined with the assignment of function there can be collective assignments of function. Status functions are pertinent to understanding professions in terms of institutions as they are special assignments of function where

> the object or person to whom the function is assigned can ... perform the function only in virtue of the fact that there is a collective assignment of a certain *status*, and the object or person performs its function only in virtue of collective acceptance by the community that the object or person has the requisite status. (p. 7)

Members of the professions have a collectively assigned status and on that basis can perform certain functions accepted by the community and assigned to the collective.

In addressing the question of 'What is an institutional fact?' Searle claims that such facts typically require rules such as '*X counts as Y in context C*' and that institutional facts only exist in virtue of collective acceptance of something having a certain status, where that status carries functions that cannot be performed without the collective acceptance of the status. 'This ... is the glue that holds society together' (pp. 9–10). However, while this account is consistent with the operation of professions, it does not tell us *how* the collective acceptance of status comes about – whether by a group of individuals who claim for themselves privileged use of what might best be referred to as dangerous knowledge or by the society at large that cedes use of this dangerous knowledge to a group to which there are significant barriers to entry.

To this point there is still not enough to explain what a profession is.

SERVING THE PUBLIC GOOD

Perhaps Davis (1988) can add something. Davis asserts that, in common usage, a profession is 'an occupational group *organized* to use the characteristic skill of its members for the *public good*' (p. 342) and in so doing distinguishes professions from other groups organized for other purposes such as making a profit. He says it is a 'conceptual truth' that professions are occupational groups that must be organized in large part 'for the purpose of serving others' 'beyond what ordinary morality requires' (although he does not offer an argument for this) and adds that a member of a profession *professes* a standard of skill and conduct. The sense of group organization around a self-professed standard of skill and conduct can be expressed in terms of Searle's notion of status function in that the professed skill and conduct can be put into practice only because there is a 'collective assignment of a certain *status*' and community acceptance that the practitioner has the requisite status. Davis asserts that some at least of the obligations of a professional, such as the obligation to give a client priority over non-clients in the normal run of things, exist as standards of practice set out by the profession, continuing adherence to these standards being a condition of remaining within the profession.

We have moved closer to understanding what a profession is, but need more.

ACT AND ACTIVITY

Let us take one occupation — teaching — that MacIntyre says is not a practice (MacIntyre & Dunne, 2002, p. 5), a claim that others have disputed (e.g., Noddings, 2003). Firstly, it is worth noting that there is a possible equivocation in the use of the term 'teaching' in MacIntyre and others. For example, is teaching being used as a verb (I am teaching John), or as a gerund (teaching is important)? One way to unravel this is to go back to Aristotle, as both Noddings (2003) and MacIntyre (2007) do, but to examine more closely a distinction between an act and an activity — as the notion of an activity is central to MacIntyre's definition of a practice.

> By a 'practice' I am going to mean any coherent and complex form of socially established cooperative human activity through which goods internal to that form of activity are realized .... (2007, p. 187)

Noddings (2003, p. 242) notes that 'Aristotle pointed out that teaching is an activity that finds its results in the learner, not the teacher'. The reference to Aristotle, although unreferenced in Noddings, is to a passage in his *Metaphysics* at 9.8 (Aristotle, 2013):

> ... matter exists in a potential state, just because it may come to its form; and when it exists actually, then it is in its form. And the same holds good in all cases, even those in which the end is a movement. And so, as teachers think they have achieved their end when they have exhibited the pupil at work, nature does likewise.

This passage raises a number of questions relevant to practices and professions. The first is whether there is a good *internal* to teaching, as the 'end' (or purpose) of teaching is to bring about a change (movement) in the student. Another is whether the 'end' for teachers comes from a single occurrence (an act) or from an ongoing activity. Yet another is whether teaching requires there to be learning.

On the first question, if the good is (only) external to the activity, can teaching be a practice in MacIntyre's sense? At first glance the answer is no, since, for MacIntyre, a practice has an internal good and teaching is a means to an end. Noddings, however, notes that if 'means-defined activities are not to be considered practices' (p. 242) then it would be hard to defend medicine being a practice as it is a means to treat illnesses.

The second and third questions can be addressed in Noddings' (p. 242) citing of John Dewey's (1933) claim that 'teaching may be compared to selling commodities [whereby] no one can sell unless someone buys'. She modifies this later – and distinguishes act from activity – in pointing out that 'Dewey did not say that every bona fide teaching act has to produce learning in every student' but also that 'teachers cannot go on claiming to teach if no-one learns' (p. 243). From this, teaching may be both an act (I taught my son the word 'dog' as a name for our four-footed pet) and an activity (I continued over the following months to teach my son other words and their referents). An *act* of teaching may not require learning, but the *activity* of teaching does.

Teaching is an act and an activity. If it is to be a practice in MacIntyre's sense then it needs to have an internal good. But if its good is deemed to be external to the activity because it requires a change in the student, then it is not a practice. However, if teaching is not a practice because of this, then for the same reasons medicine and nursing are not practices either.

Dunne (2003) offers a way through this by referring to

> Aristotle's distinction between poiesis, where the end is separable from the activity, and praxis, where the end lies in the activity itself. (p. 354)

So perhaps teaching is a mix of poiesis and praxis and thus might be a practice and a profession. Correlatively, medicine and nursing would also each be a practice and a profession.

PROFESSIONAL VIRTUES AND PROFESSIONALISM

What might be the connection, if any, between practices and professions? And is MacIntyre's version of a practice at all useful in understanding what a profession is?

In addressing this, two ideas appear relevant: MacIntyre's (2007, p. 273) requirement that the core virtues of justice, courage and honesty are necessary to achieve the goods internal to practices and Davis's assertion that 'the claim of professionalism is primarily a moral claim ...[but] is not simply a moral claim' (1988, p. 343).

MacIntyre's account of the virtues moves through a sequence of three necessary 'states': a first where virtues are necessary if agents are to achieve the internal goods of practices; a second in which the virtues are 'qualities contributing to the good of a whole life' and a third 'which relates them to the pursuit of a good for human beings the conception of which can only be elaborated and possessed within an ongoing social tradition' (2007, p. 273). However, 'where the virtues are required, the vices also may flourish' (p. 193), leaving open the possibility that those charged with using dangerous knowledge — knowledge that can harm people — may do so without primary regard for the welfare of their clients or patients.

The following elements would appear to be relevant. The virtues are necessary for an agent to realize the goods internal to a practice. Practices cannot operate in the absence of institutions or without the practices being part of a life narrative. Following Miller and Searle (above) a profession is arguably an institution. However it is an institution through which professionals make use of specialized and frequently dangerous knowledge. What is missing here, is the role of professions in monitoring and managing the use of dangerous knowledge. The professions themselves impose added unilateral obligations on professionals to serve others and to require 'a commitment to benefitting others beyond what ordinary morality requires' (Davis, 1988, p. 343). The unilateral nature of the obligations is characterized by Davis in the following terms:

> The claim of professionalism is primarily a moral claim. To be a professional is to have obligations one would not otherwise [have]. These are not mere legal obligations (although they may be that too). They are obligations one is in honor, in conscience, in decency, bound to respect ... since the claim of professionalism is primarily moral, morality must limit the content of professionalism. Professionalism can never require anything immoral.

However, Davis notes, the claim is not only a moral claim as it is a 'conceptual truth' that a profession must organize itself in such a way that its purpose includes serving others and having a commitment to others (notably clients, but also to the wider community) 'beyond what ordinary morality requires' (p. 343). There is an obligation to others beyond the requirements of ordinary morality because the professional organization makes it so as a matter of its standards of practice. The fact that the many join as one in a professional organization gives them the 'power to do good which the unorganized cannot' (Davis, 1988, p. 345).

This, though, does not tell the whole story as it does not address the question of *why* a profession makes special obligations a matter of practice standards or *why* individuals join themselves to the institution that is the profession. To answer that question requires that we go beyond practices, institutions and the virtues.

To reach a fuller understanding of what a profession is it may pay to add the notion of a tacit 'contract' that allows professionals to make use of dangerous knowledge, for the benefit of the community whilst also generating a benefit for themselves.

SOCIAL CONTRACTS

Veatch (1981) argued for three main points with respect to social contracts: that social life is contractual in nature, with the 'contract' being structured by shared values and common ethical principles; that the contents of professional ethics should be based on a 'contract' between the professions and the wider society and that professionals strike a contract with their clients. The second point about 'contracts' is most relevant to this chapter as one of the signal results of this 'contract' is an asymmetry between the ethical expectations that apply to the professional and the client. This asymmetry (following Veatch) arises from a contract between the professions and the wider society, and is not determined merely by the professions themselves. If this is so Davis's contention that the professions themselves determine that there should be special obligations to clients cannot hold. And what counts as professional conduct cannot be simply accounted for as a consequence of professional virtue as this begs the question of whether a person becomes a professional because he or she has certain virtues or maintains certain virtues as a result of their professional status. Professions will have their formal institutions, their governing structures, and their various particular roles, rules and regulations, but these will rest upon the wide acceptance of the need for professions in the general society and culture: the social institution of the professions is the result of a tacit contract predicated on adequate controls over use of dangerous knowledge by a self-organized group with special, and potentially dangerous, knowledge. The contract gives, in effect, a licence to suitably qualified people to self-organize to control the use of dangerous knowledge. The controls include

barriers to entry, the development of practice standards and the availability
of sanctions for breaches of those standards. That the practice standards
include a requirement to bring a benefit to the community and/or clients
above and beyond a commercial contract is, in part, a *quid pro quo* for the
community licence to use dangerous knowledge.

REFERENCES

Aristotle. (2013). *Metaphysics*. Adelaide: eBooks@Adelaide. Retrieved from http://ebooks.
    adelaide.edu.au/a/aristotle/metaphysics/index.html
Bourdieu, P. (1977). *Outline of a theory of practice [R. Nice, Trans.]*. Cambridge: Cambridge
    University Press.
Davis, M. (1988). Professionalism means putting your profession first. *Georgetown Journal of
    Legal Ethics, 2*(341), 341–357.
Dewey, J. (1933). *How we think: A restatement of the relation of reflective thinking to the educa-
    tive process*. Boston, MA: D.C. Heath.
Dunne, J. (2003). Arguing for teaching as a practice: A reply to Alasdair Macintyre. *Journal of
    Philosophy of Education, 37*(2), 353–369.
MacIntyre, A. (2007). *After virtue: A study in moral theory* (3rd ed.). Notre Dame: University
    of Notre Dame Press.
MacIntyre, A., & Dunne, J. (2002). Alasdair Macintyre on education: In dialogue with Joseph
    Dunne. *Journal of Philosophy of Education, 36*(1), 1–20.
Miller, S. (2009). *The moral foundations of social institutions: A philosophical study*.
    Cambridge: Cambridge University Press.
Noddings, N. (2003). Is teaching a practice? *Journal of Philosophy of Education,
    37*(2), 241–251.
Rouse, J. (2001). Two concepts of practices. In T. R. Schatzki, K. K. Cetina, & E. v. Savigny
    (Eds.), *The practice turn in contemporary theory*. New York, NY: Routledge.
Schatzki, T. R. (2001). Introduction. In T. R. Schatzki, K. K. Cetina, & E. v. Savigny (Eds.),
    The practice turn in contemporary theory. New York, NY: Routledge.
Searle, J. R. (2005). What is an institution? *Journal of Institutional Economics, 1*(1), 1–22.
Tapper, A., & Millett, S. (2015). Revisiting the concept of a profession. *Research in Ethical
    Issues in Organisations, 13*, 1–18.
Veatch, R. M. (1981). *A theory of medical ethics*. New York, NY: Basic Books.

TRANSFORMATION: AN EXAMINATION OF THE VIRTUOUS CHARACTER FROM THE PERSPECTIVE OF PROCESS PHILOSOPHY

Giuseppe Naimo

ABSTRACT

The virtuous character and the ethical agent represent mutually inclusive terms, neither of which independently, in the Aristotelian tradition, is considered an innate quality. Virtues, if not innate, are contingent; but what makes each instantiation recognisably general? Normative ethics in this sense is a dynamic process and similarly process philosophy is based on the principle that existence is dynamic and that it should be the primary focus of any philosophical account of reality. I argue that the transformative process is equally as important as the end result of realising the virtuous dispositional traits. An important criticism of virtue ethics is the focus on character and not rules such as industry practices and codes found in the professions. The criticism however is less

Contemporary Issues in Applied and Professional Ethics
Research in Ethical Issues in Organizations, Volume 15, 41–59
Copyright © 2016 by Emerald Group Publishing Limited
All rights of reproduction in any form reserved
ISSN: 1529-2096/doi:10.1108/S1529-209620160000015003

worrisome than usually accepted. The reasoning herein developed to overcome this criticism rests on the presupposition that no one exists in isolation and virtues are developed in a social context and not simply given. Using process philosophy as a methodological approach to examine virtue ethical agency and the transformative process involved in its realisation elicits insights that allow the conceptual development of a more robust account of virtue ethics. I extend this nuanced rendition, in ways already commenced by others, into areas of organisational, environmental and intergenerational ethics.

Keywords: Process philosophy; virtue ethics; process virtue ethics; transformation; environment; self-organising systems

INTRODUCTION

Why examine virtue ethics through the lens of Process Philosophy? The simple answer is, because the acquisition of virtues established as dispositional traits involves a transformative process. Indeed Process Philosophy in general maintains that:

> time and change are among the principal categories of metaphysical understanding ... that process is a principal category of ontological description ... that processes – and the force, the energy, and the power that they make manifest – are more fundamental, or at least not less fundamental, than things for the purposes of ontological theory ... that contingency, emergence, novelty, and creativity are among the fundamental categories of metaphysical understanding. (Rescher, 2013, pp. 1265–1266)

To demonstrate these parallels the following discussion will draw out the similarities between virtue ethics and process philosophy to establish a general practical ethical framework. To that end, what can process philosophy bring to the table that is not already contained in established accounts of virtue ethics? To answer this question, let us examine the most damaging criticism of virtue ethics when considered as a general ethical framework, namely that it lacks a prescriptive mechanism for decision making process required to address many ethically charged situations across broad ranging scope. However, perspective is important, particularly when examining the narrow presupposition that developing a virtuous character is instructive and ideal for the individual. This provides the critic with a riposte: if virtue ethics focuses on the individual, then its applicability is limited, too limited given the range of applicability required in the competitive world of business and corporate sectors of society and for consequent environmental concerns. That contention rests on the presupposition that an ethical theory should provide a broadly applicable mechanism to make appropriate ethical decisions and resolve ethical concerns in practical ways across broad ranging situations; foremost, to be action guiding. The standard against which any broad scale moral judgment is made requires civil acceptability as a minimum criterion. Broad acceptability requires human agreement grounded in an inclusive system linked by the concepts of 'responsibility, respect' and 'ownership'. These three affirmative ideas in conjunction with the minimum criterion of civil acceptability are pivotal in providing a linking conceptual mechanism. The application of virtue ethics I contend is dynamic and transformative through the development of dispositional character traits which through the transformative process cannot be limited to the human individual without acknowledging the encompassing condition of being a social creature.

My exploration of virtue ethics draws largely upon Aristotelian scholarship because of its far-reaching influence beyond philosophy into other realms of human inquiry. The focal point of this investigation lies in the process of transformation, of becoming the virtuous and ethical agent. No human being can develop from birth in isolation. The old adage that humans are social and political organisms is culturally manifestly true. Developing virtuous character traits, just like learning to talk, is in fact a social practice that we know in no small measure thanks to Ludwig Wittgenstein (i.e. Language Games). Examining human kind in-the-world as a subject of transformation provides an integrative way to characterise humans as self-organising systems so that activities, such as the formation of institutions, associations, organisations and business corporations, are appropriately recognised as Space-Time-Event-Motion (STEM) (Naimo, 2009) extended interactive self-organising systems. In addition, self-referential STEM systems are manifested by the variety of utilised communication mediums and exchange mechanisms which form interactive containment-fields. I employ the idea of containment-fields because it serves multiple interlinking functions. First, it marks individuals, constituted by the component biological parts and integrated systems whose physical boundaries are putatively taken as the bodily integument (your skin). Yet the consequences of any one person's actions are hardly ever confined to their own body (e.g. affects by what one communicates, leaves behind, influences, treads upon, carbon footprint etc.). Second, then the idea of containment-fields allows us to see that people are constantly interacting

through differing mediums. Those combined activities of interacting individuals in communities and societies whose impact therefore is not limited by
proximity includes environment and associations of every nature. Each
human being constitutes an ecological unit, and together they constitute an
ecological community inclusive of the environment they inhabit.

The chapter develops by firstly making the case for process philosophy,
which includes a discussion of concern for process philosophers about substance philosophy associated with Aristotle. I argue that this concern is less
worrisome with regard to Aristotle than it may be with regard to Plato.
The account is developed by examining the concept of transformation
mediated through Aristotle's interrogation of the problem of change.
Indeed, Aristotle developed his own philosophy of nature based on the outcome of that examination. I extend this treatment by drawing out the differences between Plato's realism and Aristotle's realism to demonstrate
why Aristotle's version is indeed amenable to the version of process philosophy as rendered in this chapter. This provides a perspective from which
an understanding of process virtue ethics emerges. This is then expanded
into an analysis and application of the ethical intuitions of process philosophy as developed in the recent literature on management. The central ideas
of this development are compared to Aristotle's view of the city-state
drawn from his work in the *Politics* to analogically demonstrate that both
sets of ideas are indeed amenable. From this perspective, by integrating the
two distinct schools of thought (Process Philosophy and Virtue Ethics), I
aim to produce a prescriptive ethical framework that is broadly applicable.

THE MAKING OF PROCESS PHILOSOPHY

Debate continues as to which thinkers and their respective systems or
accounts of nature belong within the classification of process philosophy
but its origin, historically in the West at least, is Heraclitus. For clarification, a sticking point about philosophers whose system of thought trades
on process philosophy needs to be addressed, namely their opposition to
substance metaphysics – the 'dominant paradigm in the history of Western
philosophy since Aristotle' (Seibt, 2013, p. 2). The early Greek philosophers
wrestled with the problem of the 'one and many' (universal and
particular) – of accounting for the plurality of things in the world by
inquiring and thinking about the most basic material out of which things
are made. They reasoned that the many different kinds of things in the

world are transformations, changes from one or more basic things. They wanted to understand the primary principles (*arche*) or causes of nature or cosmology (Shand, 1993).

They disagreed about what that thing or those things were. For example, as generally understood,[1] the Milesian philosophers commencing with Thales, regarded as the founder of natural philosophy, said *arche* was 'water', while for Anaximenes it was 'air' and for Heraclitus it was 'fire'. In terms of the acquisition of knowledge the Milesians generally granted that change occurs and that the world of sense-experience is not an illusion. Not long afterwards, philosophers started questioning the foundation of our knowledge of the external world. Are the senses to be trusted or should we base our understanding on reason alone? The articulation of these types of questions ensured that anyone enquiring into the ultimate constitution of matter first needed to consider these fundamental issues. Common sense could no longer be taken for granted and the enquirer had to provide 'an account both of the foundations of knowledge (the problem of epistemology) and the nature of change and coming-to-be' (Lloyd, 1970, p. 36).

Historically there are two pre-Socratic thinkers polemically entwined in Western philosophical tradition, namely Parmenides and Heraclitus. On the one hand, Parmenides, the Eleatic philosopher, had reasoned that 'being' should be understood as the simplest thing, that it is internally undifferentiated and unchangeable, that change is logically contradictory, and that there is only 'being' and not 'becoming'. On the other hand, Heraclitus reasoned that becoming is fundamental since change occurs (Shand, 1993, pp. 6–7). The dispute that emerges is known as the problem of change. Both Heraclitus and Parmenides raised the problem of change in specific forms and proposed diametrically opposed solutions to it (Lloyd, 1970, p. 36). Recent scholarship about the interpretation of Heraclitus offers a different picture. According to Kirk, for instance, Heraclitus maintained that things are simultaneously one and many (2010, p. 15). Modern thinkers suggest that Heraclitus had emphasised that changes and interactions occur in the world at large. Change is 'confined within certain limits or 'measures' which ensure a balance between things that interact' (Lloyd, 1970, p. 37). The important part of his idea was the understanding that a 'state of apparent rest or equilibrium may conceal an underlying tension or interaction between opposites ... illustrated by such examples as the strung bow or lyre, which while they seem at rest are in fact in a state of tension' (Lloyd, 1970, p. 37). In any case substance metaphysicians following Parmenides generally maintained that the primary units of reality (substances) are static, the same at any instant in time, immutable. In contrast, process philosophers analyse 'becoming and what is occurring as well as ways of occurring' (Seibt, 2013, p. 3).

The preceding is relevant because Aristotle's own philosophy of nature emerges from his analysis of change. To explain change or transformation, Aristotle needed to overcome Parmenides' logic that in reality there is no change. According to this account, reality is one and, counter-intuitively, change is mere appearance. Indeed for Parmenides there were only two alternatives: 'It is' or 'It is not' — so no becoming, contra Heraclitus. According to this Parmenidean logic a new being cannot be derived from a non-being since 'nothing comes from nothing' (non-existence or 'It is not') (Shand, 1993, p. 11). Furthermore a new being cannot be derived from being since what has being, already is ('It is'), and 'does not begin to be'. The missing concept in the Parmenidean account is that of potency. Since Aristotle accepted Parmenides' idea that 'nothing comes from nothing', he reasoned instead that it does not follow that being cannot come from being. One of his arguments was grounded upon his distinction between 'potentiality and actuality' (Lloyd, 1970, p. 103). Aristotle's move was to distinguish 'being-in-act' from 'being-in-potency'. He understood that 'being' can come from 'being-in-potency' and from 'being-in-potency' can come 'being-in-act'. A seed, for instance, is a tree in one sense (it is) but it is a potential tree (*is not*), not actual one (Lloyd, 1970).

In the *Categories*, Aristotle gives his account of the ontological foundations from which we understand what he described as the metaphysical basic entities, primary substances (Studtmann, 2008, p. 10). Substances as such include living members of natural kinds and parts of substances, for example 'heads and hands' ... 'bodies and bits' ... like 'logs' and 'honey'. Explicitly, though, 'all accidents inhere in primary substances while primary substances do not inhere in anything' (Studtmann, 2008, p. 10). From this schema primary substances are classified as ontological primitives and so ontologically do not admit of further constituents (Studtmann, 2008).

What is important therefore about the preceding account and marks the most significant distinguishing feature between Plato's realism and Aristotle's realism is that for Plato, forms (universals) are other-worldly, whereas for Aristotle, forms are indwelling in the particular (e.g. human being). Forms do not exist apart from the particular. The immediate question that arises therefore is: Are the concerns of process philosophers totally in conflict with Aristotle's philosophy? From a Platonist perspective, forms are eternal and exist beyond the world of appearance. Accordingly, on this account it is completely incompatible with process philosophy. But Aristotle's version is dissimilar to Plato's in very important ways which make it more amenable to process philosophy. First, and importantly, for Aristotle knowledge is derived via the senses; it is not innate as rendered in the Platonic tradition. Second, on the question of the ultimate constituents of matter Aristotle is looking for the principles of perceptible bodies which are two pairs of contrary qualities (hot/cold; wet/dry) (Lloyd, 1970, p. 102). Third, Aristotle rejects outright physical theories espoused by the atomists (Leucippus and Democritus) and by Plato according to which differences between substances are ultimately 'quantitative, mathematical differentia'. "His main objection to such theories is that they are mistaken about the nature of the problem, which is one of physics, not one of mathematics: the principles of perceptible body must themselves be perceptible contrary qualities" (Lloyd, 1970, p. 102). This rendition makes Aristotle's natural philosophy more compatible with process philosophy as herein developed.

Furthermore, linked to this account is the concept of motion. Motion is a technical concept used by Aristotle to describe changes in accidents. Categorically speaking, for Aristotle there are three kinds of motion: a change in quality (alteration); a change in quantity/size (growth or diminution) and a change in place (local motion). Motion is the process that a substance goes through, and during which it loses one accidental form or actuality and gains another. In all cases motion is defined as 'the act of being in potency insofar as it is in potency' (Studtmann, 2007).

What does Aristotle's metaphysics have to do with his ideas about virtue ethics? Aristotle's general views regarding the importance and value of the study of nature revolve around his discussion of the good life (see book 10 of the *Nicomachean Ethics*). The highest faculty man possesses is reason, *nous*. Accordingly, that which one is most capable of engaging in is 'contemplation', *theoria*. The highest *telos* is rendered through the transformative activity when engaged in the 'study of first philosophy (metaphysics) and mathematics, and second philosophy (*physike*) – the study of natural objects having a capacity for change and movement in themselves, comprising the physical sciences inclusive of the branches of biology' (Lloyd, 1970, p. 104). From here we can start the process of teasing out parallels between Aristotle's virtue ethics and process philosophy ethics to establish the grounds upon which to scaffold the framework for a process virtue ethics.

THE GROUNDING OF PROCESS VIRTUE ETHICS

Connecting the preceding to developing virtue ethics from a process philosophy perspective requires turning attention to examining Aristotle's ethics.

Since the aim is to broaden the applicability of virtue ethics as generally understood, the preliminary step is an account of how the ethical agent is to be perceived. To be sincere, respectful and responsible assumes the ability or freedom to choose among available options, or courses of action. When Aristotle asks, 'What is it that makes a human being human?', he answers: 'the mind' (based on its deliberative capacity to choose among means to an end) (Rist, 2002, p. 85). With regard to free will, Aristotle arguably falls within a compatibilist position exhorting a philosophy of active self-determinism grounded in the human capacity for self-awareness. Self-awareness enables a level of freedom to construct and articulate new and creative decisions. We can realise a degree of freedom when we deliberate about the means to achieve the ends we desire: 'We deliberate not about ends but about means ... a doctor does not deliberate whether he shall heal ... deliberation is inquiry' (Aristotle, 1998, pp. 56–57). Having chosen the means, we are responsible for our actions, and we are responsible strictly speaking only for those actions that we do voluntarily (as a result of our choices). Our freedom is an aspect of being as an activity of engagement developmentally resulting in our habits or dispositions arising from the choices we have made throughout our past. Those choices and actions based on them are voluntary, and as such Aristotle construes them as our responsibility. Ignorance is no excuse. We are equally responsible for bad actions and good actions because we have the 'power to act as it is in our power not to act' (Aristotle, 1998, p. 59). Consequently, if any reasonable person facing circumstances similar to ours could have avoided such ignorance or negligence, then the excuse would be ineffective. Moreover, Aristotle believed that we are responsible for learning how a 'reasonable' person acts according to reason by developing through our activities the character and personality traits that constitute the embodiment from which our actions stem. We are not responsible for involuntary actions, out of our control due to coercion, constraint, or indeed justifiable ignorance.

Most modern versions of virtue ethics articulate their Aristotelian heritage by employing three main concepts: *arête* (excellence or virtue) *phronesis* (practical or moral wisdom) and *eudaimonia* (happiness/flourishing) (Hursthouse, 2012, p. 2). The starting point for the acquisition of knowledge and understanding for Aristotle is the rather empirical basis of being-in-the-world. The concept of a virtue refers to that quality or property that renders its possessor good. A virtuous person is a 'morally good, excellent or admirable person who acts and feels well, rightly as one should'. Being virtuous involves the acceptance of a 'whole range of considerations as reasons for action'. Common among different versions of virtue ethics is the understanding that living a life in accordance with virtue is necessary for *eudaimonia* — it is not independent (Hursthouse, 2012, pp. 3–9).

Happiness, for Aristotle, is an activity not a state. Indeed Aristotle used the term *energeia* (root term of energy) to characterise happiness as 'inward activity' (Blair, 1967, p. 104). To qualify this idea, happiness consists of a certain way of life which reflects the soul's proper use: to think and reason. The term 'living' for Aristotle utilises two senses: the first associated with power, and the second with 'inward activity' (Blair, 1967, p. 104). Form, it should be mentioned, for the more mature Aristotle refers to a 'special kind of activity', which is quite a shift away from the Platonic static notion of form (Blair, 1967, p. 109). This is an important linking notion developed with reference to Alfred North Whitehead's process philosophy in the next section. However, in saying that happiness is *energeia*, virtue for Aristotle is contrasted by the use of *hexis*, or state of being (Blair, 1967, p. 109). Therefore developing all the right virtues disposes a person to living well, whereby happiness is understood as the activity of living well.

It follows that establishing the dispositional virtuous character traits involves responsibility for who one becomes through the transformative process. This is a principled and social process, authentically unique for each individual as an internalising aspect of becoming. To learn, if not construed as an obligation, is nonetheless a requirement to develop the appropriate character traits pursuant to reasonableness. The expression of each virtue, for example, prudence, might share similar defining characteristics, though each instantiation is singularly trope-like and uniquely individual as rendered through one's own circumstances and requirements, understanding, consequent actions and overall transformative development. While virtue ethics has a number of strands (eudaimonism, care- and agent-based theories), they nonetheless have common features as pointed out above, the most prominent being the transformation of the individual, the agent of 'intrinsic value', through a teleological process. It follows that, when examining the determining role the agent plays in one's own development as an engaged spatio-temporal individual, one must take into consideration how one navigates one's way through life and the influences of one's full complement of associations (people, period, place, environment etc.).

Ethically charged problems require solutions resulting from a process of practical reasoning. That process involves an inductive principle of 'let experience be your guide' in terms of context-specific critical reflection. A virtue-based directive or guiding principle — as articulated, for example, in the context of environmental decision-making concerns — might resemble: 'Act such that your actions generate virtuous goods for stakeholders without unnecessary detriment to the environment'. Coupled with the minimum criterion of civil acceptability, such an approach arguably extends the applicability of virtue ethics.

PROCESS PHILOSOPHY AND ETHICS

Unpacking these common features of process philosophy and virtue ethics allows us to identify the grounding connections between the two approaches. Among many, the most prominent twentieth century process philosopher was Alfred North Whitehead. It must be acknowledged that Whitehead left no developed ethical theory. Throughout his work, however, his ideas about moral experience and his criticisms of ethical theory and the moral codes it sanctions are numerous and expansive enough to produce an informative if not prescriptive framework (McRae, 2001). A snap-shot view of process philosophy seen as a research paradigm of philosophical inquiry must include the observation that it is rather broad in its systematic scope. The dynamic sense of being as becoming or occurrence is of central concern for inquiry, which include the conditions of spatio-temporal existence, relations between different dynamic entities, and relations between the mind and the world; and, for the purposes of an ethical framework, the realisation of 'values in action' (Seibt, 2013, p. 2). Whitehead's Process Philosophy advances an 'organism ontology' that stems from an 'elucidation of immediate experience' as gleaned using the method of descriptive generalisation which by and large is not that dissimilar to the Aristotelian view of human nature.

Broadly understood, the central task of process philosophy is 'to construct a cosmology in which all intuitions well-grounded in human experience can be reconciled' (Griffin, 1998, p. 1). Griffin (1998) summarises that in the past cosmologies were based on religious, ethical, aesthetic and scientific experiences. According to Griffin (1998) modern cosmology (scientific-materialism) is impoverished and incapable of accounting for the human intuitions commonly defined in terms of aesthetic, ethical, religious and more broadly common-sense beliefs presupposed in practice. For example, he cites the belief that our thoughts and actions are not wholly determined by antecedent causes. From this perspective process philosophy has a task: its role is 'the critic of abstractions'. For when the tendency of overstatement emerges from the dominant paradigms as with the physical sciences, he explains, 'the primary critical task now is to challenge the half-truths constituting the scientific first principles' (1998, p. 1). The basic error Griffin identifies is when the 'fallacy of misplaced concreteness' is committed, usually when an abstraction from something specifically particular is identified with the concrete thing itself (1998, p. 1). Scientific materialism commits the fallacy by presupposing that everything, human experience included, can be explained in 'terms of locomotion of bits of matter devoid of spontaneity, internal process and intrinsic value' (1988, p. 1).

There is no singular type of process philosophy. The term 'process' itself varies according to the specific framework. On some accounts, for example, 'becoming' 'is the mode of being common to the many kinds of occurrences or dynamic beings' (Seibt, 2013, p. 3). Others regard 'being' as ongoing self-differentiation, so that 'becoming' refers to both the 'mode of being of different kinds of dynamic beings *and* the process that generates different kinds of dynamic beings' (Seibt, 2013, p. 3). Ontologically speaking, process philosophers replace the 'descriptive concepts of substance metaphysics' with a different set of categories. Among them is the individuating idea of functionality – an entity is distinguished by what it 'does'. The adapted version advocated here, however, is consistent with all versions of process philosophy that hold that all dynamic entities labelled 'processes' 'occur' and are 'intimately connected not only to temporal extension' but also to the directionality of time (Seibt, 2013, pp. 3–4).

A strictly Whiteheadian process philosophy maintains the 'two-fold idea that the actual units comprising the universe are momentary 'occasions of experience' involving two kinds of process' (Griffin, 1998, p. 2). Whitehead, influenced to some extent by the emerging developments in quantum physics, conceived the 'fundamental units of the world ... not as enduring individuals but as momentary events' (Griffin, 1998, p. 2). He regarded enduring individuals as 'temporally ordered societies of these momentary events' (p. 2). 'Actual occasions' is the term used to describe actual entities as events understood as spatiotemporally extensive. So the two kinds of processes according to this account are described firstly as 'a process within an actual occasion, called 'concrescence' (involves moving from potentiality to concreteness); and secondly, a process between actual occasions, called 'transition'' (Griffin, 1998, p. 2). These two processes involve two kinds of causation: 'efficient causation expresses the transition from actual entity to actual entity', and 'final causation expresses the internal process the actual entity becomes itself' (Griffin, 1998, p. 2). Griffin explains that Whitehead endeavoured to fulfil a central task of philosophy, to which I add an Aristotelian legacy: 'to exhibit final and efficient causes in their proper relation to each other' (1998, p. 2). That proper relation is largely reciprocal in

that every actual occasion commences by receiving efficient causation manifested from prior actual occasions. It then completes itself by exercising
final causation, understood as self-determination, and then exercises efficient causation upon following occasions. Whether intended or not, the
connection to Aristotle's natural philosophy is clear. The 'temporal process
involves the perpetual oscillation between efficient and final causation'
(Griffin, 1998, p. 2). What is highlighted on this account is the role played
by the concept of time which for Whitehead is an integral element of being.
Whitehead understood 'becoming' and 'conformal feelings' as constitutive
elements connecting the past to the present (Whitehead, 1978, p. 238).

In one sense Whitehead provided an alternative account to materialism's
response to dualism by advancing a cosmology with one type of actual
entity. Cartesian dualism promotes the idea that minds are temporal
though not spatially extensive while material bodies are spatially extensive.
Both process philosophy and materialism share a common and central concern with substance dualism, namely with regard to the problem of causal
interaction between the two substances. Dualistic accounts negate experience over broad types of entities, moreover denying some creatures the
capacity to experience emotion. Whitehead's conception that all actual entities are spatio-temporal events overcomes substance dualism by providing
a description of actual events that involves both *concrescence and transition*
(Griffin, 1998, p. 2). What is meant by the internal process of concrescence
is that the 'process is the becoming of experience'. But that does not mean
that all actual entities are conscious, only that they have some 'degree of
feeling' (Griffin, 1998, p. 2). I find it easier to think in terms of receptivity
by functional and property means in relation to attraction and repulsion.

Whitehead, being rather critical of materialism, identified two cardinal
elements missing, which 'makes a process such as evolutionary development impossible to understand: *internal relations* and *substantial activity*'.
Substantial activity refers to an activity that is 'intrinsically active (origina-
tive) rather than passively reactive' (Weekes, 2009, p. 143). Whitehead's
argument is captured thus:

> ... from what everyone implicitly knows about consciousness (their own), we can infer
> that nonconscious, even so-called 'inanimate' nature must harbor some kind of substan-
> tial activity and be able to accumulate a plethora of internal relations if something like
> consciousness is ever to evolve from it (diachronically) or emerge from it (synchroni-
> cally) moment by moment. (Weekes, 2009, p. 143)

The inherent criticism here is aimed at both the materialist and dualist
conception of nature as containing vacuous actualities so that things that

are fully actual are construed as devoid of experience. That idea is challenged by providing a perspectival shift when considering the life of the environment (ecology) in this light.

Where process philosophy differs, one might say advances, from Aristotle is in its challenge to the 'sensationalist' theory of perception whereby knowledge of the world is derived exclusively through sensory perception. Significantly, in *De Anima iii 5* Aristotle introduces the distinction between the active intellect and the passive intellect, which has been an enduring source of conflict, firstly regarding his previous work about the soul and secondly for those who endeavour to interpret Aristotle's writings (Shields, 2016). That most significant point aside, Whitehead adds to this understanding by providing a description and analysis of a non-sensory mode of perception – 'prehension' which may or may not be conscious and as such, he suggested, is more fundamental than sensory perception (Griffin, 1998, p. 3). Griffin provides a couple of examples. The first deals with memory recollection – 'when an occasion of experience directly perceives occasions in its own past'. The second is the 'mind's direct reception of influences from its brain (which sensory perception presupposes)' (1998, p. 3). According to Griffin, this constitutes 'direct prehension of other actualities' whereby we know of the existence of the 'external world' referred to as 'perception in the mode of causal efficacy'. Griffin suggests that it 'provides the experiential basis, denied by Hume, for our idea of causation as real influence' (1998, p. 4). Non-sensory prehension is not only central to process philosophy but it is thought to constitute the presupposition in 'the acceptance of aesthetic, ethical and religious experiences as genuine apprehensions' (Griffin, 1998, p. 4).

In sum, while process philosophy and virtue ethics are distinct and differ in some important ways, mostly due to the millenniums that separate Whitehead and Aristotle, they have in common the examination of being, of human nature, via an exploration of the behavioural modes/structures of experience through the relationship of the individual among others in the world. I am advocating a nuanced approach conceptualised by synthesising aspects of both systems of thought. Process philosophy can be described as the 'ontology of becoming'. It is grounded in the physics of relativity and, as already conveyed, it holds that the fundamental entities in nature are described as 'events' and 'occasions'. Entities in the world, seen as events and occasions, 'interact with, change and are changed by, each other in a continual process of transformation' (Macklin, Mathison, & Dibben, 2014, p. 74). Considering a general ethical account, particularly where environment and intergenerational ethics are concerned, the language of 'development' and 'change' as rendered in process philosophy are taken to be more appropriate descriptors of reality than those found in the language of Platonic static being. Given Whitehead's version, we can summarise an overall picture of reality by recognising that the fabric of nature is not divided by way of some 'ontological dualism'. This is also true of Aristotle's philosophy. Spatially extensive material requires temporal extension and vice versa. There is no temporally extensive mind or spirit without spatial extension. On this account, 'humans, animals, general phenomena (rocks, plants, molecules and subatomic particles) and God are ontologically related' (Macklin et al., 2014, p. 74). That means that everything is interrelated and is part of a flow or movement of energy, but without implying that this flow of energy is necessarily an undifferentiated unity. Individuals do exist in the flow, but are described as 'series of events rather than ontologically distinct and separate things'. These events are the 'actual occasions' that Whitehead takes to be the most fundamental things in the universe: as such even God is construed as an actual entity (Macklin et al., 2014, p. 75).

ANALYSIS AND APPLICATION

The description of organisations as construed from a process perspective drawn from the literature on management is described as fundamentally dynamic and societal in nature. On some accounts, an organisation is viewed as 'a mini-society, or societal group, in which meaningful interpersonal interactions and exchange take place in order to achieve the significant advance ... that is the aim of the individuals within it' (Macklin et al., 2014, p. 75). However, Macklin et al. (2014) provide a slight departure from the general Whiteheadian position, suggesting a conception of societies as 'structured fields of activity' that are concomitantly objectively real and ordered by events occurring within them (2014, p. 76). Macklin et al. explain that from a Whiteheadian perspective an organisation is not a discrete subject of experience since there is no agency. Nonetheless, they argue, it does have 'causal laws which dominate the social environment... and is only efficient through [the actions of] its individual members' (Macklin et al., 2014, p. 76).

Members of organisations can function only 'by reasons of the laws which dominate [it], and the laws only come into being by reason of the analogous characters of the members of the society' (Bracken, cited in Macklin et al., 2014, p. 76). The laws, in this sense, pertain to 'policies', 'procedures' and 'guidelines of an organisation' as realised through the management process. Hence, when an organisation is conceptualised in terms of energy, an event, even as a containment-field, 'progressively shaped and ordered by successive generations of occasions [e.g. managerial learning]', it can be understood in terms of a 'self-referential semantic information system' (Macklin et al., 2014, p. 76). Organisations function best when they are internally cohesive and engaged through a self-organising 'stream of experiences that exhibits a defining essence of becoming' and of growth. It follows that, rather than thinking about organisations through the lens of the standard view (which is the identification of isolated individual structures through externality), the perspective instead should be the 'identification of related personal individuals through internality; they are event fields within which persons-in-communities reside' (Macklin et al., 2014, p. 76).

What emerges from such a conception is a richer vision of the nature of embodiment in organisations than rendered from the metaphysics of Platonic stasis. Organisations construed as societies of occasions of experience form part of an emerging structure of social order. From a Whiteheadian perspective, each actual occasion has intrinsic value since each has some level of experience, each exists as a member of society, and the sense of individuality is not construed as an isolated unit since its developed existence requires essential reference to others, evidently more so for human beings. Though value may be a relative term, 'one can neither be removed from the value of others nor from the value of the whole' (Macklin et al., 2014, p. 78).

In an important way this account echoes Aristotle's notion of the City-State as developed in the *Politics*. Aristotle believed that the state is a natural society. Humans are 'impelled by our very nature' to form the societies of family, village, and state. One's natural end is the good life for all the reasons outlined above and found only in the state. The state is a natural society. In *Book 1 part II* of the *Politics*, Aristotle (2009) says:

> The proof that the state is a creation of nature and prior to the individual is that the individual, when isolated, is not self-sufficing; and therefore he is like a part in relation to the whole. But he who is unable to live in society, or who has no need because he is sufficient for himself, must be either a beast or a god: he is no part of a state. A social instinct is implanted in all men by nature, and yet he who first founded the state was the greatest of benefactors. For man, when perfected, is the best of animals, but, when separated from law and justice, he is the worst of all; since armed injustice is the more dangerous, and he is equipped at birth with arms, meant to be used by intelligence and virtue, which he may use for the worst ends.

The inclusive basis of Aristotle's notion of the City-State resonates profoundly today and is worthy of revival. The account of Process Ethics developed by Macklin et al. (2014) is not aligned to any one specific major normative ethical theory. Yet the kind advocated here and elsewhere is indeed teleological. Henning (2005) advocates the pursuit of beauty for an aesthetic of morality which he describes as a state 'where there is a balance between a harmonious whole and enhanced parts, whose individuality is not sacrificed'. This work, essentially an ethics of creativity, is largely situationist, because an action is morally appropriate when 'it achieves the most beauty possible in the situation taken as a whole' (Henning, 2005, p. 190). In other words, what is right is based on and is relative to the 'beauty achievable against the circumstances and as such is not about abstractive moral laws' (cited in Macklin et al., 2014, p. 78). In one sense, the ethics of creativity defends the Kantian idea of the individual as an end in itself, since individuality is construed so as to require reference to others (Henning, 2005, p. 60).

Following Henning in the context of a process cosmos, individuality does not imply independence. The Whiteheadian 'actual occasion' begins and constitutionally develops by achieved values of the past and completes itself by enacting and internalising its relationship to each past value in the manner of either eliminating some (negative prehension) or by integrating 'them by repeating their felt value intensity (positive prehension)' (Henning, 2005, p. 60). In this way, the individual becomes what it is because it is 'internally and essentially related to other achieved values' (Henning, 2005, p. 60).

Whitehead's unique sense of intrinsic value emerges compositionally, through an axiological triad of self, other, and whole.

> To have intrinsic value is (1) to have incorporated the values of others (concrescence), (2) to subsequently become a (instrumental) value for others (principle of relativity), and (3) thereby to contribute to the value experience of the whole, that is, God. Each of these is 'on a level'. 'No one in any sense precedes the other'. (Quoting Whitehead). This triadic structure not only characterises the meaning of actuality, but also is the stimulus for the conception of morals'. (Henning, 2005, p. 63)

The Whiteheadian 'meaning of actuality is thus characterised by a triad of self, other, and whole'. Henning advances the Whiteheadian idea that each actual entity has 'self-value, is self-important', yet this understanding does not entail (as it often does in moral theory) 'that the individual is the sole locus of value that must be protected at all costs' (2005, p. 63). Most often lost in debates over 'moral considerability is that each individual, *qua* value experience, has value not only for itself, but also for others and for the whole' (2005, p. 63). Self-importance extends beyond the individual to the world or universe we inhabit. In other words, anything that exists has intrinsic value, which is inclusive of instrumental value, and religious value.

We can follow Henning, extending this understanding to the leaders and managers of organisations, to appreciate that they do have a moral responsibility to address what is good for both the actual occasions (individuals) within its organisation and the societies outside them. It means that what is selected from the environment, how it is utilised, the implications of such use, treatment of its employees and the overall effect on environment and external societies both current and future must be taken into consideration and respected. The virtuous character is captured in a more inclusive recognition of the constituent others and environment integral in the process of transformation. Several implications arise for applying this approach to human resource management and the consequent effect on organisational policy.

Consonantly, Nicholas Rescher promulgated the idea that:

> ... the key to moral objectivity lies in the very nature of the moral enterprise. For the reality of it is that morality is a functional enterprise that exists for the sake of an end and purpose: to foster modes of action and interaction that facilitate the realization of human interests and, in particular, that channel people's actions in ways that make people's lives within their communities more beneficial and pleasant. (2008, p. 395)

Rescher's point here resonates with the Aristotelian concepts of *arête* (excellence or virtue), *phronesis* (practical or moral wisdom) and *eudaimonia* (happiness/flourishing) (Hursthouse, 2012, p. 2). Broadly speaking, therefore, organisations do evolve and are inherently changeable. They are not permanent immutable structures. Human beings, actual occasions, have choices and are responsible for the person they become through their choices based on past experiences. In an important sense, humans, the actual occasions, are open-ended in their embodied experiences not measured by one's integument – indeed forming containment-fields of experiences extending beyond the skin by causal influence and extended interaction. Ethics, as it has been described here is dynamic and character-based, pointedly, not limited to the singularly embodied individual. Institutions and organisations are constituted by individuals, actual occasions developing through the processual experience of becoming that no less in practice form containment-fields of activity. Thus the characterisation of a virtue as habituated through a transforming practice should not be conceptually limited to the individual adherent as if one were an isolated unit. It is because individuals form collectives, which by extension participate in a transformative process of interaction and engagement when forming and sustaining the embodiment of organisations and societies, that makes it a sensible objective to extend the application of virtue ethics into a framework of Process Virtue Ethics.

NOTE

1. Whether correctly or not is still unsettled (Kirk, 2010, p. 365).

REFERENCES

Aristotle. (1998). The nicomachean ethics *(J. L. Ackrill and J. O. Urmson, Trans.)*. New York, NY: Oxford University Press.

Aristotle. (2009). Politics (B. Jowett, Trans.). *The Internet Classics Archives*, Book 1, Part II, Retrieved from http://classics.mit.edu/Aristotle/politics.1.one.html

Blair, G. A. (1967). The meaning of energeia and entelecheia in Aristotle. *Journal of International Philosophical Quarterly, 7*(1), 101–117.

Griffin, D. R. (1998). Process philosophy. In E. Craig (Ed.), *Routledge encyclopedia of philosophy*. London: Routledge.

Henning, B. G. (2005). *The ethics of creativity: Beauty morality and nature in a processive cosmos*. Pittsburgh, PA: University of Pittsburgh Press.

Hursthouse, R. (2012). Virtue ethics, "virtue ethics". In E. N. Zalta (Ed.), *The* Stanford encyclopedia of philosophy (Fall, 2013 ed.). Retrieved from http://plato.stanford.edu/archives/fall2013/entries/ethics-virtue/

Kirk, G. S. (2010). *Heraclitus the cosmic fragments: A critical study*. New York, NY: CUP.

Lloyd, G. E. R. (1970). *Early Greek science: Thales to Aristotle*. New York, NY: W.W Norton and Company.

Macklin, R., Mathison, K., & Dibben, M. (2014). Process ethics and business: Applying process thought to enact critiques of mind/body dualism in organizations. *Process Studies, 43*(2), 61–86.

McRae, E. S. (2001). Whitehead's theory of moral experience: Its reconstruction and importance. *The Journal of Speculative Philosophy, 15*(4), 305–320.

Naimo, J. (2009). *The primacy of consciousness: A triple aspect ontology*. Cologne: Lambert Academic Publishing.

Rescher, N. (2008). Moral objectivity. *Social Philosophy & Policy, 25*(1), 393–409.

Rescher, N. (2013). Process philosophy. In R. L. Fastiggi (Ed.), New catholic encyclopedia supplement 2012–13: *Ethics and philosophy*. Detroit: Gale.

Rist, J. M. (2002). *Real ethics: Rethinking the foundations of morality*. New York, NY: CUP.

Seibt, J. (2013). *Process philosophy*. In Stanford encyclopedia of philosophy. Retrieved from http://plato.stanford.edu/entries/process-philosophy/

Shand, J. (1993). *Philosophy and philosophers: An introduction to western philosophy*. London: Penguin Books.

Shields, C. (2016). *The active mind of De Anima iii 5*. In Stanford encyclopedia of philosophy. Retrieved from http://plato.stanford.edu/entries/aristotle-psychology/active-mind.html

Studtmann, P. (2007). *Aristotle's categories*. In Stanford encyclopedia of philosophy. Retrieved from http://plato.stanford.edu/archives/fall2007/entries/aristotle-categories/

Studtmann, P. (2008). *The foundations of Aristotle's categorical scheme*. Milwaukee, WI: Marquette University Press.

Weekes, A. (2009). Whitehead's unique approach to the topic of consciousness. In M. Weber & A. Weekes (Eds.), *Process approaches to consciousness in psychology, neuroscience, and philosophy of mind* (pp. 137–174). New York, NY: Suny Press.

Whitehead, A. N. (1978). The primary feelings. (Part III the theory of prehension) In D. R. Griffin & D. W. Sherburne (Eds.), *Process and reality* (Corrected ed.). New York, NY: The Free Press.

MODEL LITIGANT GUIDELINES – CURRENT AND EMERGING ISSUES

Ian H. Gibson

ABSTRACT

Since the mid-1990s most Australian jurisdictions have adopted, either through subordinate legislation or through internal government directives, rules regarding how government agencies should behave when participating in litigation. While these rules met an immediate need associated with the outsourcing of legal work to private law firms, this chapter argues that they are unsuited for enduring use: they lack a proper rationale, they are poorly worded and uncertain in their meaning; it is unclear whether and how courts should enforce them, and they have not been reviewed to take account of the more recent developments in civil procedure.

Keywords: Model litigant; governments as litigants; acting fairly in litigation; Australian governments as litigants

Contemporary Issues in Applied and Professional Ethics
Research in Ethical Issues in Organizations, Volume 15, 61–83
Copyright © 2016 by Emerald Group Publishing Limited
ISSN: 1529-2096/doi:10.1108/S1529-209620160000015004

INTRODUCTION

The purpose of this chapter is to show what can happen when a poorly considered code of conduct becomes entrenched by usage and law without (1) having a coherent and defensible rationale for what it does and does not cover; (2) being carefully drafted; and (3) periodic re-examination in the context of more recent obligations.

BACKGROUND AND CONTEXT

The Term 'Model Litigant'

Before the mid-1990s, there had been some judicial dicta drawing attention to the courts' expectations that governments and public bodies would conduct themselves fairly (*Kenny v South Australia*, 1986; *Melbourne Steamship v Moorehead*, 1912; *P&C Cantarella v Egg Marketing Board*, 1973)[1] both generally and as litigants, but the specific term 'model litigant' did not enter the judicial lexicon until 1996 and 1997 (*Hughes Aircraft Systems International v Airservices Australia*, 1997; *SCI Operations Pty Ltd v Commonwealth*, 1996; *Yong Jun Qin v Minister for Immigration and Multicultural Affairs*, 1997). In 1999, the Australian Law Reform Commission reported that as of that time 'several judges and barristers professed not to have heard the term "model litigant" or seen the text of the rules' (ALRC, 1999, p. 3.171). The ALRC also reported that the Australian Consumer and Competition Commission would still have preferred the term 'responsible litigant' to 'model litigant' (ALRC, 1999, p. 3.140). The earlier judicial references to fair play and good behaviour had come in contexts where the Crown's conduct was manifestly unacceptable and an adverse decision inevitable: the comments were therefore more in the nature of surprise and admonition than a reason for the outcome. Nonetheless, the Commonwealth also set out the obligations on government litigants in an instruction incorporated into the Commonwealth Policy for Handling Monetary Claims approved by the Attorney-General for the purposes of Regulation 9 of the Financial Management and Accountability Regulations (Leader, 1998).[2] It did so in the context of changes in how legal services were provided to the Commonwealth Government, specifically establishing the Australian Government Solicitor as a statutory authority (National Commission of Audit, 1996, p. s 3.4, recommendation 3.5) and providing reassurance that private law firms to which the provision of legal services was now to be outsourced would be bound by the same principles as applied to the Australian Government Solicitor (Cth Parliamentary Debates, 20 November 1997, p. 10968).

Adoption in Other Australian Jurisdictions

The Commonwealth Attorney-General issued Legal Services Directions under section 55ZF of the now-amended *Judiciary Act 1903* in September 1999 and, following the Commonwealth's initiative, the Attorney-General of Victoria introduced guidelines for that State in 2001. It seems that there may have been model litigant principles in Queensland as early as 2003 (cf. *Lamb v Department of Natural Resources and Mines*, 2005, p. 27). In 2005, the Commonwealth Attorney-General issued new Legal Services Directions and repealed the 1999 Directions. In New South Wales, a Model Litigant Policy was endorsed by Cabinet for adoption by all government agencies on 8 July 2008 (Robinson, 2009). In the Australian Capital Territory, the Attorney-General issued the guidelines in the form of an instrument.[3] At the direction of Cabinet, Queensland issued revised model litigant principles in October 2010. In South Australia, the Crown Solicitor in Legal Bulletin No. 2 has set out the duties of the Crown as a model litigant. Victoria reissued its guidelines in 2011. For convenience this chapter uses the term 'model litigant guidelines' to refer to all forms in which the standards are documented, unless it is referring to rules or policies specific to a jurisdiction. (The Commonwealth and various State rules and principles are collected under a separate heading "Australian Commonwealth and State Model Litigant Rules, Policies et cetera" in the references to this paper.)

Usage

Some research for the purposes of this chapter was done within the Victorian Government Solicitor's Office. While the results are only indicative, they suggest that across all Australian courts in the five-year period February 2010 to February 2015 the term 'model litigant' had been used in between 411 and 480 different cases, compared with about 300 cases in the preceding five-year period. Sampling of these instances suggests that the term 'model litigant' in some form is being referred to in State or territory jurisdictions in about twice as many cases as in the Commonwealth

jurisdiction, that the Crown and other government agencies are more or
less equally represented, and that the guidelines are raised by the government party about 20% of the time, and by the non-government party and
the court or tribunal each about 40% of the time. At the very least, it is
clear that there is a growing awareness of the model litigant guidelines in
the courts and amongst litigators both within and against government.

WHY HAVE MODEL LITIGANT GUIDELINES?

The Rationale for Expecting Governments to Be Model Litigants

The Productivity Commission advances a number of policy reasons for
expecting governments to act as model litigants:

— due to the inherent power of government;
— because the proper role of government is to act in the public interest (as
  it has no legitimate private interest);
— due to the large quantity of resources at governments' disposal;
— because governments also derive power from their frequent player
  status; and
— because governments can be important role models in setting bench-
  marks for behaviour and conduct across the system (Productivity
  Commission, 2014, pp. 430–431).

There are two lines of justification here: that based on a disparity of
power and that based on the duty to act in the public interest and promote
the public good. Another way of describing this is to say that one justification rests on the characteristics that a government has as a litigant, while the
other justification depends on the inherent characteristics of a government.

Justifications based on the characteristics of a government as a litigant
have several difficulties. First, they are ultimately empirical, and encounter
the problem that other litigants can be shown to have the same characteristics. For example, if the justification for the heightened expectation of governments is the imbalance of power between the government and the
citizen, why is the government expected to be a model litigant when
opposed by very rich corporations, even multi-national ones? And why is
there no consideration given in the formulation of policy to the other ways
in which the balance has been addressed or even redressed, including contingency fees, class actions and litigation funders? A similar point could be

made about the government as a frequent player. Many institutions (such as banks, insurance companies, debt collectors and property developers) are equally frequent players, and one of the espoused reasons for engaging solicitors and counsel is that they have frequent player status, even if their clients do not. (There is hardly any reference to these empirical considerations in the academic literature,[4] and none that I have found refers to contingency fees and litigation funding.)

Second, the arguments based on the disparity of resources, power or experience are hard to sustain, because they would suggest that governments need not be required to be model litigants when there is no disparity, or when the disparity is in the opposite direction. The Productivity Commission discussed whether the model litigant guidelines should be extended to well-resourced private litigants, and concluded that

> [t]he Commission's view is that the practical difficulty in establishing whether there is a situation of 'resource disparity', coupled with the special role of government, mean that model litigant rules should not be extended to private parties. (Productivity Commission, 2014, p. 442)

Of the two lines of justification referred to earlier, the better is that based on the duty to act in the public interest and promote the public good, for example, by respecting the rule of law, observing the spirit as well as the letter of the law, treating all who come within its jurisdiction with dignity and respect, being fair, honest and even-handed in dealing with their subjects and so on. The State is a 'model' litigant in acting in this way because it always does so in practice, while other litigants may or may not do so in practice, regardless of whether it might be considered desirable that they do so. This justification is consistent with some cases where the position of the courts has not found its way into the text of the guidelines, for example, the positive duty on the Crown to assist the Courts (as enunciated in *P&C Cantaella Pty Ltd* and *Mahenthiarasa* (No. 2), 2008: in both these cases the court said that when a government was party to a matter before the court, the government had a duty to assist the court to ascertain the law, and to provide appropriate assistance to the court to do so) and the duty of public bodies to administer the law as determined by the courts (*Commissioner of Taxation v Indooroopilly Children Services*, 2007). This justification is also consistent with the approach taken by the English courts.[5]

While a rationale based on the inherent status of the Crown is compelling, however, as already noted it naturally invites the question why all those who have business before our courts should not also be expected to respect the rule of law, treat other litigants with dignity and respect and be fair and honest in their dealings with each other. And as the model litigant guidelines explicitly impose duties on lawyers acting for the government as well as on their clients, the question can be framed even more strongly by asking why lawyers acting for litigants other than the government should not be expected to observe the same standards as those acting for the government.

For as long as the rationale for the guidelines leads to them applying uniquely to governments, it seems to locate that rationale in the domain of good government and public administration, and for as long as that is so it is not obvious that the courts should take on a broad responsibility for determining what conduct is in the public interest or promotes the public good, especially in view of the fine balance of considerations referred to by Appleby (2014). For the same reason, if the justification for the model litigant principle is what is properly expected of the Crown because of its inherent nature, then a better approach may be to have guidelines that include only those matters that do not also apply to all litigants (e.g. as found in the common law and in the Civil Procedure Act). The then Australian Government Solicitor, Dale Boucher, is reported to have said in 1996 that the 1995 Commonwealth guidelines (Attorney-General's Department, 1995) were intended to be an ethical code of aspirational intentions, not a strict code of conduct with sanctions for non-compliance (Cameron & Taylor-Sands, 2007, p. 507).[6]

In addition, as matters of public policy, or public good, they would more appropriately be administered by the Parliament, the Auditor-General, the Ombudsman and other similar institutions than by the courts. The larger point here is that a collection of admonitions assembled independently of any evident rationale is a poor foundation for robust and enduring public administration.

The Rationale(s) in the Context of Other Considerations

If there is some uncertainty about the rationale for the model litigant expectation, there is even more fluidity in the recognition of the competing factors that are relevant to how a government participates in litigation. Many of the early statements of the principle emphasized that the government must be 'fair but firm', and Appleby, for instance, points to the countervailing policy considerations, such as the need to protect public money. (The fact that a government is a disinterested party does not mean that it does not have something akin to a fiduciary duty in relation to public funds.[7]) Although the Crown does not have a legitimate private interest, this does not mean that the *public* interest is always best satisfied by a government accepting all claims brought against it: the ALRC said in 1999: 'The model litigant rules require fair play, but not acquiescence, and government lawyers must press hard to win points and defend decisions they believe to be correct' (ALRC, 1999, para 3.139). This is clear in the guidelines themselves.[8]

The fact that what is 'fair and firm' will always involve an eventual course of action that is the result of weighing and balancing a range of considerations again makes it hard to set out the guidelines in ways that determine what is right in a particular matter, as distinct from pointing out some guiding principles.

The Issue of Enforcement

How to achieve compliance with the model litigant guidelines has always been an issue. It was discussed by the Australian Law Reform Commission in 1999 (ALRC, 1999) and by Chami in a recent article (2010, p. 47). At the Commonwealth level, the model litigant rules do have the force of law, but are enforceable only by the Attorney-General. There is debate about whether the courts could apply and enforce these or other model litigant precepts based on the common law or the attributes of a Chapter III court. At present, the Victorian Model Litigant Guidelines are a statement of government policy and obviously cannot be enforced by the courts at the initiative of a party to litigation. At the same time, they are binding on public servants as a matter of public law or employment law and on private law firms acting for the government as a matter of contract law.

There is no agreed position on whether section 55ZG of the *Judiciary Act 1903* prevents courts from considering compliance with Appendix B of the Legal Services Directions in awarding costs in litigation to which the Commonwealth or one of its agencies is a party,[9] but in any case costs lie within the scope of judicial discretion where fairness is a consideration (*Fair Work Ombudsman v Quincolli Pty Ltd*, 2011[10]).

Following the Australian Productivity Commission's (2014) report,[11] the Administrative Law and Human Rights Section of the Law Institute of Victoria has been considering whether to advocate for 'better' enforcement of the Victorian Model Litigant Guidelines. In a submission to the Productivity Commission Maurice Blackburn Pty Ltd said:

> It is recommended that the model litigant guidelines be reinforced in a manner that gives opponents standing to complain that the guidelines have not been complied with.

This could be done by an amendment to the Judiciary Act that imposes a sanction on a government agency if a court finds non-compliance. (Maurice Blackburn Pty Ltd, 2013)

In a submission to the Royal Commission into Institutional Responses to Child Sexual Abuse, Janet Loughman, Principal Solicitor, Women's Legal Services NSW, said:

There needs to be a positive duty on government agencies and their legal advisors/representatives to turn their minds to whether action taken or advice given is in accordance with the Model Litigant Policy. Consideration should be given to requiring a declaration similar to that required by an expert witness pursuant to r 31.23(3) of the UCPR, suitable for the provision of advice. (Loughman, 2014, para 48)

Later she recommended

that consideration be given to a mechanism or mechanisms to strengthen the status of the Model Litigant Policy. For example, this could be through legislation, the Australian Solicitor Conduct Rules, or Barristers Rules. (Loughman, 2014, para 53)

At present, however, this would not appear to be the majority view. The conclusion of nearly everyone who looks at this[12] tends to be the same:

(1) The courts will continue to do what they have always done, which is to factor the heightened expectations of governments into the exercise of their discretions in relation to costs and procedural matters;
(2) There should be clear avenues of complaint to administrative bodies;
(3) The guidelines should not become an independent basis for sanctions against governments or their lawyers.

It is true, as is noted in the Productivity Commission report, that there is some disagreement about whether responsibility for enforcement should lie with the courts or the government, although to some extent this can be answered if the courts are seen as enforcing a general obligation of fairness and fair play, while the government is responsible for compliance with the more detailed obligations. This is precisely reflected in current practice: even though only the Commonwealth can enforce the text of the guidelines as set out in the Legal Service Directions, that text has obviously not displaced the obligations already recognized by the courts and applied by them in various ways.

Consistent with treating the detailed model litigant obligations as administrative rather than legal requirements, the Productivity Commission recommends establishing a 'formal avenue of complaint' to government ombudsmen. It is not clear, however, what such formal avenues of complaint might be, or whether they need to be different from the avenues of complaint to the various ombudsmen that are at present available.

The Victorian Ombudsman already has the necessary jurisdiction insofar as the administrative action involves the conduct of litigation by a government department or agency (that is, the government client), although there is no jurisdiction in relation to a person acting as legal adviser to the Crown or an authority or as counsel for the Crown or an authority (*Ombudsman Act 1973* (Vic) s 2(1) and sch. 2).[13] The Victorian Ombudsman in her 2014 Report[14] stresses 'fairness' as being the strand running through so much of her work. This is closely aligned to the paramount consideration in the model litigant principle.

It would seem that for the time being the policy, although not unchallenged, will be to strengthen the administrative and political remedies, rather than the curial ones. This is justified by Gabrielle Appleby in this way:

> [T]he courts' powers should be and are limited by a number of operational and conceptual hurdles. First, the courts operate best when they enforce the model litigant obligation in cases of extreme unfairness to an individual. In other cases, the courts' intervention carries with it the danger of substituting the government's view on whether a particular course of action was fair with a judge's view. Sometimes this will be necessary, but where the competing underlying values are delicately balanced, the intervention is inappropriate and inconsistent with the judicial function. These are questions of policy that ought to be resolved by government officers, or potentially by the Attorney-General issuing a general direction as to how such matters must be resolved in the future. (2014, p. 122)

If, however, the courts in which the government or its agency appears were to be given responsibility for enforcing the model litigant guidelines, a possible approach that seems not to have been canvassed so far is for the guidelines to be enforced against the State in the same way that the overarching obligations are enforced under Part 2.4 of the Victorian *Civil Procedure Act 2010*,[15] and such an approach would be consistent with the type of obligations involved and their purpose.

THE WORDING OF THE MODEL LITIGANT GUIDELINES

Even if there is an argument that there should be model litigant guidelines, the guidelines need to be properly expressed, in terms which give a proper account of their grounds. Here are four examples of how the current wording is unhelpful.

Technical Defences, Points and Arguments

The first issue concerns a requirement relating to technical defences or arguments. The requirement in the Commonwealth's rules, and in the NSW principles, is that those governments act honestly and fairly by 'not relying on technical defences unless the [relevant government or its] agency's interests would be prejudiced by the failure to comply with a particular requirement' (NSW Model Litigant Policy: para 3.2.g). The Victorian obligation now is that its Departments and agencies 'do not rely on technical arguments unless the State's or the agency's interests would be prejudiced by the failure to comply with a particular requirement' (Vic, Model Litigant Guidelines: para 2.i). In both cases, the obligation suggests that a technical defence or argument must depend on a failure to comply with a requirement — in other words, a defence based on a procedural failure. Instances of where courts have referred to technical defences have included:

— Defences to the effect that there were flaws in the various securities, in the notices of default and demand, and in the notices of entry into possession (*Elders Ltd v Swinbank*, 1999),
— Formal proofs of appointment of health inspectors (*Yamasa Seafood Australia Pty Ltd v Watkins*, 2000),
— The compliance of breathalyser machines with statutory requirements (*Impagnatiello v Campbell*, 2003) and
— The requirement of the Supreme Court Rules in the Northern Territory that 'a party shall, in a pleading subsequent to a statement of claim, plead specifically a fact or matter which the party alleges makes a claim ... not maintainable' (*Buric v Transfield PGM Pty Ltd*, 1992).

In the Royal Commission into Institutional Responses to Child Sexual Abuse there was some debate about what constituted a 'technical point', a different term again, and one which does not appear in the rules, policies or guidelines of any jurisdiction. Counsel assisting, Mr David Lloyd QC, asked a question that referred to 'a technical point which shouldn't have been taken if one was adhering to the model litigant policy' (Royal Commission: Institutional Responses to Child Sexual Abuse, 2014, Transcript 23 October 2014: 10191). Ms Allison, a solicitor from the NSW Crown Solicitor's Office, did not resist the proposition that, in an action where two plaintiffs had been identified in the pleadings, it was a technical point to require the front page of the statement of claim to be amended to name the second plaintiff (Transcript 23 October 2014: 10190–10192). She did not agree, however, that it was a technical point to seek to have the particulars provided by 15 different plaintiffs contained in 15 separate pleadings rather than in a single pleading, which is what was ordered by the judicial registrar (Transcript 23 October 2014: 10163). Other matters suggested as being technical points included raising a limitations defence and putting the plaintiffs strictly to their proofs (Transcript 23 October 2014: 10192) The considerable attention given in the hearings of the Royal Commission to whether conducting litigation in this way (whether characterized as relying on technical defences, technical arguments or technical points) illustrates how unsuited the guidelines are for construction as if they were drafted as legislation or rules of court.

A Requirement to Act Fairly

The Commonwealth's model litigant rules say, in paragraph 2:

> The obligation to act as a model litigant requires that the Commonwealth and its agencies act honestly and fairly in handling claims and litigation brought by or against the Commonwealth or an agency by:...

The ACT's model litigant guidelines are similar. By contrast, the Victorian Model Litigant Guidelines state:

> 2. The obligation requires that the State of Victoria, its Departments and agencies:
>
> (a) act fairly in handling claims and litigation brought by or against the State or an agency;
>
> (b) ...

The approach adopted by the Commonwealth and the ACT is to set out in sub-paragraphs the particular ways in which those governments will act honestly and fairly. As a matter of statutory interpretation it seems reasonable to conclude that those governments have sufficiently complied with the requirement to act honestly and fairly if they have complied with the various requirements set out in the paragraphs that follow.

By contrast, the Victorian approach makes the requirement to act fairly an independent obligation in its own right, meaning that the government and its agencies can fail to meet the requirements of the obligations even if they adhere scrupulously to the requirements of all the other obligations. If there are to be detailed written guidelines, they should at least have a common position on whether the obligation to act fairly exists fully in its own right or whether it is sufficiently discharged by adherence to some other specified obligations.

The Meaning of 'Acting Fairly'

In giving evidence to the Royal Commission, the New South Wales Crown Solicitor, Mr Ian Knight, struggled to explain what it meant to act fairly. He was asked by counsel assisting about the content of the word 'fair' in the NSW Model Litigant Policy (even though it is not used in the policy) and responded, 'it doesn't actually explain what "fairly" means. In fact, there are very few resources which actually tell you what "fairly" means ... "Fairly" doesn't mean sympathetically, it doesn't mean compassionately' (Royal Commission: Institutional Responses to Child Sexual Abuse, 2014, Transcript 30 October 2014: 10643–10645). A little later he said,

> The only guidance I've really seen which looks at this is Chief Justice Griffith in Melbourne Steamships, [who] I think, said, 'Yes, fairness is old-fashioned traditional fair play, almost instinctive'. Now, that's probably a good starting point.

The issue of fairness was discussed especially in *Australian Securities and Investments Commission v Hellicar* (2012), and the difficulty with that term, and especially in distinguishing procedural fairness from substantive fairness, is discussed by Le Mire in her article (2014). However, it is possible that the focus on 'fairness' is misleading. As Mr Knight says, the term used by Griffiths CJ was 'fair play',[16] and the expression in the model litigant guidelines is 'act fairly'. In both cases, the words 'fair' or 'fairly' are used to describe actions or conduct; in other words, the focus is not on the result, but on how it is achieved. Indeed, 'fair play' suggests a reference to sport and to not cheating. Justice McClelland in the passage just quoted and many other times in relation to the Bethcar matter talked about 'litigating with your cards on the table' and 'not keep[ing] a card up your sleeve'. Farwell LJ put it bluntly in *In re Tyler*:

> As I understand the principle laid down in the cases to which my Lord has referred, it comes to this, that the officer of the Court is bound to be even more straightforward and honest than the ordinary person in the affairs of every-day life. It would be insufferable for this Court to have it said of it that it has been guilty by its officer of a dirty trick. (In re Tyler, 1907, p. 871)

Much of what the courts, and maybe the guidelines too, are saying could be summarized in the proposition that governments may play hard, but must play fair.

Another raised in Mr Knight's evidence in the Bethcar case study was that of compassion. He said, 'My officers are constrained that they can't provide legal services having regard to compassion or having regard to disadvantage of people. They are matters that the client should be looking at'. While this is a clear claim that compassion and a regard for disadvantage is not part of a lawyer's role, it also suggests that such matters should be considered by the client department, although Mr Knight did not say whether they should do so as model litigants or merely as a matter of good government.

In *Pinot Nominees Pty Ltd v Commissioner of Taxation* (2009), Siopis J was referring to the client when he said,

> [A]lthough compassionate considerations may from time to time, as a practical matter, weigh with the Commissioner in determining how to deal with the taxation liability of a taxpayer, the question of whether the Commissioner has acted with compassion, is not, without more, a relevant factor in considering whether he has acted unreasonably or failed to act as a model litigant in the conduct and settlement of litigation. Appendix B to the Legal Services Directions 2005 (Cth) which describes the Commonwealth's obligation to act as a model litigant, makes no reference to the Commonwealth having to have regard to compassionate considerations which may affect the other party to the litigation. (Pinot Nominees Pty Ltd: 41)

Going beyond the Law and Ethics

An example which demonstrates how immature the guidelines are as anything more than an indication of a broad aspiration is to be found in one of the notes to the guidelines. It has to be assumed that the notes form part of the guidelines and rules – there is certainly nothing to suggest that they do not. Note 3 in the Commonwealth's rules states: 'The obligation to act as a model litigant may require more than merely acting honestly and in accordance with the law and court rules. It also goes beyond the requirement for lawyers to act in accordance with their ethical obligations'. Note 8 to the Victorian model litigant guidelines is identical. By contrast, the NSW policy state:

> The obligation to act as a model litigant requires more than merely acting honestly and in accordance with the law and court rules. It also goes beyond the requirement for lawyers to act in accordance with their ethical obligations. Essentially it requires that the State and its agencies act with complete propriety, fairly and in accordance with the highest professional standards. (NSW, Model Litigant Policy: para 3.1).[17]

The South Australian Crown Solicitor's position is:

> The obligation to act as a model litigant may often require more than merely acting honestly and in accordance with the law and court rules. It also goes beyond the requirement for lawyers to act in accordance with their ethical obligations and the Rules of Professional Conduct and Practice. It requires that the Crown act with complete propriety, fairly and in accordance with the highest professional standards. (SA: 'The Duties of the Crown as Model Litigant': 2)

What do these paragraphs mean? As we have already seen, the requirement to act 'in accordance with the law and the court rules' includes the common law requirement to act fairly when a party to litigation. In addition, the Commonwealth's model litigant rules are themselves in subordinate legislation, and therefore part of the law of the Commonwealth. In Victoria the overarching obligations have the force of law. The note says that the obligation to act as a model litigant *may* require more than 'merely' acting honestly and adhering to the law relating to civil procedure and conduct as a model litigant. However, the second sentence in this note does not contain the word 'may', but rather sets out a positive obligation: 'The obligation to act as a model litigant ... goes beyond the requirement for lawyers to act in accordance with their ethical obligations'. It is difficult to know what to make of this requirement. To begin with, in the Commonwealth context[18] it contains a logical impossibility, since every effort to comply with the note by doing more than merely acting in accordance with the law will necessarily represent compliance with the law.[19]

In addition, however, these various statements require lawyers not only to act honestly and adhere to the rules of court, but also to go beyond the requirements of their ethical obligations. Once lawyers have exhausted the requirements of law and ethics, to what else might they refer as a basis for establishing the content of this obligation?

New South Wales attempts to answer this question by implying, at least in the juxtaposition of the third sentence in relation to the two that precede it, that there is a requirement of complete propriety, fairness and the highest professional standards that cannot be located in the law, the rules of court and ethics. However, the New South Wales approach seems merely to push the question back a step. If lawyers cannot identify what constitutes propriety, fairness and professional standards through what is required by law, the rules of court and ethics, where else should they look?

It is interesting to see how the South Australian Crown Solicitor has stated that the obligation goes beyond the requirement for lawyers to act in accordance with their ethical obligations *and* the Rules of Professional Conduct and Practice. In doing so, he has made it clear that the term 'ethical obligations' is not to be interpreted as referring to the rules of professional conduct. We seem, then, to be left with a positive obligation on those acting for government to pursue what is firm and fair beyond what can be established as fair and firm by reference to the law, to the rules of court, to rules of professional conduct and to ethics.

A possible approach to how this might be achieved was suggested by Mr David Lloyd QC, counsel assisting the Royal Commission. He asked,

> [i]sn't one of the things the model litigant policy is designed to do, in your understanding, to introduce a human or moral dimension to the decisions that the state takes in relation to plaintiffs just like these ones? (Royal Commission: Institutional Responses to Child Sexual Abuse, 2014, Transcript 30 October 2014: 10584)

However, an obligation to introduce a human or moral dimension seems to take us into strange territory, and especially strange given that it is not a requirement that government lawyers act compassionately and that it is a requirement that government act consistently in handling claims and litigation. There is a real challenge for good government and good public administration, and for a reasonable level of predictability and certainty in the lawyer-client relationship, if lawyers are positively required to act in ways not referable to law, rules and ethics, especially when the wording of the obligation seems to be imposed on lawyers independently of (and therefore presumably independently of the instructions, wishes and obligations of) their clients.

As a rhetorical flourish this requirement has clearly found favour across most Australian jurisdictions, but as a statement of legal obligation it appears most ill-considered; and yet the Chair of the Royal Commission asked a lawyer within the Crown Solicitor's Office (Transcript 23 October 2014: 10180):

Q. The model litigant obligation extends beyond merely acting honestly, doesn't it?

A. I'm not sure, your Honour.

Q. Have you looked at −

A. Yes, I have.

Q. It goes beyond acting in accordance with the law and the court rules, doesn't it?

A. I might need to be taken to that, your Honour. I'm not sure.

Q. And it goes beyond any requirement for lawyers to act in accordance with their ethical obligations, doesn't it?

A. I'm not sure, your Honour.

Q. And, indeed, do you know this, that it requires complete propriety, fairly and in accordance with the highest professional standards?

A. Yes.

Nonetheless, my own view is that the model litigant guidelines are best regarded as a legal obligation: in the case of the Commonwealth because they are subordinate legislation; in other States because they are a decision of the Cabinet and binding on Ministers and other Crown servants, and because lawyers in private practice are required to adhere to them by the contract with the government through which they are engaged.

ARE GUIDELINES STILL NEEDED?

While there has been considerable discussion, including in judgments, speeches and academic articles, about the reasons why governments should have high expectations placed on them as litigants, no reasons are offered as to why government should seek to set out those expectations in writing.

The current guidelines began as another instance of governments developing policies and guidelines about how their officers and agencies should undertake public administration, and understandably so. As noted earlier, the then Australian Government Solicitor, Dale Boucher, is reported to have said in 1996 that the 1995 Commonwealth guidelines were intended to be an ethical code of aspirational intentions, not a strict code of conduct with sanctions for non-compliance (Cameron and Taylor-Sands, 2007, p. 507).

Since then there have been considerable attempts in other ways as well to change the culture and practice of litigation. Across Australia this has happened notably through the evolution of case management (Barker, 2009; Croft, 2010a, 2010b; Warren, 2014). In various jurisdictions, there has been new legislation relating to civil procedure, and notably in Victoria the *Civil Procedure Act 2010* contains overarching principles binding all parties to civil litigation.

As the Productivity Commission has put it:

> While courts traditionally allowed parties free rein to run a dispute, this approach is giving way to one in which judges and courts exercise greater control to ensure that resources are used efficiently and proportionately. More active judicial case management is part of this cultural change (chapter 11).
>
> A related set of initiatives seek to directly influence behaviour by placing duties and obligations on parties and their representatives. In addition to promoting more efficient dispute resolution and a less adversarial culture, taming overly adversarial behaviour can reduce the extent to which resource disparities between parties affect the outcome of a dispute. (Productivity Commission, 2014, p. 420)

Cameron and Taylor-Sands have gone a step further in suggesting that reinforcing the themes in the Model Litigant Rules could create an informal 'reform partnership' between courts and government litigants, enhancing the prospects for the desired change in litigation culture (2007, p. 521).

At least some of the matters addressed by the guidelines are now also dealt with through these other laws and mechanisms. An analysis of the areas of overlap and difference between the overarching obligations in the Civil Procedure Act reveals that the matters that are covered in the guidelines but not by the overarching obligations relate to internal government administration rather than to the conduct of the parties in the litigation itself.[20]

At the same time, as La Mire has pointed out, '[t]he claim of unfairness may even be asserted for tactical reasons in the cut and thrust of litigation' (2014, p. 470). It might be added that such claims are even more easily asserted when they can be referenced to particular text in the guidelines, especially where the text is relied on independently of a consideration of what is fair but firm in the context of that particular matter. This can be seen vividly in the consideration of the *Bethcar* litigation by the Royal Commission into Institutional Responses to Child Sexual Abuse.

If the question can be asked, 'In a world of active case management and the overarching obligations, is there any work left for the model litigant guidelines to do'?, the converse question can also be asked: In a world in which all litigants are required to co-operate with the courts in the conduct of litigation and to observe the overarching obligations, why should any principles applicable to government litigants not apply to *all* litigants? In *Priest v NSW*, Johnson J pointed to this very question:

> In a sense, s. 56 [of the *Civil Procedure Act 2005* (NSW)] has the result that every litigant in civil proceedings in this Court is now a model litigant. (*Priest v NSW*, 2007, 34t).

In this context, it is also relevant to note that courts are now seeing the judicial system as a public resource, and a publicly funded resource, that should and must be available to parties for the resolution of disputes, but need not therefore be infinitely available regardless of the cost to the state and to litigants in other matters. This reasoning makes all litigants accountable for their use of a limited public resource (Barker, 2009; *Haset Sali v SPC Limited*, 1993).

Brian Mason in an article in the *Law Institute Journal* in September 2014 (Mason, 2014) also referred to the overlap between the overarching obligations and the model litigant guidelines. He argued that the courts would now apply even higher standards to governments; he referred to the guidelines as being 'supercharged'. It would certainly appear that we are nearing something of a choice point: either to assume the detailed articulation and codification of the government's undisputed obligations has done its work, or to impose on governments and their lawyers requirements that are stricter than what is required of all other litigants.

CONCLUSION

The growing reference to the model litigant principles in and by courts, and by government commissions and academic commentators, means that they are of present importance and need to be more closely considered.

In fact, however, before the mid-1990s the courts had developed an adequate and robust basis for imposing high standards on government as a litigant, and the courts have continued to apply those standards without needing to have recourse to the ways in which governments have subsequently chosen to detail for themselves what those standards may mean in practice.

Given the more recent introduction of overarching obligations in the Civil Procedure Act of Victoria, and related obligations in NSW and Queensland (though not the Commonwealth) and the development of case management by the courts, it has to be asked whether this attempt at codification serves any useful ongoing purpose. If it does, and certainly if the guidelines were to be accorded any more status than they have now, the reason for them needs to be properly considered, and they should then be drafted afresh.

NOTES

1. The full citation of each case referred to is in the references.

2. It has not been possible to establish the precise relationship (both in time and in content) between the Legal Practice Guidelines and the Policy for Handling Monetary Claims as the latter seems to be unavailable.

3. Law Officer (Model Litigant) Guidelines 2010 (ACT).

4. See, however, Cameron and Taylor-Sands (2007, p. 506): 'Government litigants can be 'out-resourced' in court by opponents who are large corporate litigants with significant commercial interests at stake. Class actions also have the capacity to blur the lines between repeat players and one-shotters and to neutralize asymmetries between well-resourced defendants and individual claimants who are members of a class. It is also possible for individuals who litigant against the government to hire specialist lawyers or law firms who are so experienced that they fit into the repeat player category and change the one-shotter status of their clients'.

5. 'But Baron Atkyns was strongly of the opinion, that the party ought in this case to be relieved against the King, because the King is the fountain and head of justice and equity; and it shall not be presumed, that he will be defective in either. And it would derogate from the King's honour to imagine, that what is equity against a common person, should not be equity against him' (*Pawlett v The Attorney-General*, 1635, p. 552); '[T]he defendants, being an emanation of the Crown, which is the source and fountain of justice, are in my opinion bound to maintain the highest standards of probity and fair dealing, comparable to those which the courts, which derive their authority from the same source and fountain, impose on the officers under their control ...' (*Sebel Products Ltd v Commissioners of Customs and Excise*, 1949, p. 413).

6. Neither Cameron and Taylor-Sands nor the current author have been able locate Boucher (1996).

7. Cf. submission by the State of Victoria in *Slaveski v State of Victoria* (2013) that '[t]he State is a model litigant and, as such, has responsibilities to the State of Victoria'. Under s 44(1) of the *Financial Management and*

Accountability Act 1997 (Cth), a Chief Executive must manage the affairs of the Agency in a way that promotes proper use of the Commonwealth resources for which the Chief Executive is responsible, 'proper use' being defined in sub-section (3) to mean 'efficient, effective, economical and ethical use that is not inconsistent with the policies of the Commonwealth'. Similarly, under s 13 of the *Public Administration Act 2004* (Vic) a Department Head is responsible to the public service body Minister or Ministers for the general conduct and the effective, efficient and economical management of the functions and activities of the Department and any Administrative Office existing in relation to the Department, and under s 14(1) an Administrative Office Head has the same responsibilities in relation to their Administrative Office.

8. Cth. Legal Services Directions para 2, note 4: The obligation does not pre-vent the Commonwealth and its agencies from acting firmly and properly to protect their interests. It does not therefore preclude all legitimate steps being taken to pur-sue claims by the Commonwealth and its agencies and testing or defending claims against them.

9. Consideration of compliance possible: *Australian Competition and Consumer Commission v ANZ Banking Group Limited (No. 2)* (2010), *Nelipa v Robertson* (2009), *Re Brown v Comcare* (2011). Consideration of compliance not possible: *Australian Competition & Consumer Commission v Leahy Petroleum Pty Ltd* (2007).

10. Appleby says, 'While section 55ZG limits the enforceability of the model liti-gant rules articulated in the Legal Services Directions, it is silent in relation to the courts enforcing common law obligations that rest on government officers and agencies in the conduct of litigation' (Appleby, 2014, p. 113).

11. Chapter 12 of the report is concerned with the duties on parties, and in part 12.2 of that chapter the topic 'Model litigant rules to address power imbalances' is discussed.

12. Including Appleby (2014), Chami (2010), the Productivity Commission, and those commenting to the Administrative Law and Human Rights Section of the Law Institute of Victoria.

13. It is not clear whether or in what circumstances the Ombudsman's jurisdic-tion should be considered to extend to in-house lawyers in departments and agencies.

14. See for example 'Fairness is at the heart of the role of VO and a key consid-eration in looking at complaints we receive. We not only look at whether an agency has acted lawfully and in accordance with its policies and procedures, but also whether its actions were fair and reasonable in the circumstances' (Victorian Ombudsman, 2014, p. 18).

15. Largely through the payment of the costs of the non-State litigant or of a third party, and through financial compensation – see s 29.

16. As did Finn J in *Hughes Aircraft Systems*.

17. The document has no date, author or other provenance. The Ministry of Justice website states, 'The Model Litigant Policy was approved for adoption by all government agencies on 8 July 2008', but does not state who approved the policy.

18. This is because the Commonwealth's guidelines are contained in subordinate legislation, being directions made by the Attorney-General under section 55ZF of the *Judiciary Act 1903*.

19. The same could be said for the guidelines and principles adopted by the governments of Victoria, NSW and Queensland which, it has already been noted, are binding on public servants as a matter of public law or employment law, and on private law firms acting for the government as a matter of contract law.

20. Namely, the obligations to act fairly, to act consistently; make an early assessment; pay legitimate claims without litigation, when participating in ADR or settlement negotiations, to ensure that as far as practicable the representatives of the State or the agency have authority to settle the matter so as to facilitate appropriate and timely resolution and participate fully and effectively, not to rely on technical arguments unless the State's or the agency's interests would be prejudiced by the failure to comply with a particular requirement, not to take advantage of a claimant who lacks the resources to litigate a legitimate claim, not to undertake and to pursue appeals unless the State or the agency believes that it has reasonable prospects for success or the appeal is otherwise justified in the public interest; to consider apologizing.

REFERENCES

Articles

Appleby, G. (2014). The government as litigant. *UNSW Law Journal, 37*, 94.

Attorney-General's Department. (1995, November). *The attorney-general's legal practice: Guidelines on our values, ethics and conduct.*

Australian Law Reform Commission (ALRC). (1999). *Managing justice: A review of the federal civil justice system.* ALRC 89.

Barker, J. M. (2009). *The duty of parties and their lawyers to co-operate and act in good faith in civil proceedings.* Federal Judicial Scholarship 17.

Cameron, C., & Taylor-Sands, M. (2007). "Playing Fair": Governments as litigants'. *Civil Justice Quarterly, 26*, 497.

Chami, Z. (2010). The obligation to act as a model litigant. *AIAL Forum No 64.* Commonwealth House of Representatives *Hansard.*

Croft, The Hon Justice Clyde. (2010a, August 19). Aon and its implications for the Commercial Court. A paper presented at the Commercial Court CPD and CLE Seminar — Aon Risk Services Australia Ltd v ANU [2009] HCA 27: What does this mean for litigation and how will it affected trial preparation?

Croft, The Hon Justice Clyde. (2010b, November 30). Case management in the Commercial Court and under the Civil Procedure Act. A presentation given at Civil Procedure Act 2010 Conference presented by the Department of Justice, the Supreme Court, the County Court and the Magistrates' Court on.

Le Mire, S. (2014). 'It's not fair!': The duty of fairness and the corporate regulator. *Sydney Law Review, 36*(3), 445.

Leader, B. (1998). The model litigant principle: Can the AGS stay competitive? *Australian Law Reform Commission Reform Journal, 73*, 52.

Loughman, J. (2014). Submission to the Royal Commission into Institutional Responses to Child Sexual Abuse, SUBM.1019.005.0014, December 16, 2014.

Mason, B. (2014, September). The principles of propriety, 88 (09) LIJ 44.

Maurice Blackburn Pty Ltd. (2013). Submission to Australian productivity commission. Submission No. 59. November 8, 2013.

National Commission of Audit. (1996, June). *Report of the commonwealth government.* Retrieved from http://www.finance.gov.au/archive/archive-of-publications/ncoa/coaintro.htm

Productivity Commission. (2014, September 5). *Access to Justice Arrangements.* Report No. 72.

Robinson, M. A. (2009, November 5). Administrative law update. Paper for ADT Annual Members Conference on in Sydney.

Royal Commission into Institutional Responses to Child Sexual Abuse. (2014). *Case study 19.* Retrieved from http://www.childabuseroyalcommission.gov.au/case-study/a83cd4b4-1c68-4233-953c-a7da8e3cfa8b/case-study-19,-october-2014,-sydney. Accessed on February 25, 2015.

Victorian Ombudsman. (2014). Annual Report.

Warren (2014, October 17), The Hon. Chief Justice Marilyn AC, *The litigation contract: The future roles of judges, counsel and lawyers in litigation.* Victorian Bar and Law Institute of Victoria Joint Conference High Stakes Law in Practice and the Courts.

Australian Commonwealth and State Model Litigant Rules, Polices, et cetera

Australian Capital Territory: Law Officer (Model Litigant) Guidelines. (2010). (No 1).

Commonwealth: Legal Services Directions, s.55ZF Judiciary Act (1903) (Cth), app B.

New South Wales: Legal Services Coordination, Model Litigant Policy for Civil Litigation (2008, July 8) New South Wales Attorney General & Justice Law Link.

Queensland: Department of Justice and Attorney-General, Government of Queensland, Cabinet Direction: Model Litigant Principles (2010, October 4).

South Australia: Greg Parker, 'The Duties of the Crown as Model Litigant. Legal Bulletin No. 2, Attorney-General's Department (SA), (2011, June 10).

Victoria: Department of Justice, Government of Victoria, Victorian Model Litigant Guidelines (March 2011).

Cases

Australian Competition & Consumer Commission v Leahy Petroleum Pty Ltd (2007) FCA 1844.

Australian Competition and Consumer Commission v Australia and New Zealand Banking Group Limited ACN 005 357 522 (No. 2) (2010) FCA 567.

Australian Securities and Investments Commission v Hellicar 247 CLR 345, (2012) HCA 17.

Re Brown v Comcare (2011) AATA 606.

Buric v Transfield PGM Pty Ltd (1992) 112 FLR 189.

Commissioner of Taxation v Indooroopilly Children Services (Qld) Pty Ltd (2007) FCAFC 16.

Elders Ltd v Swinbank [1999] FCA 798 (16 June 1999).

Fair Work Ombudsman v Quincolli Pty Ltd (2011) FMCA 139.

Haset Sali v SPC Limited (1993) HCA 47; 67 ALJR 841.

Hughes Aircraft Systems International v Airservices Australia (1997) FCA 558.

Impagnatiello v Campbell [2003] VSCA 154 (26 September 2003).

In re Tyler ex parte The Official Receiver (1907) 1 KB 865.

Kenny v State of South Australia (1986) 46 SASR 268.

Lamb v Department of Natural Resources and Mines (2005) QLC 0019.

Mahenthiarasa v State Rail Authority of New South Wales (No 2) (2008) 72 NSWLR 273.

Melbourne Steamship Co Ltd v Moorehead (1912) 15 CLR 333.

Nelipa v Robertson (2009) ACTSC 16.

Pawlett v The Attorney-General (1635) 145 ER 550.

P&C Cantaella Pty Ltd v Egg Marketing Board (NSW) (1973) 2 NSWLR 366.

Pinot Nominees Pty Ltd v Commissioner of Taxation (2009) FCA 1508.

Priest v NSW (2007) NSWSC 41.

SCI Operations Pty Ltd v Commonwealth (1996) 69 FCR 346.

Sebel Products Ltd v Commissioners of Customs and Excise (1949) Ch 409.

Slaveski v State of Victoria [2013] VSC 76 (28 February 2013).

Yamasa Seafood Australia Pty Ltd v Watkins [2000] VSC 156 (28 April 2000).

Yong Jun Qin v The Minister for Immigration and Multicultural Affairs (1997) 75 FCR 155.

LOCAL ACTION, GLOBAL SHAME

Nicholas Munn

ABSTRACT

How we should behave online is an issue that is deceptively complex. The online community, whether in a professional or a personal context, is much broader than the communities in which all but the youngest of us grew up. As such, the standards of propriety in this space can differ, in ways unexpected and dramatic, from those we are used to. In this chapter I ask whether and when we are under an obligation to conform to the expectations of the dominant groups within the online communities we participate in, and argue that there are at least some times when it is defensible to conform to one's own local norms and expectations rather than subordinating these to the broader online community.

Keywords: Internet; activism; social norms; local/global; conflict

INTRODUCTION

As we become more and more embedded in digital environments, we face ever greater challenges in ensuring that what we do online, and how we do these things, are not used against us. These challenges were initially faced by large entities such as states and multinational corporations, who found that their actions were followed by a wider audience than was previously possible, and that this audience had a different set of standards to apply to

Contemporary Issues in Applied and Professional Ethics
Research in Ethical Issues in Organizations, Volume 15, 85–102
Copyright © 2016 by Emerald Group Publishing Limited
All rights of reproduction in any form reserved
ISSN: 1529-2096/doi:10.1108/S1529-209620160000015005

judgement of their actions. In contexts such as these, there has been significant support for the rise of online activism. However, as the ubiquity of online communication and technology has increased, the same set of challenges is now felt by everyone who acts online, whether as a private or public individual, a large or a small business, a political actor or a representative of an NGO. It is unclear whether the power of the internet, lauded in criticising large organisations, is similarly praiseworthy when used against smaller businesses or private individuals.

Here, I focus on instances of popular online criticism, and attempt to establish a set of considerations that can be applied in determining whether any particular instance of such criticism is warranted or defensible. In order to establish this, I utilise a range of examples, both of successful instances of the harnessing of the power of the internet to generate positive changes, and of instances where that same power has been used (or has been attempted to be used) in service of less defensible ends.

I begin with a brief description of the various ways in which online interactions have expanded the scope of our social interactions and enabled a broader range of actions to come under criticism. I then analyse some positive (or at least less controversial) instances of this form of social criticism, discussing the benefits that have arisen from it, before moving on to an analysis of recent, controversial cases of online criticism. I suggest and defend a number of considerations, which I argue work so as to legitimise certain forms of online criticism while undermining others. These include considerations of proportionality in the response to the action being criticised; the nature of the perceived wrongdoing (i.e. whether it is moral wrongdoing or mere breach of etiquette); the relative power and position of the agent being criticised and the scope of the action. I argue that utilising these considerations, we can draw a reasoned distinction between cases that have the same form, such that we are not acting inconsistently in praising some cases of online activism, while damning others that look, at first glance, to be operating in just the same manner.

EXPANDING OUR SOCIAL CIRCLES

It can be difficult to do justice to the extent to which online communications have expanded the scope of our social interactions. Anyone with access to the internet now has the ability to connect to others anywhere in the world, to a degree that no nation could envisage even a few decades ago. Further, this ability is not simply peer to peer. That is, we do not just have the ability to contact those we know, regardless of their location. We can, and do, broadcast huge amounts of information via the internet, such that it is available, in the public domain, for anyone with internet access to see, if they so choose. Every one of us has the power to reach a global audience, the vast majority of whom are complete strangers to us, who may have very little in common in terms of social background, beliefs, customs, standards or behaviours. Services such as Facebook, Twitter and Instagram both provide us with this global reach for our online actions, and with the means to access the information uploaded through these channels by other users of them.[1] But these services are not solely used by private individuals. They also provide platforms for businesses (large and small), NGOs, and even states to broadcast information, and for these users, the very point of the platform is that it provides an efficient means of letting as many people as possible know what you are doing.

The services I have described above are new to the internet age, but they have not completely replaced more traditional means of communication. These traditional means have, however, similarly had their scope broadened. New media outlets (webpages, streaming content online) provide traditional media outlets with global exposure and its accompanying risks in far greater measure than classic forms of distribution. The smallest local newspaper's online edition can be viewed by more people than the print edition of the New York Times. A video from a local television news station, embedded into their website, is both more readily available and more persistent than the biggest evening news story, broadcast via traditional means. The result of this is that any story, no matter how small, when made available in virtual space, has the potential to become a global story. Increasingly, news media actively encourage this sort of behaviour. So, for example, breakfast news shows will feature segments on social media posts/features that have 'gone viral', thereby both legitimating these as worthy objects of discussion, and exposing them to that segment of the population who both watches morning television and doesn't pay attention to new media. Sites like Reddit actively collate funny, interesting, or merely odd news stories from around the world and display them for a massive global community, thereby driving unintended and unexpected audiences to the least likely of places.

Regardless of the form taken by our actions online, they share a common feature of having dramatically expanded the reach of our social interactions. Each of these domains offers us a reach beyond what we are used to, and beyond what we know enough about to act properly in except by chance. It exposes ourselves and our content to others whose habits and biases we know nothing of, and who we ought not to be expected to know anything of. This is true for public and private users of these online communication systems. So, for example, tweets by any private individual have the potential to travel as far as tweets by the President of the United States. That is not to say it is likely, merely possible. Similarly, a news report by any small town reporter can be picked up globally and retransmitted, whether as evidence of excellent reporting, or of stereotypical small town parochialism. What this all means for social criticism is that we are all more susceptible to it, from a wider range of sources, than we expect or intend. The question I address in what follows is whether the internet, in its majestic equality, does harm to some of us in treating the private individual and the public figure alike,[2] in subjecting them to the weight of the world's criticism for what they say or do online.

EARLY ONLINE ACTIVISM

The increased scope discussed above manifested first in movements, organised and co-ordinated online, to criticise powerful organisations. Many such organisations were used to acting with impunity, whether because, as in the case of state actors breaching human rights norms, they saw themselves as being above criticism (DeMeritt, 2012; Krain, 2012) or, as in the case of breaches of environmental regulations by companies in a variety of industries, exposing these practices had been difficult if not impossible. Organisations engaged in this kind of criticism had, of course, existed without the internet (Amnesty International is a famous example of the first, and Greenpeace similarly of the second), but their power only grew with the communicative possibilities provided by the move online. Shame, always a powerful tool in the hands of a protest movement, is easier to wield in the digital age as the dissemination of evidence of wrongdoing is so much easier to engage in, and harder to suppress than it has previously been. Research into the scope and effectiveness of online campaigns targeting states, NGOs and corporations is comparatively widespread (Murdie & Urpelainen, 2015), but it is only recently that the power of the internet as a tool used by and for private individuals on the global stage has been harnessed, and there is little discussion of this new phenomenon. What discussion there is, is often focused on behaviour such as private online crime investigations, particularly in instances where public opinion coalesces around the idea that the police aren't trying their best to discover the truth (Armstrong, Hull, & Saunders, 2015; Kushner, 2013; Woods, 2014).

It seems clear that the practice of harnessing the power of the internet to challenge the practices of large organisations can be beneficial. In many instances, the internet serves to redress a power asymmetry in positive ways. For example, online campaigns against contested business practices have been helpful in shaming industries into changing their behaviours to reduce the harms done to workers within these industries, or to the environment, or both. Bloomfield (2014) describes the 'No Dirty Gold' campaign, targeted at jewellers, and intended to improve work conditions and reduce the environmental impact of gold mining by shaming those in all levels of the industry into improving their practices. While this kind of campaign doesn't exist solely online, its efficacy is enhanced by the presence of new communications technologies, and the ease with which campaigns of this sort can be undertaken, including by those with comparatively few resources available to them, is a benefit in itself (at least, when the campaigns are undertaken responsibly). We can see the progression of this kind of campaign by comparing the frequency and spread of these campaigns now to the earlier instances of similar attempts, such as the campaigns against the use of sweatshop labour in the apparel industry, in the 1990s. The internet has massively increased the power of campaigns of this sort, simply by making them easier to develop and sustain (Bartley & Child, 2014).

In a similar vein, the mere fact of public exposure of state action to the global community is effective (to some degree) in changing the behaviour of states. NGOs such as Amnesty International and Human Rights Watch have benefitted greatly by being able to rapidly disseminate evidence of human rights breaches to areas beyond the control of the states practising them. From these kinds of examples, we can begin to establish an idea of the conditions under which online activism is positive, to be then compared, in the following section, to cases where the worth of the behaviour is less clear. The first of these is that online activism redresses power imbalances between protest movements and offenders, by decreasing the costs of publication and dissemination of information regarding the behaviour of the organisations being criticised. Secondly, the status of the complainants themselves is important. When NGOs such as those I have been discussing in this section are involved in online activism, they need to protect their reputations as reliable sources of information, as their legitimacy and power to mobilise public opinion depend on a reputation for accuracy. This need for verifiability in claiming injustice serves as a bulwark against false accusations or exaggerations. By contrast, while organisations such as Anonymous have had some notable successes in bringing the power of the internet to bear to catch criminals who were not being pursued by law enforcement, the disparate nature of the Anonymous membership, and the comparative lack of concern for verifying the reliability of their information, amongst at least some of those involved, has undermined their behaviour, despite the positive outcomes in many cases (Bazelon, 2014; Filipovic, 2013; Trottier & Fuchs, 2014; Wong & Brown, 2013). As I will discuss in the next section, this worry is heightened when we move from investigations of criminal behaviour to online activism focused on social norms; that is, to the criticism of behaviour that merely deviates from socially expected practice in particular jurisdictions.

CURRENT ONLINE ACTIVISM

The kinds of online activism I am primarily concerned with here have two dominant features. They are at most loosely organised, often by coalitions of private individuals acting semi-independently, and they are targeting private individuals as a result of non-criminal behaviour. A further common, although not necessary feature of this kind of criticism is that it arises organically, rather than deliberately, such that whether for any given act it will be the subject of a widespread social backlash is, if not random, at least incredibly difficult to predict in advance. There are, however, some factors which seem to trigger the relevant kinds of response.

One such factor is the clash between standards for a given locale, and the standards of the global community. While in the past an online presence was more important for larger businesses, and for other large actors such as states and NGOs, local businesses and private individuals did not commonly engage in much online activity. Now that small businesses and private individuals also commonly act online, the clash between the standards taken by these small-scale actors to be appropriate, and the standards of the global internet community, occurs more frequently. A seemingly trivial example, yet one fraught with tension, is linguistic variation between communities. Some phrases have stronger negative connotations in locale A than in locale B, and sometimes it is the case that a term in common and unconsidered usage in locale A is forbidden in locale B. Yet, the internet means that inhabitants of locale A are not transmitting their usage of these terms solely to co-inhabitants, but to the world at large, which includes people who will react in unexpected ways to these terms.

This raises questions regarding when it is appropriate for inhabitants of B to criticise inhabitants of A for their terminology, when it is legitimate for inhabitants of A to rely on a defence of locality in arguing for the legitimacy of this usage, and how the comparative size/power/history of the various locales weighs on these questions. While all the actors involved in such a situation are members of a shared online community, it isn't clear that this community membership does or ought to trump their local community membership and the norms in place within it.

There is a growing body of research examining the ways in which online communities criticise each other, both internally and externally, and also the ways in which businesses and individuals are becoming increasingly vulnerable to criticisms of this sort (Trottier & Fuchs, 2014). What is missing is an analysis of the extent to which either individuals or businesses deserve the critiques they receive. While it might be tempting to take the position that it is a moral requirement on anyone to call out wrongdoing and injustice wherever it is perceived, in the case of online interactions, for the majority of those who spend significant time online, this option is not available. It is unavailable simply because of the frequency with which outrageous wrongdoing, in various forms and degrees, perpetrated by a range of agents (large and small, public and private, corporate and state), is presented to us online. So rather than engaging in the Sisyphean task of appropriately objecting to all of this in all its forms, we must have some decision-procedure for determining when and how to respond.

We cannot, I believe, rely simply on intuition to generate such a procedure. The reasons why particular problematic behaviours catch the interest of the internet public (go viral) are not particularly well studied, but it is nevertheless clear that the presence of viral criticism bears no direct relationship to the severity of the harms being identified and criticised. For every Martin Shkreli who generates massive global outrage with a plan to hike the price of a 62-year-old drug 5000% (Ramsey, 2015), and is rapidly forced to backtrack from this plan by the collective enmity of the internet public, there is a Lindsey Stone who is driven into hiding and threatened for the sake of a trivially silly photograph that was mistakenly made publicly available on Facebook (Ronson, 2015). Yet in both these cases, significant numbers of those driving the reaction are at most tangentially affected by the action. The criticism comes both from those who (in legal parlance) have standing, and those who do not, and there is little or no mechanism for determining who is who.

It is tempting to say that, when some agent acts in a way that their local community takes to be perfectly reasonable, and this action generates a global backlash, the agent is perfectly entitled to double down, to defend themselves by appeal to local standards and norms. They have done nothing wrong, and if their behaviour causes a number of people on the other side of the globe to go into convulsions, well so be it. But this type of response is seldom convincing. When a local politician rallies support behind a confederate flag, or when the Dutch celebrate Christmas using racist caricatures of Africans (Helsloot, 2012), there is a harm being done, regardless of how well received this is at the local level. The question is to what level that wrong generates obligations or entitlements on the part of the global community to criticise it.

There is a significant danger of piling on in cases of this nature, where the response of the massively populous global community simply swamps and massively outweighs the harm of the initial act. In the remainder of this piece, I will suggest that merely being placed so as to be able to respond to a given action is insufficient to generate either an obligation or entitlement to respond. Before engaging, one ought to consider the source of the harm. Some targets are more legitimate than others, as a result of a variety of considerations (such as proportionality, reach, the public or private nature of the actor causing the harm, and the status of the act, that is, whether it merely breaches local norms of etiquette, or does something more deeply problematic). As a general rule of thumb, larger actors (States, NGOs, large corporations) are more likely to be legitimate targets of global criticism than smaller actors (private individuals, small businesses).

HARD(ER) EXAMPLES

One way to illustrate the difficulty posed by the new media world in which we operate is to look at examples of misguided criticism: instances wherein it is at least arguable that a misunderstanding of the structural features of a situation lead someone to object forcefully to a perceived injustice, when that injustice didn't exist, or at least, didn't exist in the way it was being accused of. Lorde's 2013 song Royals featured a passage that makes reference to gold teeth, alcohol and drugs, luxury cars and diamond-studded watches, jet planes and exotic pets (tigers on gold leashes) (for details visit http://www.lyricsfreak.com/l/lorde/royals_21064144.html second verse).

The song was unexpectedly successful, reaching far beyond the New Zealand market and achieving massive international success, including becoming the first song by a solo New Zealand artist to top the US

Billboard Hot 100 chart. This success was made possible, beyond the song itself, by the development of new media such that more people could hear the song than was previously possible. It also meant that a song by a teenager from Auckland was heard by millions of people who had little or no understanding of New Zealand in general or her background in particular. Disappointingly, but perhaps not surprisingly, criticism followed, with Veronica Bayetti Flores, a blogger for Feministing, saying that 'While I love a good critique of wealth accumulation and inequity, this song is not one; in fact, it is deeply racist. Because we all know who she's thinking when we're talking gold teeth, Cristal and Maybachs' (Flores, 2013a, 2013b). Essentially, the objection is that there are racist overtones (or explicitly racist references, depending on how bluntly one wishes to make the case) in the lyrics of the song, as certain of the features alluded to by Lorde of the rock star life, were stereotypes of African-Americans, and portrayed in a negative light, such that the song itself could be construed as racist.

Setting aside whether this criticism is merited within the context in which Flores was embedded, I will focus in this example on the context in which Lorde was operating when writing and recording the song. In particular, as a teenager in New Zealand, her exposure to American culture occurs primarily through exposure to US exports of cultural commodities (movies, television, music, and the associated concepts). One feature of successful US cultural exports is that they are coded, in the eyes of their non-US recipients, not as 'White', 'Hispanic', 'African-American' and so on, in discrete sections, but as 'American'. The Offspring, Snoop Dog and Dr. Dre are all examples of American musicians of a particular era, and for non-Americans, the idea that there is a functional and important further division to be made according to racial origin is not intuitive.[3]

This type of response to the allegation was widespread, with Brendish (2013) responding that '[n]ot everything in this world should be viewed through the lens of Americans, particularly when it comes to race and cultures of other countries. To insist otherwise is ignorant at best and imperialistic at worst'.

Flores (2013a, 2013b) attempted to respond to these criticisms of her attack on Lorde by appealing to her place within a particular geographically bounded community, and to the narrower intended scope of her criticism. She said that 'Feministing is a U.S.-based site and has a predominantly U.S.-based readership' and that as such, '[b]ecause that is the audience of this blog, it is the audience I believed would be reading my initial post. Clearly it has reached a much wider audience now, one that does not necessarily have a full understanding of the context from which I am writing'. Of course, it is exactly her lack of understanding of the context in which Lorde was writing that caused her initial attack to miss its mark.

So, Lorde appears to have a legitimate response available to her in the face of allegations such as these, namely that her lyrics (even taking just the verse which was the subject of the criticism, and ignoring the broader context in which other verses shaded features that aren't identifiably 'African-American') merely described common tropes of successful American pop-cultural exports. As such, the perception of them as racist by someone who is treating Lorde as a stereotypical white American, rather than as a member of a distinct culture, in which the various components of the song appealed to have different meanings, lacking the racial tension that undergirds the criticism, is misguided. The presumption that one's own biases and experiences will have been paralleled in the life of the one you are criticising is problematic in the new media environment, where this assumption of equivalence is far less likely to be true at even the most general level.

We can contrast the failed attempt to engage in online shaming of Lorde with the effective criticism of Mark Coffey, an Indigenous Affairs advisor to Tony Abbott (at that time, the Prime Minister of Australia) who in July 2015 wore a confederate flag shirt to a 4th of July themed dinner, at which he won best dressed. Photographs of him in the shirt were published online, thus generating the global reach which we have been considering (Wright, 2015). While no time is ideal for wearing a confederate flag shirt, this particular time was worse than most, being both the 4 July, and closely following the killing of nine African American churchgoers by a gunman in a church in Charlotte, North Carolina. Unsurprisingly, Coffey's choice of attire drew widespread international criticism, and while he claimed to be 'unaware' of the flags connection to racial tension in the United States, it does not seem that he is entitled to ignorance as a defence. I claim this for a number of reasons. We may be willing to grant that, even so shortly after the shootings in Charlotte, it is not reasonable to expect the average Australian to know about the issues with the confederate flag, but for an Indigenous Affairs adviser to the Prime Minister, to make this claim on 4 July, suggests rather that he is incapable of doing his job. Even if the loaded nature of the flag is outside his own cultural sphere, the relevance of this example to concerns in Australia is such that we ought reasonably to expect one in his position to be aware of the problematic nature of the garment. The global response here seems to be appropriate in pointing out the wrongness of the act.

The arrest of Dominique Strauss-Kahn in New York provides another interesting case study of the difficulty in balancing norms and expectations for a global audience. The process of arrest followed standard US practice, but this practice is itself rejected by other states, and the publicising of Kahn's name while he was only a suspect in the investigation is itself illegal in other jurisdictions, including France. However, DSK as a public figure and presidential candidate is, in many ways, the kind of person who the broader global public does have a reasonable interest in knowing about, and the offences in question were relevant such that his global shaming could be defended, whether successfully or not (Boudana, 2014).

ISSUES ARISING

Proportionality

We may be worried about the shift in focus of online activism due to concerns regarding the proportionality of response. When disparate groups of activists from around the world chose to target a particular state, NGO, or large corporation, the relative power of the activist group and the target was rarely, if ever, skewed in favour of the activists (Jochnick, 2014). Much more commonly, the group engaged in the protest/criticism was at a significant disadvantage with regard to message reach, media contacts, and so on (Bakardjieva, Svensson, & Skoric, 2012). However, as the ubiquity of online interaction has grown, and as private individuals and small organisations have increasingly shifted much of their activity online, potential has arisen for an inversion of this standard power dynamic. A key feature of the situations which I am labelling as problematic is that they involve a power imbalance in favour of the activists, rather than in favour of the targets.

While I am not yet convinced that the appropriate response in instances like this is to avoid joining in the criticism, it is at least, I think, incumbent upon us as internet-involved citizens to critically analyse whether further condemnation of an individual or small business is either necessary or helpful. Harmful instances of online activism appear to be characterised by a bandwagon or piling-on effect, wherein the sheer volume of criticism is disproportionate to the scope of the offence/harm, and indeed, where at times the offence/harm caused by the initial act is increased by the process of criticism. Instances of the second are those wherein, for example, offensive statements, originally seen by a small number of people, have their reach and scope amplified such that significant numbers of those who would not otherwise have been exposed to them, see them and are subjected to the relevant offence. In an instance such as this, the act of public shaming is causing more problems for those who are ostensibly being protected by it, than the act which they are ostensibly being protected from.

We can make a further analysis of the appropriateness of global criticism to localised instances of bad behaviour by considering the roles of those targeted by the criticism. When an individual in a position of relative power, such as Tony Abbott (when he was Prime Minister of Australia), makes public comments that are reasonably interpreted as undermining the equal status of women in society, his role as Prime Minister is such that a much greater response is proportional than if a local mayoral candidate made the same comments on Facebook. In the first instance, global criticism serves a defensible purpose of pointing out to Australians as a whole the harm done to their image by the comments of their leader. In the second case, where the candidate is running for local office, and their influence even if elected is comparatively small, the full weight of the international community in criticising their claims is overkill, and counter-productive. Similarly, in a business context, widespread international criticism of Martin Shkreli is much more defensible than the same criticism applied to a local hairdresser for an offensive advertisement.

Reach

The issue of the reach of one's actions arises both in the context of the action and in that of the response to these initial acts. In many cases the issues are one and the same, but the possibility of harm arises from asymmetries in expectation regarding reach; that is, in the intended or anticipated scope of one's acts. The initial actor is often caught out by the unanticipated scope of a quote, photograph or video they upload. It goes viral, against or beyond their expectations. By contrast, the respondents to such viral imagery are already drawn from the global community, and intend their responses as such.

It is also the case that the differing expectations of reach are justifiable depending on the standpoint of the original actor. While companies are used to having global reach, in the form of curated web presences and international or global marketing departments, they expect it to occur in forms they can control. Increasingly, they come under unexpected (although arguably it ought increasingly to be anticipated) global criticism for a wider range of actions than ever previously.

The expansion of criticism against companies is mirrored in the experience of everyone who operates online. Everyone online has (potentially) global reach, and comparatively little control over what components of their online presence, if any, become globally known. A depressing example of this type of concern arises in the case of Ariel Ronis, an Israeli government official who became a target of social media activists after a Facebook post accused him of being racist. Two days later, under a barrage of criticism, he wrote a suicide note in which he noted that his life's work, including a book he published on treating people equally, and an organisation dedicated to, in his words, 'equality between all citizens, especially minorities, and their integration into a homogenous Israeli society' had all been swept aside by this accusation. Unable to cope with the now widespread belief that he was all these things he had tried not to be in his life, he killed himself (Jpost.com Staff, 2015).

Private/Public

The appropriateness of a global reaction could also depend on the role of the target. When discussions of online activism first came to the forefront, they did so in the context of activist groups protesting against governments, against NGOs, and against large corporations. In instances such as these, the bodies being targeted have public roles, such that the argument can be made that their exposure in wrongdoing is in the public interest. By contrast, in the hard cases under discussion here, private individuals are being targeted by the same type of campaigns, albeit organically arising rather than deliberately organised, and it is by no means clear that the public interest rationale is sufficient to warrant the response.

The morally relevant distinctions between, on the one hand, large businesses, states, and NGO's, and on the other hand, small local businesses and private individuals, are largely to do with what constitute reasonable expectations for each of the potential targets to have, along two paths. Firstly, one could focus on the expectations of privacy held by the target. It is much more plausible that a private individual expects their personal communications to remain personal, even if transmitted in a relatively public space, such as via Twitter/Instagram/Facebook. State actors, businesses and NGOs are both more used to, and more expected to, operate in the public domain, and as such the threshold for them being called out on their behaviour can defensibly be lower than that for private individuals. In the second instance, we can examine what it is reasonable to expect each

potential target to know, regarding the likelihood of some behaviour causing offence/harm. Private individuals again have (or should have) lower
expectations placed on them for avoiding causing offence to those they
don't intend to interact with, whereas businesses and other organisations
ought as a matter of good public relations do research to reduce the likelihood of inadvertently causing offence. An inadvertently offensive holiday
photograph posted on a private Instagram account is much less culpable
than an inadvertently offensive advertisement on a company Instagram.
The differential culpability ought to be but is not always reflected in a difference in reaction to the offence.

Of course, the separation of public and private selves is becoming
harder, as the Lindsey Stone case referenced earlier makes clear. In this
case, photographs posted to a personal Facebook page became public, as
the page was not set to be private. These photographs, featuring Stone
making a (mildly) obscene gesture and pretending to yell, in front of a sign
asking for silence and respect, drove her from her job (despite them being
only tangentially related to the job), and caused her to be subject to a variety of threats. This type of distinction is also made more difficult by the
increasing ease of connecting individuals to their employers, such that private activity can generate a backlash against one's employer, regardless of
whether the activity was done in work time, or while the private individual
reasonably expected their employer's identity to be discernible.

Etiquette versus Morality

Finally, one might consider whether the behaviour being considered in
these contexts constitutes breaches of moral norms, or simply of etiquette.
It seems like it would be wrong, or at least in need of justification, to globa-
lise etiquette, as etiquette is relativised to particular domains, and it is not
obviously wrong to do in context A what is inappropriate in context B,
regardless of whether those in context B will be able to come to know of
your actions in A. That is, the content of norms of etiquette is not such
that failures to abide by them are problematic outside of the context in
which they are undertaken. However, it looks like, in at least some of the
cases I have been considering, such as the criticism of Lorde, it is failures
of etiquette that motivate the attacks.

We should bear in mind that the boundaries between etiquette and morality are fluid. So, for example, certain language becomes 'bad form' and
then becomes 'wrong', and whether it is either, or which it is, differs at any

time between local contexts. The internet, in its various forms, strips away this localisation, and raises for us the question of whether there is a sense in which we can decide which context to privilege. I have been suggesting throughout that it is defensible to privilege the local context in at least many of these cases, such that, again, because Lorde is who she is, a criticism that would work against someone else (differently situated), does not work, and ought not to be made, against her.

CONCLUSIONS

The modern functioning of the internet has globalised shaming mechanisms, such that any material posted publicly online, in any online domain, is at least in principle accessible by anyone, anywhere, with internet access. This provides opportunities for widespread social criticism, and dangers for both private individuals, and companies. For example, labour practices anywhere can be used to reflect badly on the companies concerned, whereas it was historically easier to disguise differential conditions between states. Similarly, what would historically have been minor gaffes, ignored by the world, can become public relations disasters, both public and private. By contrast to this, our knowledge and actions remain importantly local. We don't necessarily know how others treat things we take as standard practice. Furthermore, it isn't clear that we ought to know, particularly when we are doing these things within familiar contexts, and the degree to which these contexts is exposed to outside examination is all that has changed. So we have a greatly increased opportunity to engage in online activism, as we have access to knowledge that certain actions are occurring, globally. But we have not had a parallel or equal increase in our knowledge of the background conditions in which these actions are occurring.

A common default position when faced with injustice is to claim that there is a duty inherent on witnesses of injustice to oppose it, and that the means by which any individual opposes it will depend on their circumstances. But while this may work well in a local context, where one's exposure to different kinds of injustice is bounded by the limits of physical space, and of access to local, regional, national information via traditional news media, the development of new media technologies has massively increased our exposure to instances of injustice. There are two ways in which this causes problems for a traditional approach to confronting injustice. Firstly, it is trivially easy to be exposed to sufficient injustice that one must make meaningful choices regarding which instances of it to actively oppose, and which to leave aside. Secondly, comparatively trivial instances of injustice, whether because they are only slightly harmful, or because their effects are highly localised, are at least potentially apparent to a much larger class of potential objectors than has historically been common, such that a much greater risk of disproportional response arises, if even a moderate percentage of those made aware of the injustice, respond to it.

So, in the first instance, we ought to be more wary about engaging in online activism, particularly against private individuals, as we can be less certain of the appropriateness of our response to particular actions, than we would be if those actions had occurred within a context we are familiar with. In considering whether to direct one's outrage at any particular instance of injustice one comes across online, one ought to determine who the action harms; who the action refers to, whether harmful or not; who the action could harm; the intended scope of the action; and the actual/ projected scope of the action. By looking at these criteria, one will find that in many instances, the fact of taking offence is insufficient to ground a meaningful reaction to the action under consideration.

Businesses, by contrast, both are increasingly vulnerable to criticism in the same manner as private individuals, and do not have recourse to the objections against that criticism that are available to private individuals. Unlike private individuals, businesses must own the greater risks that come with these new technologies, and as such, there is a stronger obligation on them to ensure that their actions online are carefully considered. It seems like there is nothing inherently problematic about a widespread internet action campaign, targeted at a large multinational corporation, calling on it to admit wrongdoing in some domain, or to refrain from engaging in a planned project which will if undertaken cause significant identifiable harms. But at the same time, it seems that there is a problem with a similar widespread internet action campaign, when the campaign targets either private individuals acting in their personal capacity, or small local businesses whose presence online makes them subject to scrutiny that extends far beyond their sphere of activity.

I have throughout this piece been focussing on the negative side of online action. There is much to say about the positive contributions we can make online, and the various ways in which online activity opens up new areas for positive contributions to the world. Others have done so in depth (Freelon, 2014; Halupka, 2014; Rotman et al., 2011; Zuckerman, 2014).

NOTES

1. That is not to say that all this information must be broadcast globally. One can choose, with some but not all social media services to restrict the availability of one's content to only certain people. Facebook, for example, allows you to restrict to 'friends' or 'friends of friends', amongst other options.

2. Or indeed, in treating the small and large business alike.

3. That many of these tropes are identified within the United States as being 'African-American' rather than 'American' may be explained in many ways, whether as evidence that A-A cultural exports are more successful externally than internally, or that observers external to the US underestimate the extent of ongoing racial discrimination within the United States, in part because it is less visible in the cultural exports of the United States to the world at large than it is in day-to-day life.

REFERENCES

Armstrong, C. L., Hull, K., & Saunders, L. (2015). Victimized on plain sites: Social and alternative media's impact on the Steubenville rape case. *Digital Journalism, 4*(2), 247–265.

Bakardjieva, M., Svensson, J., & Skoric, M. (2012). Digital citizenship and activism: Questions of power and participation online. *eJournal of eDemocracy & Open Government, 4*(1), i–iv.

Bartley, T., & Child, C. (2014). Shaming the corporation: The social production of targets and the anti-sweatshop movement. *American Sociological Review, 79*(4), 653–679.

Bazelon, E. (2014). The online avengers. *The New York Times Magazine*, January 15, 28–33.

Bloomfield, M. J. (2014). Shame campaigns and environmental justice: Corporate shaming as activist strategy. *Environmental Politics, 23*(2), 263–281.

Boudana, S. (2014). Shaming rituals in the age of global media: How DSK's perp walk generated estrangement. *European Journal of Communication, 29*(1), 50–67.

Brendish, L. (2013). *No feministing, Lorde's 'Royals' is not a racist song*. Retrieved from http://livinlavidalynda.com/2013/10/no-feministing-lordes-royals-is-not-a-racist-song

DeMeritt, J. H. R. (2012). International organisations and government killing: Does naming and shaming save lives? *International Interactions: Empirical and Theoretical Research in International Relations, 38*(5), 597–621.

Filipovic, J. (2013). In Maryville, anonymous must beware the risk of vigilantism. *The Guardian*. Retrieved from http://www.theguardian.com/commentisfree/2013/oct/18/maryville-anonymousbeware-risk-vigilantism

Flores, V. B. (2013a). A little more on Lorde, Royals and racism. *Feministing*. Retrieved from http://feministing.com/2013/10/10/a-little-more-on-lorde-royals-and-racism

Flores, V. B. (2013b). Wow, that Lorde song Royals is racist. *Feministing*. Retrieved from http://feministing.com/2013/10/03/wow-that-lorde-song-royals-is-racist

Freelon, D. (2014). Online civic activism: Where does it fit? *Policy & Internet, 6*(2), 192–198.

Halupka, M. (2014). Clicktivism: A systematic heuristic. *Policy & Internet, 6*(2), 115–132.

Helsloot, J. I. A. (2012). Zwarte piet and cultural aphasia in the Netherlands. *Quotidian. Journal for the Study of Everyday Life, 3*, 1–20.

Jochnick, C. (2014). Challenging corporate power through human rights. In C. Rodriguez-Garavito (Ed.), *Business and human rights: Beyond the end of the beginning*. Retrieved from http://ssrn.com/abstract = 2501084

Jpost.com Staff. (2015). Interior ministry official commits suicide after accusation of racism goes viral. *The Jerusalem Post*. Retrieved from http://www.jpost.com/Israel-News/Interior-Ministry-official-commits-suicide-after-accusation-of-racism-goes-viral-403924. Accessed on May 24.

Krain, M. (2012). J'Accuse! Does naming and shaming perpetrators reduce the severity of genocides or politicides? *International Studies Quarterly, 56*(3), 574–589.

Kushner, D. (2013). Anonymous vs. Steubenville. *Rolling Stone*. Retrieved from http://www.rollingstone.com/culture/news/anonymous-vs-steubenville-20131127.   Accessed   on November 27.

Lyricsfreaks. (2015). Retrieved from http://www.lyricsfreak.com/l/lorde/royals_21064144.html

Murdie, A., & Urpelainen, J. (2015). Why pick on us? Environmental INGOs and state shaming as a strategic substitute. *Political Studies, 63*, 353–372.

Ramsey, L. (2015). *We called Martin Shkreli … Business Insider*. Retrieved from http://www.businessinsider.com.au/martin-shkreli-q-and-a-2015-10. Accessed on October 14.

Ronson, J. (2015). The Internet Shaming of Lyndsey Stone. *The Guardian*. Retrieved from http://www.theguardian.com/technology/2015/feb/21/internet-shaming-lindsey-stone-jon-ronson. Accessed on February 21.

Rotman, D., Preece, J., Viewig, S., Shneiderman, B., Yardi, S., Pirolli, P., ... Glaisyer, T. (2011). From slacktivism to activism: Participatory culture in the age of social media. *CHI 2011 Extended Abstracts on Human Factors in Computing Systems*, 819–822.

Trottier, D., & Fuchs, C. (Eds.). (2014). *Social media, politics and the state: Protests, revolutions, riots, crime and policing in the age of Facebook, twitter and YouTube*. New York, NY: Routledge.

Wong, W. H., & Brown, P. A. (2013). E-bandits in global activism: WikiLeaks, anonymous, and the politics of no one. *Perspectives on Politics, 11*(04), 1015–1033.

Woods, H. S. (2014). Anonymous, Steubenville, and the politics of visibility: Questions of virality and exposure in the case of #OPRollRedRoll and #OccupySteubenville. *Feminist Media Studies, 14*(6), 1096–1098.

Wright, T. (2015). Abbott bureaucrat flaunts Confederate flag in Alice Springs, wins first prize. *Sydney Morning Herald*. Retrieved from http://www.smh.com.au/federal-politics/political-news/abbott-bureaucrat-flaunts-confederate-flag-in-alice-springs-wins-first-prize-2015 0707-gi7596.html. Accessed on July 7.

Zuckerman, E. (2014). New media, new civics? *Policy & Internet, 6*(2), 151–168.

POSTHUMOUS DONATION AND CONSENT

Frederick Kroon

ABSTRACT

In this chapter I consider the need for consent in two cases of posthumous donation of parts of one's body: organ donation and the donation of sperm to allow one's partner to conceive a child after one's death. What kind of consent is appropriate in these cases and why? In both cases, jurisdictions tend to prefer explicit consent, although many countries now adopt presumed consent (opt-out) in the case of organ donation, and there has been a recent plea for presumed consent in the case of sperm donation as well. In this chapter I first argue that arguments in favour of presumed consent are inadequate as they stand, and then describe another way of understanding opt-out schemes, one that focuses on different models of what is at stake and on the ethical requirements incurred on such models.

Keywords: Posthumous sperm procurement; organ donation; consent

Contemporary Issues in Applied and Professional Ethics
Research in Ethical Issues in Organizations, Volume 15, 103–119
ISSN: 1529-2096/doi:10.1108/S1529-209620160000015006

INTRODUCTION

Posthumous organ procurement or donation faces a familiar problem. Explicit consent to such a procedure seems to be the consent regime that best supports the idea of agent autonomy, but there is an increasing need for organs available for transplantation, and a regime of explicit consent tends to go hand-in-hand with a low rate of organ donation. That has been an important driver behind the move in many countries to a regime of presumed consent, implemented by an opt-out system rather than an opt-in system. By contrast, there had been no great demand for posthumous sperm procurement (and for posthumous conception arising out it), and the debates around the kind of consent required have mostly focused on whether explicit consent should be liberalised to implied or hypothetical consent. Recently, however, some have argued that there would be a greater demand, and a corresponding ability to meet this demand, if presumed consent was adopted as the appropriate notion of consent in this case as well.

In this chapter I argue that an important aspect about the debate about presumed consent in these two cases is misplaced. There is something at stake in the demand for a more liberal regime, and the notion of opt-out versus opt-in catches the mechanics of what is at stake; but it is misleading to call this a debate about whether we need a more liberal notion of consent. Another account of the debate is needed, especially if we are going to understand the case for an opt-out system for posthumous sperm procurement.

The chapter is structured as follows. In the next section I briefly describe the debate about the various notions of consent as they have been applied to the two cases of posthumous organ procurement and posthumous sperm procurement. The section 'An Argument for Presumed Consent in the Case of PSP' provides a critique of the notions of implied and especially presumed consent, and in particular the way a recent argument has applied the notion of presumed consent to the case of posthumous sperm procurement. The section 'Deconstructing the argument' offers a reconstruction of this argument in terms that don't mention consent, suggesting that underlying the argument is an unarticulated preference for a kind of 'pure resource' model of sperm. I claim that a similar model can be seen to underlie a preference for a policy of presumed consent in the case of posthumous organ donation. The final section 'Where to Next?' offers an evaluation of this argument, suggesting why in the former case, but not in the latter, a kind of relationship-centred model is likely to seem more plausible.

POSTHUMOUS DONATION: EXPLICIT, IMPLIED AND PRESUMED CONSENT

There are two widespread systems for posthumous organ procurement: explicit and presumed consent. Explicit consent, generally implemented as a simple opt-in system, is defined by the WHO as a system in which 'cells, tissues or organs may be removed from a deceased person if the person had expressly consented to such removal during his or her lifetime'. Such a system is based on something like the ideal of agent autonomy − it is my body to dispose of at will, so I will choose whether to donate parts of it. The fact that there is a global organ shortage, however, has led many countries to adopt in its place a system of presumed consent, defined by the WHO as one that 'permits material to be removed from the body of a deceased person for transplantation and, in some countries, for anatomical study or research, unless the person had expressed his or her opposition before death by filing an objection with an identified office or an informed party reports that the deceased definitely voiced an objection to donation'.[1]

The situation is markedly different in the case of posthumous sperm procurement, even if the language of consent dominates the debate there as well. The salient features of this case are as follows. Posthumous sperm procurement (PSP) involves the collection of sperm from a recently deceased male for the purpose of posthumous reproduction.[2] Since 1980, advances in Assisted Reproductive Technology, have made PSP increasingly feasible as a way to allow someone to conceive a child despite the death of the biological father. But it has also highlighted a number of ethical issues. One such issue is whether such a procedure shows proper regard for the well-being, needs and dignity of the child, an issue I am putting aside in this chapter.[3] But no less fundamental to the ethics of PSP is the question of consent, in particular whether explicit consent is always necessary for such a procedure to be morally permissible.

Explicit consent to the procedure prior to death is certainly the test insisted on in most western legal jurisdictions that permit PSP. Explicit consent in this sense should be understood as *informed* consent, where this includes competency, disclosure, understanding voluntariness, and consent (Beauchamp & Childress, 2012). (This is also the notion at play in opt-in systems case for posthumous organ procurement; the fact that consent is so easily registered, say by ticking the appropriate box on a driver's license, is because of the widespread assumption that people asked to consent know the relevant facts about the procedure and its consequences.) Of course, explicit consent of this type is not intended to override all other considerations. It may turn out that the situation the partner is in after the man's death is so different that it is no longer likely that he would have consented to having a child under the new circumstances (imagine that the partner applies to have the deceased's frozen sperm released for posthumous conception only after she has entered into a new and abusive relationship). In that case a request may well not be granted. So while explicit consent is necessary in most legal jurisdictions where PSP and posthumous conception are permitted, it is not considered sufficient.

But some ethicists also consider the test of explicit consent to be too demanding. Men who die suddenly in accidents, for example, may not have thought about giving explicit consent to such a procedure, even though they may well have wanted their partners to have their child under these circumstances. There may even be good evidence of this: it may be known, for example, that the couple had actively discussed this possibility. This has led a number of ethicists to propose another model of consent: *implied, inferred* or *hypothetical* consent, here understood as the idea that it is enough that the person concerned would, on the balance of probabilities, have consented to the course of action in question − in this case, that the deceased would have consented to the procedure had he been presented with the relevant facts pre-mortem and been able to discuss the matter with his partner.[4]

Note that a system based on implied consent is much more stringent than one based on presumed consent. Implied consent requires evidence that the deceased wished a certain thing to happen after death, not merely evidence that the deceased failed to lodge an objection to this thing happening. Not surprisingly much of the debate around the issue of consent in the case of PSP and posthumous conception has revolved around the question of whether the difficulty of verifying implied consent condemns such a system, seemingly leaving the field to a system based on explicit consent. But presumed consent has recently been advocated as the appropriate notion of consent in the case of PSP as well. In a recent article, Kelton Tremellen and Julian Savulescu have argued that the standard two-option debate is seriously flawed (Tremellen & Savulescu, 2015), and that a strong case can be made for a regime of presumed consent: they think there are few significant moral differences between the case of posthumous organ procurement for the purpose of transplantation and posthumous sperm procurement for the purpose of posthumous artificial conception. The next section addresses their argument.

AN ARGUMENT FOR PRESUMED CONSENT IN THE CASE OF PSP

Tremellen and Savulescu begin their rather complex, multi-pronged argument by providing a number of reasons for taking PSP without explicit consent to be ethically justifiable. First, as noted above many countries already allow for organ donation on the basis of presumed consent. Secondly, PSP benefits the donor (they cite an analogy with life insurance), since the deceased gains a benefit prior to death through the benefit of motherhood gained by his partner after his death. (They also suggest as an alternative and seemingly weaker version of this claim: the benefit is to others' *view* of his legacy.)[5] Third, where there is a tension between an individual's self-interest and a demand of morality such as consideration for others, the individual has a moral duty to follow this demand; it follows that, since he is in an optimal position to support his partner in her wish for a child at minimal cost to himself (a minor surgical procedure), the deceased has a duty – the duty of 'easy rescue' (Howard, 2006) – to assist his partner in this. They insist that 'it is hard to see how [he] can be meaningfully harmed by such an action at that time, as he has no interests' (Tremellen & Savulescu, 2015, p. 8).

They also provide a set of reasons that specifically support the option of presumed consent. First, they contend that the available evidence suggest that 'most men surveyed actually support their partners having access to their sperm after death', so that 'it is a failure to respect their autonomy to fail to engage in PSP and conception' (Tremellen & Savulescu, 2015, p. 8). Implementing a policy of presumed consent would be an easy way to allow the wishes of the majority to be respected. Secondly, they reject the middle road of implied consent.[6] They point out that in most cases there will be no substantial evidence supporting a man's desire to become a father. Much of the supposed evidence will be hearsay, a problem compounded by the fact that both the widow and parents have an obvious vested interest in the outcome. This might lead to unwarranted reports of what the deceased had said,[7] but also has the potential to lead to familial conflict.

Before considering this argument in some detail, it is worth reminding ourselves of the reasons why there is (growing) support for a notion of presumed consent in the case of the posthumous donation of body parts, now to include sperm if Tremellen and Savulescu have their way. Roughly speaking, the argument for moving to a notion of presumed consent is based on the claim that the ideal of agent autonomy and explicit consent is outweighed by the benefits that donation would bring if we were not to insist on system of explicit consent, in conjunction with the thought that agent autonomy (a less ideal version) is sufficiently served in such cases by giving the agent the chance to opt out. (This latter thought is not explicit in the argument given by Tremellen and Savulescu, but it is hard to make sense of the idea of opt-out without something like this in place – if agent autonomy is given low weight, why not simply presume consent without the chance of opting out?) We can take Tremellen and Savulescu's argument to be one that fleshes out these schematic considerations.

I want to offer some general criticisms of the idea of presumed consent, before offering some more specific criticisms of Tremellen and Savulescu's argument in particular. But before I do so, I want to endorse part of Tremellen and Savulescu's argument: their scepticism about the notion of implied consent as it has been applied to the case of PSP. To begin with, note that neither implied nor presumed consent is a genuine notion of consent; they are replacement notions that fulfil some of the roles that genuine consent – an (illocutionary) act of granting permission – plays. Importantly, they are claimed to be notions that, in the circumstances, are adequate moral replacements of the notion of genuine consent.

In the case of implied consent, the standard of adequacy is set high: there is implied consent if the agent *would* have wanted the procedure to go ahead, and so would have consented, given familiarity with the situation. What is difficult in this case is knowing when the standard is met. Here is how Jones and Gillett put the problem:

> ... the difficulty lies with satisfactorily ascertaining the views of those who can neither confirm nor deny assumptions or inferences made about them ... [I]t is difficult to imagine that all men in serious relationships would desire posthumous reproduction. Even if a man was eager to be a father, in the normal sense, that would normally include both begetting a child (biological fatherhood) and contributing to its upbringing (social fatherhood) and to disconnect the two could conceivably undermine his paternal desires. (Jones & Gillett, 2008, p. 282)

The matter may be put in more direct epistemological terms. The evidence for the subjunctive that an agent *would* have consented will in many cases be far from reliable. For one thing, the partner as well as other family members have a clear conflict of interest, and so may simply hide the truth, or put a certain spin on things the deceased might have said or done. Furthermore, as Jones and Gillett point out

> [t]here is ... no empirical evidence demonstrating which character traits are correlated with a wish to proceed with PSP; nor is there any way of disentangling these wishes without an explicit statement about the exact terms of fatherhood contemplated and desired by the deceased. That crucial ambiguity makes it quite unclear

what would constitute reasonable grounds for determining that a man had wanted posthumous reproduction, if he had never discussed the matter. (Jones & Gillett, 2008, p. 282)[8]

What is needed, they think, is a study that is able to ascertain

the hypothetical desires of men who are still alive in relation to the possibility of (biologically) fathering children after death. Such a study would then help to establish an objective reasonable patient standard of wishes about posthumous reproduction that could serve as a fall-back position in the absence of a specific determination of the father's pre-mortem wishes. (Jones & Gillett, 2008, p. 282)

Note that the idea of implied or hypothetical consent − the thought that the subject *would* have consented to the procedure had the matter been put to the subject prior to death − is rarely presented as an option in the case of organ donation. Should family be consulted in the absence of explicit consent, this is typically seen as a matter of seeking *proxy* consent (determining the deceased's wishes can be part of this consent process). By contrast, presumed consent, implemented by means of an opt-out system, is a common option in the case of organ donation.

It is important to stress once again, however, that presumed consent is not a notion of genuine consent. To presume consent to a procedure is to act *as if* explicit consent had been given, in the absence of a deliberate refusal to permit the procedure. We can't even say that the deceased *would* have consented to the procedure under conditions of full disclosure, although this is no doubt often the case. The failure to opt out might simply be due to ignorance or forgetfulness or deciding one has more important things to worry about at the time.[9] So someone might be presumed to have consented to a procedure even if there is good indirect evidence that there was not even *implied* consent to the procedure.

As I suggested earlier, however, it is often assumed that giving the agent the chance to opt out means that agent autonomy is sufficiently served in a system of presumed consent, even if this falls short of upholding the *ideal* of agent autonomy. I think this is indeed an attractive thought in the case of posthumous organ donation,[10] but whether the same can be said about PSP is doubtful. To see why, I turn finally to Tremellen and Savulescu's argument for presumed consent in the case of PSP. My criticisms of their argument turns on one main point: the fact that the argument depends on assigning low weight to the ideal of agent autonomy, for reasons that lack any cogency (for further discussion, see Kroon, 2015).

First note a subsidiary point. Tremellen and Savulescu appeal in their argument to statistical evidence concerning what men want. This evidence is quite uncompelling, however. Recall Jones and Gillett's call for surveys that 'ascertain the hypothetical desires of men who are still alive in relation to the possibility of (biologically) fathering children after death ... [which] would then help to establish an objective reasonable patient standard of wishes about posthumous reproduction' (2008, p. 282). The surveys to which Tremellen and Savulescu appeal establish no such standard. These involve men who have had their sperm frozen as well as couples trying to conceive, groups that are dissimilar from the general population in ways that are clearly relevant to the issue.

But even if there are surveys that clearly show that the majority of men have a preference that PSP be available in the event of their death, it is hard to see how this constitutes evidence for a more liberal standard, unless the agent's autonomy is assigned low or negligible weight. After all, the majority's wishes are taken to be the decider, not the wishes of the individual. So a great deal of the force of their appeal to what men demonstrably want depends on the view that considerations of agent autonomy are swamped by other-regarding considerations, a view that also motivates the various deontological considerations that Tremellen and Savulescu appeal to, such as satisfying the duty of easy rescue and preventing harm to the man's partner.

It is at this point that the overall argument for their position is at its most unsatisfactory. Although it is not easy to be sure (there are tensions in the argument at this point, to be discussed below), it seems that the low or negligible weight assigned to the deceased man's autonomy is explained in terms of the metaphysical basis of talk of interests, rights, and duties. Thus, they claim that 'it is important to remember that the dead person no longer exists, so at that time cannot have interests or be autonomous' (9). This is a familiar claim, often called the *existence condition* on the ascription of morally significant properties to an entity. It is well known, however, that the existence condition has strikingly counter-intuitive consequences; it implies, for example, that instantaneous killings do not harm, and do not affect the interests, of their victims. The condition also cuts across conventional wisdom, both legal and moral, about signed deeds that concern events in which the signer has an interest but which will occur after the death of the person signing. Wills and life insurance policies are an example. Even though the person will no longer exist at the time at which such a deed is actioned, there is a strong intuition that the no-longer-existing person continues to have interests that we are morally and legally required to take into account, and that the person is harmed if his or her interests are not taken into account.[11]

Tremellen and Savulescu seem to think that such attributions of interests and harm are bound to be metaphysically flawed — unless a subject exists there simply is no subject to worry about, and so we can't be said to harm anyone or infringe anyone's interests. But that claim seems to rest on a particularly strong metaphysical principle: we can stand in no relation now to something that does not exist now. The metaphysical consensus overwhelmingly goes the other way, however. We can surely admire Socrates *now* even if he doesn't exist now;[12] and if Socrates has the property of being someone whose past actions make him *currently* deserving of our admiration, then there can be no metaphysical barrier to a deceased man's having the property of being someone whose past wishes or interests make them *currently* deserving of respect. In fact, some of the other arguments that Tremellen and Savulescu use depend on the very possibility of other cross-temporal attributions to humans who no longer exist. How else can a deceased person 'gain benefit prior to death from actions taken after death'? (Prior to death, there are no actions that can confer a benefit; and after death there is no person to benefit.) And how else can a husband 'be harming his wife' by not allowing his widow access to his sperm after death? (Whatever harm there is, it is not inflicted until after the man has died and his widow makes a request that is then denied; and at this point there is no person to inflict the harm.)

Tremellen and Savulescu's argument for a system of presumed consent thus seems seriously flawed. Their treatment of the interests of the deceased appears to be based on a simplistic metaphysics, and their consequent assignment of low weight to agent autonomy entirely uncompelling. Furthermore, because of the way this assignment of low weight depends on a fraught metaphysics there is nothing in the argument to suggest that the provision of opt-out in a presumed-consent system serves the ideal of agent autonomy. Indeed, the idea of opt-out now seems quite problematic, given their argument. According to the argument, once the agent is dead, he lacks interests that should be taken into account, and hence there is every reason to let his partner's wishes trump any wishes he might have expressed prior to death. On Tremellen and Savulescu's argument, the provision of opt-out looks like a practical move designed to make agents think their wishes will be taken into account (including the provision might even make help to make the policy of presumed consent more politically palatable as a result), even though there is nothing in theory that would support taking these wishes seriously.

DECONSTRUCTING THE ARGUMENT

Even though I take there to be compelling reason to reject Tremellen and Savulescu's defence of presumed consent in the case of PSP, nothing I have said shows that the position they espouse is indefensible. Indeed, I think there is something to be said in favour of something like Tremellen and Savulescu's position, but not on the grounds they give. What really undergirds their argument, in my view, is an unspoken assumption that the argument relies but doesn't defend or even articulate; this unspoken assumption is a distinctive but contestable view about how we should view the nature of gametes, including sperm, and their potential for use.

Something similar can be said about the case of posthumous organ donation and the role of presumed consent. This is a simpler case, so I will consider it first. The intuitive reason why a system of presumed consent has so much appeal, especially given its apparent ability to make up some of the short-fall in organs needed for transplantation, has much to do with *what* is being donated. Given the nature of what is being donated, it really does look as if agent autonomy is sufficiently served by giving the agent the chance to opt out. In brief, organs able to be transplanted become a pure resource once their possessor has died. None of these things can be used to their possessor's benefit after death, and not merely because there is no one to benefit at that point. As a result, any duties the agent has as a moral agent prior to death can only involve the way she might enable this resource to confer a benefit to others, and any rights she has qua possessor of this resource are sufficiently acknowledged by allowing her the right of refusal. (Here is a close analogy. Suppose it is clear that you no longer want a certain object. It would be gratuitous to insist that if another person badly needs the object it should come to him as a gift, rather than as a result of his asking 'Do you mind if I take it?' and your not objecting. Matters are very different if it is clear that you still want the object.) In practical terms, this understanding of organs as a pure resource is best done through a regime of presumed consent with an opt-out clause.

I take it that some conception like this underlies people's generally tolerant attitude to opt-out schemes for organ procurement, and their broad acceptance once they become established. Although we appreciate the need to let people refuse to donate their organs if they so choose (for cultural reasons, say), we by and large don't think that such reasons have the weight (moral or otherwise) to warrant a system of explicit consent; nor do they have the kind of popularity that might warrant such a system.

Now consider Tremellen and Savulescu's position on presumed consent for the case of PSP. I suspect that something similar to the 'pure resource' model of what is at stake in posthumous organ donation lies behind their argument. On this model, a man's viable sperm is a pure genetic resource, usable by his partner, and benefiting both man and partner if he is alive and a child is produced, but his partner alone if he is deceased and the sperm is released to her for purposes of artificial conception. But as a pure genetic resource, the sperm is something the deceased has no interests in, apart from its being part of his body. This limits his autonomy, since none of these things can be used to his benefit after death (and not simply because there is no 'him' to benefit). What we have instead are desires that the man had for the future, including desires that his sperm be used a certain way, but satisfaction of such desires does not confer a benefit on him since they are not desires for himself, not being centred on him. As a result, any duties he has as a moral agent prior to death can only involve the way he might enable this resource to confer a benefit to others, especially to his partner since she is the one who can benefit most directly through artificial conception (hence the duty of 'easy rescue').

We can now see the moral upshot of the man's finding himself in this situation. As a pure genetic resource, viable sperm is much like a bodily organ apt for transplanting; all things being equal, the moral thing for men is to facilitate donation. Now, an opt-in scheme would severely limit the use of sperm as a genetic resource, to the detriment of the potentially many partners of deceased men who would benefit from a more liberal scheme. (This would even be true, although to a lesser extent, if the condition of consent was changed to implied consent.) But recall our earlier analogy of an object that you no longer want or need. Going for an opt-in scheme is akin to insisting that if another person badly needs this object it should come to him as a gift, rather than as a result of his asking 'Do you mind if I take it?' and your not objecting. Presumed consent with an opt-out scheme is akin to the latter way of understanding the morality of the situation, and so is surely to be preferred.

The crucial element in this model is the idea of sperm as a pure genetic resource, so we might call it the *pure resource* model. Much more could be said in elaboration of this model and the ethical principles that sustain claims about how sperm on this model can, or should be, dealt with. Instead of providing more detail, I'll simply contrast the model with an alternative model that I'll call the *relational* model.

I take the relational model to be the model at play in the debate between the two 'standard' positions discussed earlier: explicit versus implied consent as a necessary condition on PSP. On the relational model, gametes, including sperm, are invested with what I'll call centred relationship potential: we care about our potential offspring, seeing them as *our* offspring, a relationship that is centred on us. For that reason, we don't consider sperm to be a pure genetic resource in which we can't sensibly be said to have interests after death. If the sperm are used to conceive a child, the child is ours, even if we are not around to help rear the child. Because of its relationship to us, we have a vested interest in what happens to that child. That is precisely why we might refuse to give explicit consent to having our sperm used for purposes of artificial conception. Whether or not this is rational, we may not want a child of ours to be brought up in a way, or under constraints, that we would not accept for someone who is *our* child, someone to whom we stand in a centred relationship. That is also why there is no clear duty of 'easy rescue': a man may have a prima facie duty to help his partner achieve happiness through helping her conceive a child, but since it is also *his* child it is morally appropriate for him to make sure his interests are protected, something that he may recognise cannot be guaranteed if he consents to PSP. This is also why agent autonomy and the quality of the consent matters so much, and why there is a legitimate debate about the respective merits of explicit versus implied consent.

Let me make one final point before asking how the choice between these models affects what we make of Tremellen and Savulescu's presumed consent option. My claim is not that the ethics of PSP is somehow determined by these models, but only that they make certain ethical prescriptions attractive. In particular, there is no thought of trying to derive an *ought* from an *is*. Thus, someone might accept the pure resource model and still think that, independently of the model, explicit informed consent is needed if sperm to be taken from a person's body after death (Björkman & Hansson, 2006).[13] (While such a combination of views is logically coherent, to what extent it can count as reasonable is, of course, a very different matter.)

WHERE TO NEXT?

I have suggested that Tremellen and Savulescu's argument for letting presumed consent suffice for PSP is beset by serious difficulties, but that the option *might* be defended by seeing it as based on a certain unspoken assumption: the assumption that sperm should be viewed as a pure genetic resource rather than as something that, in my terms, has centred relationship potential. I also suggested that a similar assumption underlies a system of presumed consent in the case of posthumous organ procurement, and that such an assumption seemed defensible in that case. Is it also defensible in the case of PSP? That is a difficult question, in part because it is even clearer here that the question may not be a purely factual one. It is more a question about, so to speak, one's *attitude* to sperm and its potential: it is a question about how we take this potential to affect us and others and thereby to affect decisions we might make. To take sperm as a pure genetic resource is just that: it is to *take* it as a pure genetic resource, and not as anything more. Similarly, to take sperm as having centred relationship potential is to take it in a way that incorporates much more: in particular, as supporting concern for any future offspring because of their relationship to us. It is scarcely surprising that such different attitudes should inspire different answers to the question of what is ethically permissible or required in the case of PSP and posthumous conception.

The focus on attitudes makes it clear that the question of the correctness (or appropriateness) of one or another model is a philosophically complex one. I here want to set it aside in favour of another (easier?) question. We should ask which model best accommodates the way people actually think when they worry about an issue like PSP. The question is worth asking, for if it is true that something like these two models underlie people's preferences for the various consent options, or do for many people, then we need to ask whether a pure resource model is one that people would (by and large) accept as reflecting their attitude to sperm and its potential use. And it is certainly not clear that the pure resource model has such acceptance.[14] The very fact that explicit and implied consent have been the only forms of consent that have featured in discussions of PSP is strong evidence of this; the focus on such forms of consent suggests that we think that where sperm donation is concerned, even donation after death, men have a more intimate stake in the decision than they have in the case of a decision to be an organ donor, say. Of course, the only way to find out with a reasonable degree of confidence how men really feel about this would be to survey a representative sample in order to 'ascertain the hypothetical desires of men who are still alive in relation to the possibility of (biologically) fathering children after death' (Jones & Gillett, 2008), although in a way that allows us to determine the basis of these hypothetical desires. Until that time, we should remain sceptical of the view that the attitudes of (most) men towards sperm and its potential use after death reflect something like the pure resource model rather than the centred relationship model. If so, we should be correspondingly sceptical of the political-sociological acceptability of a regime of presumed consent in the case of posthumous sperm procurement, no matter how sanguine we are about the prospect of such schemes in the case of posthumous organ procurement.

NOTES

1. Although countries with this more liberal consent policy have markedly higher rates of organ donation, note that even in circumstances of presumed consent relatives are often able to override it, just as happens under a regime of explicit consent (Rosenblum et al., 2012).

2. There are two procedures – procurement of the sperm and use of the sperm in artificial conception – and one but not the other may be permissible in law (e.g. Kroon, Kroon, Holt, Wong, & Yazdani, 2012). In this chapter what is under discussion is the package as a whole: posthumous procurement of sperm for the purpose of artificial reproduction or conception.

3. Everyone agrees that where the child is put at high risk from genetically inheritable problems or is likely to be brought up in an environment that is a clear danger to his wellbeing, there is good reason not to allow PSP. But some commentators also worry about the more general potential of such a procedure to harm the child (Landau, 2004; Pobjoy, 2007). Others think the risks are overstated (Tremellen & Savulescu, 2015). All agree that more studies are needed to determine the impact on the well-being of children born from the procedure.

4. The terminology in this area is far from consistent. What I have labelled *implied* consent is sometimes called *hypothetical consent*, with implied consent reserved for acceptance or agreement evident in a person's behaviour (e.g. rolling up one's sleeve when a nurse suggests taking one's blood pressure). Another kind of 'consent' (again, not a type of explicit, self-conscious consent) is the legal notion of imputed consent, assigned to someone who behaved in a way a reasonable person would take to be evidence of acceptance or agreement. Presumed consent as understood in the bioethical literature is distinct from all these notions.

5. It is difficult to make sense of this: it scarcely makes sense to say that peoples' *view* of the man's legacy gains a benefit. Presumably they mean that people gain an improved opinion of the man's legacy (a *reputational* benefit) once PSP-based conception results in a child, and that this benefits the man after his death.

6. They take this to mean that 'in the view of the widow and the deceased's family, it is more than likely that he would have wanted his sperm to be used for posthumous conception purposes'. But by including the phrase 'in the view of ...' this makes implied consent too easy to establish. I think the notion they are really after uses the cleaner subjunctive conditional 'had the deceased known of his impending death, he would have wanted his sperm to be used for posthumous

conception purposes'. This notion of consent is often called 'hypothetical consent', with 'implied consent' used for a notion of tacit consent (Saunders, 2012a, p. 70ff).

7. Perhaps on the basis of having an honest but wrong view of what the deceased would have wanted. Tremellen and Savulescu cite a recent survey in which couples were separated from each other, and then asked about their partners' wishes for the use of their gametes in posthumous reproduction. Nearly a quarter of women incorrectly guessed the wishes of their partners (Nakhuda, Wang, & Sauer, 2011).

8. This epistemological conundrum is confirmed by the survey results in Nakhuda et al. (2011); see the preceding note. A far more radical kind of doubt about the idea of implied consent comes from the thought that, by their nature, counterfactuals are rarely true, as argued by a foremost philosopher of probability Alan Hajék (http://philrsss.anu.edu.au/people-defaults/alanh/papers/MCF.pdf).

9. Saunders thinks that, rightly understood, an opt-out system for organ donation is one of tacit consent rather than presumed consent, and that tacit consent is a proper notion of consent (Saunders, 2012a, 2012b). I am sceptical. For some well-placed doubts, see De Wispelaere (2012).

10. Even in this case, more argument is needed. One problem is that in presuming consent it is easy to presume too much. Thus consider perimortem interventions to preserve organs in optimal condition for donation. Such interventions are not straightforwardly in the patient's immediate best medical interests, so should it be presumed that the patient has consented to such interventions as well? Many will deny this. A system of explicit consent is able to handle such complexities more easily than a system of presumed consent.

11. A number of moral philosophers make room for such intuitions in their own account of posthumous harm (Feinberg, 1984; Grover, 1989).

12. Some philosophical logicians think that Socrates can be a constituent of a singular proposition that denies his existence (Soames, 2002; appendix to Chapter 3). While this view is contestable, it is certainly respectable. On this view, nothing will prevent Socrates from figuring in a proposition that attests to our current admiration for him. Similarly, nothing will prevent a deceased man from figuring in a proposition concerning the obligations we currently have to him.

13. This follows from what Björkman and Hansson call the first principle of bodily rights ('No material may be taken from a person's body without that person's informed consent'), which they present in terms of a treatment of property relations as socially constructed bundles of rights (Björkman & Hansson, 2006). Their argument for the principle is woefully short on detail, however, and what I have said on behalf of the pure resource model can be considered a challenge to that argument.

14. In the past one might have said that sperm donors are the clearest examples of people who accept a pure resource model of sperm and its potential for use. But things were never quite so simple, of course, since donors gained a pecuniary advantage from donation. With the removal in many countries of the requirement of anonymity, there has been a general decline in the availability of donors, but this has also been accompanied by a general strengthening of the social bonds between

donors and their offspring and families (Fine, 2015; Freeman, Graham, Ebtehaj, & Richards, 2014). If anything, such developments provide further reason for doubting the broad acceptance of a pure resource model.

ACKNOWLEDGEMENTS

I am grateful to Hugh Breakey, Tim Dare, Marco Grix, Ben Kroon, as well as an anonymous referee for this book, for helpful comments.

REFERENCES

Beauchamp, T., & Childress, J. (2012). *Principles of biomedical ethics* (7th ed.). Oxford: Oxford University Press.
Björkman, B., & Hansson, S. O. (2006). Bodily rights and property rights. *Journal of Medical Ethics, 32*, 209–214.
De Wispelaere, J. (2012). Tacitly opting out of organ donation: Too presumptuous by far? *Journal of Medical Ethics, 38*, 743–774.
Feinberg, J. (1984). *Harm to others*. New York, NY: Oxford University Press.
Fine, K. (Ed.). (2015). *Donor conception for life: Psychoanalytic reflections on new ways of conceiving the family*. London: Karnac Books.
Freeman, T., Graham, S., Ebtehaj, F., & Richards, M. (Eds.). (2014). *Relatedness in assisted reproduction: Families, origins and identities*. Cambridge: Cambridge University Press.
Grover, D. (1989). Posthumous harm. *The Philosophical Quarterly, 39*, 334–353.
Howard, R. J. (2006). We have an obligation to provide organs for transplantation after we die. *American Journal of Transplantation, 6*(8), 1786–1789.
Jones, S., & Gillett, G. (2008). Posthumous reproduction: Consent and its limitations. *Journal of Law, Medicine, 16*(2), 279–287.
Kroon, B., Kroon, F., Holt, S., Wong, B., & Yazdani, A. (2012). Post-mortem sperm retrieval in Australasia. *Australian and New Zealand Journal of Obstetrics and Gynaecology, 52*(5), 487–490.
Kroon, F. (2015). Presuming consent in the ethics of posthumous sperm procurement and conception. *Reproductive Biomedicine & Society Online, 1*(2), 123–130.
Landau, R. (2004). Posthumous sperm retrieval for the purpose of later insemination or IVF in Israel: An ethical and psychosocial critique. *Human Reproduction, 19*, 1952–1956.
Nakhuda, G. S., Wang, J. G., & Sauer, M. V. (2011). Posthumous assisted reproduction: A survey of attitudes of couples seeking fertility treatment and the degree of agreement between intimate partners. *Fertility and Sterility, 96*(6), 1463–1466.
Pobjoy, J. (2007). Medically mediated reproduction: posthumous conception and the best interests of the child. *Journal of Law and Medicine, 15*, 450–468.
Rosenblum, A., Horvat, L., Siminoff, L., Prakash, V., Beitel, J., & Garg, A. (2012). The authority of next-of-kin in explicit and presumed consent systems for deceased organ donation: an analysis of 54 nations. *Nephrology Dialysis Transplantation, 27*, 2533–2546.

Saunders, B. (2012a). Opt-out organ donation without presumptions. *Journal of Medical Ethics, 38*, 69–72.

Saunders, B. (2012b). Opt-out organ donation and tacit consent: A reply to Wilkinson and De Wispelaere. *Journal of Medical Ethics, 38*, 75–76.

Soames, S. (2002). Beyond rigidity: The unfinished agenda of *naming and necessity*. Oxford: Oxford University Press.

Tremellen, K., & Savulescu, J. (2015). A discussion supporting presumed consent for posthumous sperm procurement and conception. *Reproductive BioMedicine Online, 30*, 6–13.

ALTRUISM AND GENEROSITY IN SURROGATE MOTHERHOOD

Ruth Walker and Liezl van Zyl

ABSTRACT

In this chapter we address the problematic nature of altruistic motivation, commonly required of surrogate mothers, live organ donors, clinical research participants and health professionals. Altruism, understood as involving a desire to help others, often to a self-sacrificing degree, gives rise to various conceptual and ethical difficulties. We argue that encouraging the virtue of generosity is preferable to requiring altruistic motivation, because generosity is consistent with reciprocation as well as legitimate concern for self. A correct understanding of generosity also alleviates concerns about exploitation and commodification. Our focus in this chapter is on surrogacy, but our arguments apply to other domains as well.

Keywords: Surrogate motherhood; altruism; generosity; exploitation; compensation

INTRODUCTION

Surrogate mothers, live organ donors, and clinical research participants are expected to act from purely altruistic motives, and in most jurisdictions this

Contemporary Issues in Applied and Professional Ethics
Research in Ethical Issues in Organizations, Volume 15, 121–133
Copyright © 2016 by Emerald Group Publishing Limited
All rights of reproduction in any form reserved
ISSN: 1529-2096/doi:10.1108/S1529-209620160000015007

expectation translates into a requirement that they not be compensated for participating. However, medical professionals and other members of the helping professions are also exhorted to act altruistically, even though they do receive payment. In the case of nursing the appropriate motivation is thought to be the desire to help others, often to a self-sacrificing degree. In this chapter we address the problematic nature of altruistic motivation. Our focus is on surrogacy but *mutatis mutandis* the arguments apply in other contexts as well, in particular live organ donation.

It is common to distinguish between two forms of surrogacy: unpaid or 'altruistic' surrogacy, and paid or 'commercial' surrogacy. In the United Kingdom, Australia and New Zealand, only altruistic surrogacy is permitted. Typically, surrogates are reimbursed for actual expenses related to the pregnancy, but are not allowed to receive 'valuable consideration' in exchange for their labour.[1] One of the main arguments against commercial surrogacy is that it involves exploitation of vulnerable women, for whom payment acts as undue incentive and leads them to ignore their other interests (Wilkinson, 2003). It is believed that the requirement of altruistic motivation allows us to avoid the exploitation objection by ensuring that only women who truly want to help others form a family end up acting as surrogate mothers. Against this we argue that altruistic surrogacy can be exploitative as well. An altruistic act is supposed to be a selfless act − altruism involves a desire to help others, often to a self-sacrificing degree. The requirement of altruism often goes hand in hand with a failure to acknowledge the surrogate mother's legitimate needs for self-care and also makes her vulnerable to exploitation. We argue in favour of a professional model for surrogacy which encourages the virtue of generosity rather than altruism. Unlike altruism, generosity is consistent with reciprocation as well as legitimate concern for self. Further, we argue that justice or fairness requires that surrogates be compensated for their labour, and that receiving compensation is consistent with acting generously.

THE PROBLEMS WITH ALTRUISM

Altruistic surrogacy is widely regarded as the ideal form of surrogacy. Many advocates believe that surrogate mothers who are primarily motivated by altruism are not exploited and are not treated as objects or commodities.[2] However, we believe that far from solving ethical problems, the requirement of altruism generates its own problems as well as some that it is meant to prevent.

To begin with, altruism is difficult to define. Although there is widespread agreement that altruistic actions are unpaid forms of giving, there is less consensus over the finer details of what counts as altruism. There is also disagreement over whether altruism can be measured, and whether it is desirable to require it. For example, Bishop and Rees (2007) note that altruism appears to mean 'utter self-sacrifice' and applies to motivation rather than action. It is, thus, unmeasurable − because motivation cannot be observed − and undesirable − because it prevents individuals from meeting legitimate needs for self-care and having a proper regard for self-interest. In any domain in which altruism is expected from paid professionals (e.g. nursing or medicine) the measurement problem is insurmountable. For this reason non-payment has become a proxy measure of altruism in the case of surrogacy, organ donation and clinical research because it appears that the donors get nothing out of it for themselves other than the satisfaction of helping others. Fortin, Dion-Labrie, Hébert, and Doucet (2010) found that some transplant specialists thought that even this compromised the altruistic nature of donation, while others thought it was acceptable as long as it was not the main motivation for donating. Similar disagreements exist in surrogacy. Women who participate in paid surrogacy often emphasize that they don't care about the payment and are motivated purely by altruism, but many people find this implausible as altruistic motivation is thought to be incompatible with payment. Even in cases of unpaid surrogacy, women who receive gifts from intended parents often have their motives regarded with suspicion. For this reason, intended parents are often hesitant to offer, and surrogates to accept, gifts.

Where altruism is defined very narrowly as 'gratuitous (selfless, uncalculated acts of kindness)' (Fortin et al., 2010, p. 216), or as 'spontaneous, selfless, and unconditional action' (Hem, Halvorsen, & Nortvedt, 2014), there is a significant ethical problem, namely that it leads to a denial of the giver's legitimate needs for self-care. To expect a person to be indifferent to their act of giving places an impossible and undesirable psychological burden on them. In the case of surrogacy, we hope that women *do* feel good about what they have done and think it's a sign that something has gone wrong if they do not. Furthermore, we think that ethical difficulties remain even when altruism is defined more broadly, as including all acts of giving where the donor neither receives, nor expects to receive, any form of material reward. We certainly do not want to object to altruistic acts such as baby-sitting for a friend or helping a neighbour with their washing, but we would argue that merely feeling good about what you have done in carrying a baby for someone (or donating a kidney, for example) is insufficient reward, if it is a reward at all. Unreciprocated giving can be exploitative in itself. Altruistic surrogacy can be exploitative given that there are significant benefits that accrue solely to the intended parents and significant risks and costs faced solely by the surrogate. It is important to be clear about what counts as a benefit. Feelings of satisfaction or pleasure are not benefits. Feeling good about oneself as a result of doing something for someone else is a normal reaction and functions as a reinforcement of pro-social behaviour. It is the pleasure of acting virtuously. A benefit is something over and above that, something that can be weighed in the balance when doing a harm/benefit analysis. In altruistic surrogacy the intended parents gain a child. The surrogate has enabled them to form a family when they would not otherwise have been able to. The intended mother might have supplied the eggs, in which case she has been exposed to some risk, but it is the surrogate who has taken all the risks of pregnancy and childbirth. It is her body that has been permanently affected by carrying and delivering the baby for someone else.

Wilkinson (2003) defines exploitation as the unjust distribution of benefits and harms in the absence of valid consent. Supporters of altruistic surrogacy often emphasize the point that when surrogates are not paid for their labour we can be sure that their participation is free and voluntary. So even though there is an unequal distribution of harms and benefits, this is justifiable given that the surrogate consents to it. Arguably, however, valid consent is problematic in this context. Where paid surrogacy is prohibited, women who are interested in helping others form a family must consent to unpaid surrogacy. That is, they either have to consent to an unfair distribution of benefits and harms or be prevented from participating altogether. Mere reimbursement of expenses is inadequate if the benefits and harms are to be balanced out in a way that prevents exploitation. Otherwise we are simply taking advantage of givers' goodwill.[3]

In addition, an altruistic framework obscures the harms and risks to the surrogate. Surrogates suffer discomfort and worse even during normal pregnancies and it doesn't take much to go wrong for them to be burdened with significant physical hardship (e.g. infection, haemorrhage, emergency caesarean). Their service to others disrupts their family and working life. Many of the negative consequences they face arise after they have relinquished the baby. There is, however, no conceptual room to factor their needs in because what they have done is regarded as 'selfless'. Surrogates often report being abandoned to cope as best they can after the event (Teman, 2010).[4]

ALTRUISM AND GIFT-GIVING

Although altruism is widely equated with gift-giving (Shaw & Webb, 2015) there is a clear tension between the two concepts. Pure altruism is entirely selfless. If the best form of donating is purely altruistic then any benefit the donor derives lowers the moral status of the action. In practice this means that the donor cannot expect any form of reciprocation because reciprocation renders the altruism less pure. Yet, if the donation is also considered to be a gift then the donor can legitimately expect reciprocation because gifts are given in a context of exchange (Fortin et al., 2010). They should be received, acknowledged and reciprocated. In this context donors do not sully their actions by wishing to be thanked; rather the recipients fail in their obligations if they do not acknowledge the gift. In short, then, altruism requires that there be no reciprocation; gift-giving requires that there is.

The conceptual confusion surrounding altruism and gift-giving is also reflected in the practice of surrogacy. Unpaid surrogates are described as selfless women who expect nothing in return. At the same time, gift language is also prevalent in this context, with surrogates praised for giving the 'gift of love'. Accordingly, some agencies actively encourage intended parents to express their gratitude by giving a valuable gift. For example, in an important anthropological study conducted in the United States, Helena Ragoné (2003, pp. 212–217) found that many agencies encourage intended parents to give jewellery that feature the baby's birthstone. This is meant to symbolize the 'preciousness' of the child, and to validate the special connection between the surrogate and child. By reciprocating in this way, the intended parents are thought to acknowledge that gifts are mere tokens of appreciation and that the intended parents cannot repay the surrogate for her extraordinary kindness. However, other agencies discourage or even prevent intended parents from giving valuable gifts or even flowers, as they consider it inappropriate or fear that it would violate the prohibition against acting as a surrogate in exchange for 'valuable consideration'.

Unpaid surrogacy is often equated with altruistic surrogacy, but we think it is useful to distinguish between two forms of unpaid surrogacy, as there are important differences between these two practices. In the first, altruistic surrogacy, the surrogate does not receive anything in return a although she may be reimbursed for actual expenses related to the pregnancy any material form of reciprocation is discouraged or prohibited. We hope to have shown, in the previous section, that this form of surrogacy is morally objectionable. The second form of unpaid surrogacy can be called 'gift surrogacy', where, in addition to reimbursement for expenses, some material form of reciprocation is not only allowed but expected and encouraged, although the intended parents are free to decide the form it takes. Gift surrogacy is clearly preferable to altruistic surrogacy. If it is appropriate to give blood donors tea and chocolate biscuits, it is surely appropriate to do something rather more for gestational surrogates given the risks they undergo for the recipients' benefit.

The core value in gift surrogacy is *generosity* rather than altruism.[5] As we argue in the following section, the virtue of generosity provides a better ethical and conceptual basis for surrogacy because it allows a rich and comprehensive account of giving and receiving that fully captures the essentially moral nature of the practice. Generosity can accommodate reciprocation, and allows us to retain the idea of gift-giving and eliminate the requirement for selflessness.

GENEROSITY

Generosity involves giving more than is owed. We are generous when we give something we value to benefit someone else. Agreeing to act as a surrogate is, first and foremost, a generous thing to do. Given the risks and cost to the surrogate it goes well beyond the call of duty. Once she enters the agreement and becomes pregnant, a surrogate assumes a number of responsibilities. For example, she has a duty to avoid harming the intended baby in utero, to promote its best interests and to relinquish it after birth. But while duties are created within the arrangement, these usually fall far short of the intended parents' expectations. As we argue more fully elsewhere (Walker & Van Zyl, 2015), the surrogate retains all her rights as a pregnant woman and autonomous agent, so cannot be required to share intimate information or to involve the intended parents in the pregnancy and decision-making about medical care. If she chooses to do these things she is acting generously.

Kupfer (1998) identifies two dimensions of generosity: corporeal generosity and generosity of spirit. The corporeal dimension is particularly important in surrogacy. The surrogate gives of her body continuously and the intended baby is the primary recipient of her corporeal generosity. A significant advantage of using the concept of generosity is that it focuses attention on the intended baby as the recipient of the surrogate's generosity rather than on the intended parents as the recipients of the surrogate's 'gift'. This allows for independent consideration of the intended baby's interests and mitigates the worry that the baby is being objectified as a gift to the intended parents.

Generosity of spirit, which involves psychological giving, is as important as corporeal generosity. Kupfer (1998) distinguishes between generous-minded actions, such as making favourable judgments rather than unfavourable ones, and generous-hearted actions, which refers to emotional giving such as forgiveness. Members of the caring professions have many opportunities to be generous-minded given the vulnerability of many of their clients or patients who are under stress. Their behaviour can often be difficult, unreasonable or hostile. Nurses show generous-mindedness when they interpret patients' apparently difficult behaviour in neutral or positive ways, for example, judging a patient as 'anxious' rather than 'aggressive and complaining' (Arber & Gallagher, 2009).

Women who act as surrogate mothers have many occasions for acting in ways that are generous-minded. Intended parents can be so anxious that they risk overwhelming the surrogate with their fears and desire to control all aspects of the pregnancy. Services should be in place to prevent the surrogate from being victimized but the need for her to put positive interpretations on their behaviour does not diminish. Behind every surrogacy is a tragic story of lost pregnancies, infertility or illness. To see the intended mother as understandably anxious rather than aggressive is an act of generosity (unless, of course, the intended mother is in fact being aggressive and intervention is needed).

Although intended parents often assume that they have a right to information about the pregnancy, the surrogate has a moral (and often also a legal) right to medical confidentiality. She is the patient and, as with any pregnant woman, does not have to share information with anyone. She must consent to any disclosures. In addition, she retains the right to make all decisions regarding the pregnancy, including whether to terminate it. So when surrogates share intimate information about themselves and the progress of the pregnancy with the intended parents they are being generous-hearted. Surrogates also manifest generous-heartedness when helping intended mothers encompass the pregnancy and bond with the unborn child. This frequently leads to an intense and intimate bond. For instance, in her study of Jewish Israeli surrogates, Teman (2010) found that surrogates use a range of metaphors to describe the bond, including marriage. One woman used the phrase 'flesh of my flesh' to convey the idea of the two becoming one.

But if surrogates are this generous to their intended parents, how should that generosity be received? Kupfer's answer is 'gratefully' and generous-heartedly: 'Because we view what we receive as freely bestowed, we are grateful for a gift instead of simply satisfied that we have received our due' (Kupfer, 1998). This neatly encapsulates the reciprocal nature of the relationship. The intended parents should receive and acknowledge the surrogate's generosity of spirit towards them. They should also acknowledge her corporeal generosity to their baby.

GIFT SURROGACY AND EXPLOITATION

Although gift surrogacy is certainly preferable to altruistic surrogacy, we believe that the norms of gift-giving are inappropriate for surrogacy as it still leaves the surrogate vulnerable to exploitation. Gift relationships are characterized by a high degree of voluntariness. The giver is free to give, in the sense that the recipient does not have a right to a gift or benefit, and although the recipient incurs a 'debt of gratitude' he or she is free to determine its nature or form. Importantly, the aim of reciprocating is not to achieve distributive justice, but merely to express one's gratitude or appreciation. For the reciprocating act to be successful or appropriate it should be in proportion to the original gift, or it should at least be evident that some thought and effort went into it. Gift relationships are governed by a set of social norms, but these are typically fairly vague and flexible; someone who takes them too seriously and applies them too rigidly can rightly be accused of 'missing the point', the point being that an act of giving is an expression of love or care (Van Zyl & Walker, 2013).

When surrogacy is organized or modelled according to the norms of the gift relationship the risk is that the surrogate's generosity may go unreciprocated. Surrogates who view themselves as giving the 'gift of love' are unlikely to make their expectations clear, given that a gift loses much of its symbolic value when it is given in response to a request or demand. Of course, the risk of being disappointed is not unique to surrogacy. Relationships often go sour, with one party feeling that their generosity is not reciprocated or appreciated. However, in most contexts there are numerous ways in which one can safeguard against the risk of being exploited by friends. For example, the benefactor can usually decide to stop giving, or to give less. In the case of surrogacy, however, these safeguards do not exist. Once the surrogate is pregnant, she is no longer free to decide what or how much to give, or to stop giving. She could have an abortion or refuse to relinquish the child, but this would be completely disproportionate to any kind of insult or ill-treatment she might have suffered.

She could decide to be less careful with diet, medication, and so on, but by taking this route she risks violating her obligations to the intended baby. In short then, although a woman may be free to decide to act as a surrogate, once she is pregnant her freedom is restricted in a number of ways. Insisting that the intended parents should nevertheless be free to decide how and even whether to reciprocate – to give flowers, jewellery, or a simple 'thank you' – allows a considerable imbalance in power and makes the surrogate vulnerable to exploitation. This is one of the reasons why we believe that a better model for surrogacy would be one in which the rights, obligations and legitimate expectations of each party are made explicit, and where the surrogate receives fair compensation for her labour (Van Zyl & Walker, 2013).

GENEROSITY AND PAYMENT

In commercial surrogacy rights and obligations are established by contract, including entitlements to compensation. While commercial surrogacy has some advantages over both altruistic and gift surrogacy, we have a number of objections to the practice, which we will not repeat here (Van Zyl & Walker, 2013). Instead, we support a professional model for surrogacy, which requires both compensation and reciprocation. Compensation here refers to the fee for service (plus expenses) and reciprocation takes the form of an appropriate expression of gratitude. The professional model requires surrogates to be registered and clinics to be licensed and regulated through an independent body responsible for setting the fees surrogates receive as well as the professional standards, rights and duties of all parties. Instead of being negotiated between contracting parties, as is the case in commercial surrogacy, fees are set to be reasonable, fair compensation for time and service. Intended parents have obligations to the surrogate that go beyond merely paying the fees as if it is a purely commercial transaction. For example, they have to respect her right to privacy and confidentiality and also have to avoid compromising her autonomy. The surrogate does not and cannot negotiate away her human rights.

As argued above, we believe that generosity rather than altruism should be the fundamental value in surrogacy, as it can accommodate reciprocation and is also consistent with appropriate care for self. But we also think that justice or fairness requires that surrogates be compensated for their labour. The most obvious objection to this proposal is that if people are paid for the services they provide they are no longer being generous because they are doing what they owe in exchange for compensation. Against this we want to argue that generosity is compatible with receiving compensation. To see how this is possible it is important to make a distinction between what is owed in order to prevent exploitation and what is appropriate in the context of reciprocation.

In occupations such as nursing, midwifery and social work, payment serves two functions: it compensates the individual for their time and services, and it prevents them from being exploited because of an unjust distribution of harms and benefits. However, even though they are compensated for their labour there is still a significant amount of scope for generosity in the way these practitioners carry out their work. Generosity of spirit is particularly important in these occupations as it makes a discernible difference to recipients of the services. Consider, for example, the nurse who interprets difficult behaviour in a generous-minded way. It is impossible − or at least inappropriate − to try to compensate a nurse for her generosity, but this does not mean that she should not be paid at all. Instead, an appropriate response to her generosity is acknowledgement and an attempt to reciprocate. In the same way, women who act as surrogates deserve recognition for their generosity, but should also be paid. Payment does not, in other words, serve as reciprocation but rather as compensation. This leaves scope for appropriate acknowledgement and gratitude for what they are actually giving.

As we have seen, altruism leaves no space for self-care. By contrast, generosity need not be self-sacrificing in order to count as other-directed. On the contrary, it encompasses the smallest action over and above what is owed up to the greatest. Within that space the caring professions are now advocating 'mature care' of clients and patients rather than 'altruistic care' because the latter is damaging to the health and welfare of practitioners. Mature care requires the exercise of prudence to achieve the right balance between care of others and care of self (Hem et al., 2014). This provides more than enough scope for working generously. Given that practitioners have legitimate needs these must be accommodated in the structure of the workplace and the profession. The responsibility for that lies outside the individual. We argue that surrogate mothers have the same entitlements to self-care and it is the duty of the intended parents as well as the other professionals involved in the arrangement to ensure that these are respected. To claim these entitlements does not lower the moral status of her action and does not make her motivation suspect.

Advocates of altruistic surrogacy worry that payment undermines the voluntariness of the action. They argue that if surrogate mothers are paid women will enter into surrogacy arrangements for that reason and will do so even if it is not in their interests to do so. They will be 'doing it for the money' rather than freely choosing it. Money is an incentive and may even be coercive. But again, similarity to the caring professions shows that this worry is misplaced. Some fields in medicine are far more demanding and onerous than others. Emergency medicine, for example, exposes staff to every horror that can come into the hospital. Moreover it is an increasingly dangerous place to work as physical abuse of personnel becomes more common. Nurses and doctors who opt to specialize in the field will not normally be paid higher salaries than their colleagues – and in some cases will earn less than they might have. No one has to work in emergency medicine; it is purely voluntary and the payment cannot be taken as a significant factor in the decision. Surrogacy is similar in that the fees envisaged in the professional model would be fair compensation rather than excessive and hence would not entice women into surrogacy. Many women would like to act as surrogate mothers but are prevented from doing so because they cannot afford to undertake unpaid surrogacy. Compensation would enable them to do the generous thing they are already disposed to do. That is very different from saying that they would be 'doing it for the money'. There are indeed problems when the market sets the price because the price will increase until demand is met, potentially making women act against their own interests. However, opting for unpaid surrogacy is not the solution because it creates its own serious problems for surrogates.

CONCLUSION

The idea of helping someone to have a baby when they cannot do this for themselves is much better accommodated by generosity than altruism. In ordinary life, when we receive a gift we say thank you. And the more generous the gift, all things being equal, the more grateful we are or should be. The acknowledgement of that gift and our reciprocation either in a continuing gift-exchange or, as in donation, a chain of giving (Shaw, 2014) should be appropriate to the magnitude of the gift. Acknowledgement alone is insufficient to prevent exploitation. Appropriate compensation and care for the giver are also required.

NOTES

1. See, for example, the Human Assisted Reproductive Technology Act (2004) (NZ), s.14.

2. Similarly, in live organ donation motivation to help others without benefit to self is believed to remove worries about the commodification of body parts and exploitation of people. Because live organ donors undergo significantly risky and unpleasant procedures with sometimes protracted recovery periods, they are analogous to surrogates, and like surrogates, are most affected by the unintended negative consequences of requiring altruism.

3. Many scholars reject the assumption that surrogacy is morally appropriate if it is done 'for free' rather than for money. For example, Raymond (1990) argues that altruism has been one of the most effective blocks to women's self-awareness and demand for self-determination, and that the potential for woman's exploitation is not necessarily less because no money is involved and because reproductive arrangements may take place within a family setting. Narayan (1995) argues that the surrogate's relationship and emotional ties to the intended parents may make her more vulnerable to emotional pressure and coercion concerning the conditions of pregnancy and childbirth.

4. Shaw (2014) makes a similar point in the context of live organ donation.

5. Some writers refer to the central value in these kinds of exchanges as 'reciprocal altruism', which refers to instances where one person performs a service or makes a sacrifice for another, who then reciprocates in a way that balances the service or sacrifice of the provider (Trivers, 1971; Badcock, 1986; Blum, 1980).

REFERENCES

Arber, A., & Gallagher, A. (2009). Generosity and the moral imagination in the practice of teamwork. *Nursing Ethics, 16*(6), 775–785.

Badcock, C. R. (1986). *The problem of altruism*. Oxford: Basil Blackwell.

Bishop, J. P., & Rees, C. E. (2007). Hero or has-been: Is there a future for altruism in medical education? *Advances in Health Sciences Education, 12*(3), 391–399.

Blum, L. (1980). *Friendship, altruism and morality*. London: Routledge & Kegan Paul.

Fortin, M.-C., Dion-Labrie, M., Hébert, M.-J., & Doucet, H. (2010). The enigmatic nature of altruism in organ transplantation: A cross-cultural study of transplant physicians' views on altruism. *BMC Research Notes, 3*(216), 1–5.

Hem, M. H., Halvorsen, K., & Nortvedt, P. (2014). Altruism and mature care: Some rival moral considerations in care ethics. *Nursing Ethics, 21*(7), 794–802.

Kupfer, J. (1998). Generosity of spirit. *The Journal of Value Inquiry, 32*, 357–368.

Narayan, U. (1995). The 'gift' of a child: Commercial surrogacy, gift surrogacy and motherhood. In P. Boling (Ed.), *Expecting trouble: Surrogacy, fetal abuse and new reproductive technologies* (pp. 177–202). Oxford: Westview Press.

Ragoné, R. (2003). Gift of life: Surrogate motherhood, gamete donation, altruism. In R. Cook & S. Day Sclater (Eds.), *Surrogate motherhood: International perspectives* (pp. 212–217). Oxford: Hart Publishing.

Raymond, J. G. (1990). *Reproductive gifts and gift giving: The altruistic woman*. Hastings Center Report, November/December 7–11.

Shaw, R. M. (2014). Live kidney donation as body work. *Critical Social Policy, 34*(4), 495–514.

Shaw, R. M., & Webb, R. (2015). Multiple meanings of 'gift' and its value for organ donation. *Qualitative Health Research, 25*(5), 600–611.

Teman, E. (2010). *Birthing a mother: The surrogate body and the pregnant self.* Berkeley, CA: University of California Press.

Trivers, R. (1971). The evolution of reciprocal altruism. *Quarterly Review of Biology, 46*, 35–57.

Van Zyl, L., & Walker, R. (2013). Beyond altruistic and commercial contract motherhood: The professional model. *Bioethics, 27*(7), 373–381.

Walker, R., & Van Zyl, L. (2015). Surrogate motherhood and abortion for fetal abnormality. *Bioethics, 29*(8), 529–535.

Wilkinson, S. (2003). The exploitation argument against commercial surrogacy. *Bioethics, 17*(2), 169–187.

CONTEMPORARY ISSUES IN THE PROFESSIONALISATION OF CHILD CARE IN AUSTRALIA

Stephen Kemp

ABSTRACT

The purpose of this chapter is to examine how the paid care of children, and assisting with their development, is increasingly coming to resemble a professional activity in Australia. The commodification of child care has tended to create a profession of carers of children, not only by virtue of more formalized qualifications and role descriptions for carers, but also by establishing a potential framework within which a profession may be practiced. I examine how paid child caring in Australia increasingly conforms in many respects with various criteria commonly associated with a professional activity. This evolution within the child care field however is creating tension between the traditional nurturing role of child care and the more formal requirements of a "professional" carer. This process of professionalisation also has significant implications, not only for the care providers, but also for those who are receiving care — the children and their families. It also has important implications for society itself.

Keywords: Child; care; commodification; professionalization; Australia

Contemporary Issues in Applied and Professional Ethics
Research in Ethical Issues in Organizations, Volume 15, 135–147
Copyright © 2016 by Emerald Group Publishing Limited
All rights of reproduction in any form reserved
ISSN: 1529-2096/doi:10.1108/S1529-209620160000015008

INTRODUCTION

This chapter is drawn from a thesis on ethical issues surrounding the commodification of child care. Typically, one of the outcomes of commodifying a service is to create a group or profession of people whose job it is to provide the commodified service. The term "professional" however implies more than just a person who earns a living providing a certain service. Even though the term, on occasions, may be used euphemistically to portray certain occupations, such as "sanitary professional" instead of "cleaner," there are important elements which are needed to satisfy the description of "professional" when it comes to practising in certain specialized occupations such as medicine, engineering, legal practice and so on.

In this chapter, I will show how the practice of caring for children and assisting with their development is increasingly coming to resemble a professional activity. I examine various criteria which are commonly associated with professional practice, and seek to demonstrate how the commodification of child care has tended to create a profession of carers of young, preschool age children, not only by virtue of more formalized qualifications and role descriptions for carers, but also by establishing the framework within which a profession may be practiced. I also examine how this process of professionalization is creating tension between the traditional nurturing role of child care and the more formal or educational requirements of a "professional" carer that some consider may displace the nurturing aspects of caring for children. While I acknowledge the importance of traditional love and nurture in child care, I show that there are also good grounds for developing the more professional attributes of the child care workforce. I argue that this is good not only for the care providers themselves, but also for those who are receiving care, the children and their families. It also has important implications for society itself. I will endeavor to show how those involved in the care and education of children have a particularly significant relationship with the general community through the immediate and extended families of those in their care. This effectively means that the community places its trust in the carers and teachers of children to support and guide young citizens for the benefit of society in the future.

CHILD CARE AS A PROFESSION

In Australia during the past 10–20 years, there's been an increase in the qualifications required by law for child care workers to perform certain duties within licensed or approved child care services. In the three years to 2013, the proportion of the child care workforce with a Certificate III or Certificate IV qualification increased from 29−36 percent, while the unqualified proportion of the workforce fell from 30 to just 18 percent (The Social Research Center, 2014, p. 40). So, this trend toward increasingly more qualified workers might tend to support the notion of the professionalization of the child care workforce. But can child carers really be considered *true* professionals in the same way as doctors or lawyers?

The necessary attributes of a professional are debatable, but there are some which appear most commonly in the literature (Wueste, 2013, p. 3). These include:

- substantial knowledge of a field often acquired through tertiary study and training;
- significant social and community standing of the tasks performed by the professional;
- professional practice governed by role specific norms and regulated by peer group;
- motivated primarily by altruism rather than personal profit.

Let us briefly consider each of these attributes.

Professional Knowledge

First, child carers are increasingly being required to attain higher formal qualifications, at least to obtain positions with formal child care services. In addition, there are a growing number of in-service training programs to help keep practitioners abreast of recent developments in the field. Research and development in the field of early education is substantial and it is as important for child carers, as for practitioners in other fields, to update their knowledge and skills. Hence, it would appear that the first of the attributes listed above could arguably be applied to child carers, at least those employed in formal licensed or "authorized" child care services. However, those carers working with children in home-based or other care settings, may not be required to attain the same level of formal qualifications as center-based carers. So they may not possess this attribute. It is important for the potential professional standing of child care that a clear distinction is made regarding the type of caring work which might constitute professional practice. Most professions seek to maintain standards by controlling entry into the practice domain, and the existence of practitioners without the requisite qualifications or skills brings into question the entire occupation's status as a profession.

One problem is that the term child carer might be applied to a number of activities across a broad spectrum. People working in the child care field may be involved in one or all of three types of work involving young children: care, development, or learning. In this context, "care" is most closely associated with the notion of "babysitting", concerned primarily with the child's health and safety, and their emerging social/emotional abilities. "Development," on the other hand, involves assisting the child with changes as he grows and develops his physical, emotional, social, and intellectual attributes in increasingly complex ways. "Learning," meanwhile, concerns the acquisition of knowledge, skills, values, and behavioral attributes appropriate to their age through various activities, experiences, observation, and instruction, and helping them prepare for the next stage of their life.

Some observers, such as Michael Lyons, believe this role uncertainty leads to those involved in the occupation of child care suffering more from an ambiguity about their role than practitioners in other "'professionalized' feminized occupations (such as) nursing, social work, teaching and the like." He observes that there is still a "close association of the work in long day care to the 'every day' tasks of child rearing (which) formal qualifications attainable from educational institutions have only partly addressed" (Lyons, 2011, p. 124). However for some carers, particularly those tertiary qualified carers employed within formal child care services, the perception of the significance of their role is changing (Sims, 2010). This is particularly so for those involved in preparing older children in those years immediately prior to commencing formal schooling. In Australia in recent years, many more people undertaking the role of child carer for children in the four to six years age group and even younger, are holders of university degrees and commonly called "kindergarten teachers" with formal registration as a teacher.

Community Standing of Role

The second attribute relating to the significance and standing of the role of child carer within the community, might also be questionable. The activity of child care would certainly not be considered comparable to that of, say, a doctor or a lawyer, or probably even for that matter, that of a school teacher. Child carers were traditionally just considered to be mere "babysitters" and, certainly for some people involved in child care, that is a reasonably apt description of their role. Some might argue that the role undertaken by child carers is really not all that different from that of a parent — preparing children physically, intellectually, socially, emotionally and in other respects for their life ahead. This would be a situation not likely to occur in any other profession, except perhaps that of teaching to a limited degree. While this objection has some merit, it could be countered by making the distinction between raising one's own children as a parent and the raising of many children of different parents which occurs in the practice of commodified child care and early education. But while it is probably still debatable whether the role of child carer generally has attained significant enough standing to be occupied by a "professional," it is likely certain practitioners, such as kindergarten teachers, could be considered to have attained that level. Additionally, as research increasingly highlights the importance of the earliest years of a child's life to the child's later development, the role of those involved with the care and nurture of young children is likely to become progressively more highly regarded.

Role Specific Norms and Peer Group Regulation

Looking at the third attribute, the practice of child care as already noted has evolved considerably in recent decades, from something akin to a babysitting service, to that now provided by trained and qualified people in formal caring settings. There is increasing evidence of norms emerging which could be regarded as specific to the role of child carer. However, there are few examples of peer group associations of child care practitioners other than those established by operators of child care services whether from the public, private or community sectors, which might satisfy the third attribute of professionalization. In Australia, there are a number of groups including the Australian Early Childhood Association, the Australian Federation of Child Care Associations, and the Creche and Kindergarten Association, which offer some peer group affiliation for child care practitioners. However, these bodies have little or no role in setting or reviewing professional practice in the manner of associations or institutions in other fields such as the Australian Medical Association, legal bodies such as the Bar Association or a body such as the Institution of Engineers. It would appear that, in relation to this particular attribute of professionalism, the practice of child care would fail to qualify.

However, it could be argued that there are some fields where practitioners are still regarded as professionals despite their activities not being specifically subject to peer review. For example, some of those who are included under the broad term of "scientists" may certainly be regarded as professionals, but not necessarily affiliated with, nor governed by, any particular peer scientific body. Many of these people would be likely to possess most, if not all, of the other attributes of a professional apart from the peer group affiliation. Child care practitioners might therefore be considered professionals in the same way as some scientists not affiliated with a professional peer group. It's also conceivable that for child care practitioners, this deficiency may be addressed in the foreseeable future, either through government policy settings or by further maturing of the roles of existing industry representative bodies.

Motivated by Altruism Not Profit

The fourth attribute of a professional listed above relates to an issue which I've examined in some detail in my thesis concerning the ethical implications of the commodification of early childhood care. I explore the question of the motives of those paid to care for children, particularly the question of the tension between altruistic motives and any financial rewards obtained by carers. While I don't have sufficient space to go into the full details of those arguments here, I concluded among other things that those who are paid to care for children as an occupation would generally be considered to be primarily motivated by altruistic intentions rather than a desire to profit for profit's sake. In the sense of altruism as relating to the degree of care or concern for the subject of professional practice, there's little doubt that the majority of those involved in child care would meet this particular criterion.

Overall then, there appear to be good grounds for those involved in child care, particularly those with advanced qualifications and training, to be considered eligible to be termed "professionals," insofar as some of the common attributes of a professional are concerned. However, the failure of child care to conform completely with some of the common attributes of a profession suggests that it may yet fall short of what one might regard as a paradigm case of professionalism. Certainly, I would argue that it is important that the practice of child care comes to possess as many of the attributes of professionalism as possible, to enhance the quality and ethical standards of child care services. Achieving higher professional standing is important both for the providers of, and for the recipients of, a service, as well as for the community in which the service is provided, even if child care only comes to be regarded as a "quasi-professional" occupation. The creation of even quasi-professionals, if indeed it is one of the outcomes of the commodification of child care, could be regarded as a significant moral virtue associated with such a commodification.

QUALIFICATIONS VERSUS NURTURE

However, the tendency towards increased formal qualifications for child carers may involve tension with the notion of loving, nurturing care which is fundamental in matters of caring for very young children. This tension was noted in a Senate Committee report on the provision of child care in Australia:

> Those who are sceptical about qualifications stress that 'experience' is the main qualification required. Maturity and what may be described as 'motherliness' are said to be among the best qualifications. The committee noted elements of disdain in references to the willingness of young graduates to deal with the mess that comes with the care of young children. (Senate References Committee, 2009, p. 53)

Margaret Sims argues that attempts to divorce what early childhood workers do from the work of mothers is a possible driver towards higher qualifications (Sims, 2012). However, Sims questions what she claims is an underlying assumption that the early childhood workforce is comprised only of "educators" and that improvements to the workforce therefore requires higher educational qualifications. Sims argues that an overwhelming focus on only educational aspects of early childhood care is misguided and should not be regarded as "the only pathway to professionalization." She rejects attempts by others, such as Michael Lyons, to exclude from professional status those in related fields like Family Day Care, which takes place in the carer's home. Lyons argues that the co-existence of family day care, side by side with center-based children's services "diminishes the status of long day care workers and their labour." Sims, however, believes the focus on just the educational aspects of early childhood care work overlooks the equally important relationship work which she says is "fundamental in high quality early childhood practice." She argues that the role of early childhood carer involves much more than just the teaching of children, and cautions against allowing the pursuit of professionalism to devalue "the care component of our work."

However, I believe that the focus on the educational, rather than the caring, aspects of early childhood care as an occupation, in some respects, is not surprising. One of the common notions of a "professional" is that of a qualified expert, highly trained in a particular field, who provides specialized services in a careful but clinical manner, without unnecessary feeling or emotion. So, for example, medical professionals working with the very sick or dying might remain emotionally removed from the plight of their patients to ensure their judgments about necessary treatments are not clouded by emotional influences. Or, the legal practitioner acting as prosecutor might need to repress feelings of empathy towards an accused person to ensure such emotions do not affect the mounting of a thorough and effective prosecution. In the same way, a child care professional might therefore be expected to maintain a certain degree of emotional detachment from children in her care to concentrate on her teaching and child development role. This is particularly an issue in matters of discipline, when carers are faced with misbehavior by children and must act to curb the behavior while maintaining a caring and nurturing relationship with the child.

However, for child care "professionals," it is arguable that feelings of care and love are intrinsically "part of the service" and, as such, cannot be set aside in the same way as for other professionals in the performance of their duties. Even compared with other caring occupations, the role of child carer would seem to imply a certain degree of emotional attachment between the carer and the child. Children require care for all sorts of everyday living needs and this very dependency creates an attachment or bond between the child and the carer. As Margaret Sims observes: "If we are to successfully pursue professionalism and not lose elements of our work then we need to find alternative discourses that recognize the totality of our occupation and what we feel is important in that labour" (Sims, 2012). There are other caring occupations, notably certain areas of nursing, where such emotional attachments would be expected to be found.

But it could also be argued that the potential for the development of strong emotional responses and attachments on the part of carers, of itself, provides good grounds for the adoption of a professional approach to such caring occupations. There are a number of professions, including medicine, law and teaching, where the development of personal relationships between the professional and the "client" are considered improper and contrary to accepted professional conduct. These rules generally prohibit or restrict personal relationships between, for example, doctors and their patients, or school teachers and their students. However, the situation is not black and white and there are many shades of gray when it comes to relationships involving some professionals and their clients. It's not uncommon for lawyers, for example, to have personal relationships with their clients, particularly in establishing and maintaining arrangements for an ongoing business or commercial relationship.

But the key factor in most of these relationships is whether any personal connection is, or is likely to be, prejudicial to strictly professional conduct on the part of the practitioner towards his client. This is a question which I believe is relevant to the performance of the role of a child carer. It's important for the child carer to behave in a professional manner toward those in her care irrespective of the emotional responses occurring between carer and child. This becomes even more evident when one considers the alternative scenario to that where a carer has a strong emotional attachment to a child. That is, where a carer, for some reason, has developed a strong *dislike* toward a child. It is obviously most important under those circumstances that the carer ensures her personal feelings towards the child do not affect her undertaking her professional responsibilities of caring for the child. In fact, it may require a carer to maintain a suitable degree of separation in cases where there appears to be a particularly severe or intractable aversion towards a child. While strong feelings towards children in their care, one way or another, is likely to be a common experience for most child carers, this does provide a strong argument for a professional approach to their role.

PROFESSIONAL CHILD CARE AND THE COMMUNITY

Daniel Wueste makes the important point that the professional relationship is one which is based on trust and reliance. He says "… because they profess, professionals ask that they be trusted" (Wueste, 2013, pp. 2–3). But in the case of child care, the relationship is not the usual two-way relationship of, say, doctor and patient, or lawyer and client, but a three-way relationship involving the carer, the child, and the parents. The trust involved in a parent placing her child in the care of another is certainly comparable to that involved in seeking treatment from a doctor or legal advice from a lawyer even though it appears to be fundamentally different in nature. In the case of legal medical professionals, we usually have to trust their advice because we don't usually have the expertise ourselves to make a judgment about the matter at hand. In the case of child carers, it is usually not the case that we are relying on their superior or special knowledge, but instead we are trusting that they will carry out their duties competently, nurturing and not harming the child, and so on. The relationship the professional carer has with a child may also differ in that it often involves love and nurture, while the relationship between the carer and the parent is more akin to that of other professionals with their "clients." But the issue of trust is nevertheless extremely important in any professional relationship and no less so in child care. Moreover, as Daniel Wueste observes, trust is what makes a professional service "viable." That is, if you don't trust the service, you won't buy or use it (Wueste, 2013, pp. 4–5). It is reasonable to conclude from this then that a commodified child care service would not be viable without a significant degree of trust between the parties.

There is also a broader relationship involving most professional practitioners which is their relationship with the wider community. Those involved in the care and education of children have a particularly significant relationship with the general community through the immediate and extended families of those in their care. This effectively means that the community places its trust in the carers and teachers of children to support and guide young citizens for the benefit of society in the future. An important element of the trust that exists in a professional relationship stems from the perception of the moral standards of the practitioner. A medical patient relies on an assumption that her doctor will exercise good moral judgment in making decisions about her treatment in the same way that a person seeking legal advice will expect certain moral standards from a lawyer. Child care professionals must not only possess good moral standards and judgment to meet their obligations as professional practitioners, but also provide appropriate role modeling for the children in their care. Daniel Wueste argues that professionals operate within a set of moral constraints which attach to their position or role, and thereby to the individual occupying that role (Wueste, 2013). This idea of a "role morality" while applicable to many situations is, according to John Boatright, "especially applicable to the situation of *professionals*" (2007, p. 20).

Child carers are teachers of very young children who are learning about moral choices and moral behavior. The notion of a role morality for child carers is therefore much more than that of a professional behaving morally in the exercise of her professional duties. It is in fact part of the role of child carers to help guide and develop the emerging moral awareness of the child in the same way as they develop the physical, intellectual, and emotional attributes of the child. Child carers also have a moral responsibility to the parents of the child to behave appropriately toward the child and ensure the parents are fully informed on all aspects of the child's care.

This moral obligation also involves ensuring proper standards are maintained in the care of the child, for example, in the adherence to regulatory standards and requirements which may be applicable. Such role morality by professional carers is one of the strongest means of ensuring good moral outcomes within a commodified child care market. In recent years, it has become more common for authorities to require commodified child care services to adopt a comprehensive code of ethics for their staff. Early Childhood Australia, for example, developed a Code of Ethics in 2006 which closely resembles that of the British Association for Early Childhood Education. These are comprehensive statements of ethical principles to guide child carers in their relationships with children, families, fellow child carers, service providers and the community at large. These codes stress the obligations of carers to "adhere to lawful policies and procedures and, when there is conflict, attempt to effect change through constructive action within the organization or seek change through appropriate procedures" (Early Childhood Australia, 2006).

So the adoption of a professional approach to the role of child carer is likely to produce heightened awareness among carers of their "role morality" responsibilities leading to a more active pursuit of appropriate standards via various means including, on occasions, the practice of whistle-blowing. This is in the interests not only of the children and their families receiving care, but also of the community as a whole. Some, like Paul Zak, argue that it is "moral markets" which ensure good moral outcomes in the buying and selling of goods and services in the marketplace (Zak, 2011). An argument can be made that highly informed parents making choices within an open and accountable environment of child care services provides the potential to have a moral market. In this case, the morality of the market is determined by the collective morality of the consumers of the services whose response to the nature of the services is, in part, a moral response. But that does not diminish the importance of individual role morality on the part of child care "professionals" in providing good moral outcomes. The very basis of a moral society depends to a large extent on the development of good moral behavior and practice among its youngest citizens.

Child care professionals play a vital role in providing the earliest moral guidance and teaching to the future adult citizens of a society and the environment in which they do this must support the achievement of good moral outcomes. David Schumaker and Robert Heckel claim it is "one of the more robust findings in the moral development literature that children with the most advanced moral development at all stages of life are those with close and strong bonds with primary caregivers" (Shumaker & Heckel, 2007, p. 195). While these caregivers may be either parents, child carers, teachers or others, they say the findings are also clear regarding the importance of the quality of external caregivers. Schumaker and Heckel say the training of the child carers should be one of the most important considerations for any parents using child care services: "The negative consequences associated with consistently sending a child to be cared for by individuals who provide substandard care will ... have far reaching consequences as the child continues to develop" (Shumaker & Heckel, 2007, p. 54). Hence, the development of the professional skills of the child care workforce appears to be closely linked to beneficial outcomes for children which must also be beneficial for society as a whole.

CONCLUSION

I have shown how the practice of caring for children and assisting with their development is increasingly coming to resemble a professional activity. We've looked at four of the fundamental attributes of being a professional and seen how child care practitioners could be considered to meet these criteria with the possible exception of having an overarching peer group or professional association for their activities. However, the process of professionalization is still in the relatively early stages of evolution, and we've seen how this process is creating tension between the traditional nurturing role of child care and the more formal requirements of a "professional" carer. It appears that, while the traditional nurturing aspects of caring for children continue to be important, it is also necessary that more professional attributes of child carers be developed and promulgated.

I've shown how commodifying child care has tended to foster this development of a profession of carers of young, preschool age children through higher formal qualifications and providing a framework within which a profession can be practiced. I've argued that this is good not only for the care providers but also for those receiving care – the children and their families. It also has important implications for society itself. Those involved in the care and education of children have a particularly significant relationship with the general community through the families of those in their care. The community places its trust in the carers and teachers of children to support and guide young citizens for the benefit of society in the future.

REFERENCES

Boatright, J. R. (2007). *Ethics and the conduct of business* (5th ed.). Upper Saddle River, NJ: Pearson Prentice Hall.

Early Childhood Australia. (2006). *Code of ethics*. Deakin West: ECA.

Lyons, M. (2011). The professionalization of children's services in Australia. *Journal of Sociology, 48*(2), 115–131.

Senate References Committee. (2009). *Provision of childcare*. Canberra: Australian Senate.

Shumaker, D. M., & Heckel, R. V. (2007). *Kids of character: A guide to promoting moral development*. Westport, CT: Greenwood Publishing Group.

Sims, M. (2010). What does being an early childhood "teacher" mean in tomorrow's world of children and family services? *Australasian Journal of Early Childhood, 35*(3), 111–114.

Sims, M. (2012). *The early childhood workforce: Who are we and what do we want to be? National symposium: Early childhood development an emerging profession*. South Australia: Adelaide.

The Social Research Centre. (2014). *2013 National early childhood education and care workforce census*. Victoria, Australia.

Wueste, D. (2013). Trust me I'm a professional: Exploring the conditions and implications of trust for professions. *Research in Ethical Issues in Organizations, 9*, 1–12.

Zak, P. J. (2011). Moral markets. *Journal of Economic Behaviour and Organisation, 77*(2), 212–233.

MEASURING ETHICAL AND EMPIRICAL CONSEQUENCES OF DE-INSTITUTIONALISATION

Paul Jewell, Matthew Dent and Ruth Crocker

ABSTRACT

The purpose of this chapter is to examine the consequences of closing institutions for people with disabilities and accommodating them in Supported Residential Services. Issues that had been raised by an advocacy movement included shortcomings in privacy, dignity, control and meaningful activity in institutions, which led to their closure. The study applied a quality of life measurement which was commensurate with the ethical paradigms of welfare, autonomy and communitarianism to investigate whether community living in supported residences produced fulfilling lives and better outcomes than the institutions they replaced. Twenty-seven people with a disability and/or mental health issue in Supported Residential Services in Victoria, Australia were interviewed using the 'Lehman Quality of Life Questionnaire'. An investigation into the Quality of Life of one group of de-institutionalised residents revealed that issues remain. People in the Supported Residences appear to be no better off than when they were in institutions. The study identified that it was common for a resident to have no phone, no friends outside the residence,

Contemporary Issues in Applied and Professional Ethics
Research in Ethical Issues in Organizations, Volume 15, 149–167
ISSN: 1529-2096/doi:10.1108/S1529-209620160000015009

little or no family contact, no disposable money and no job. However, since there was no research conducted before de-institutionalisation, the impact of the policy change is difficult to determine. Applying ethical measures, such as the Capabilities approach, reveals that issues remain. Practical implications from this study are first, that positive measures need to be added to de-institutionalisation to achieve satisfactory outcomes and second, that policy makers would be better informed and likely more effective if data were collected before and after significant changes.

Keywords: Quality of life; de-institutionalisation; disability ethics

THE QUESTION

Crafting public policy that is a practical application of ethical theory is a challenge. Hume believed people could form communities driven by sympathy but Rousseau was keen to preserve freedom (Hume, 1978; Rousseau, 1983). Bentham and Mill thought the whole point is to maximise well-being while Kant maintained that it is imperative to treat people as ends in themselves (Bentham, 1965; Kant, 1981; Mill, 1984). Rawls argued that social arrangements should be fair and Nussbaum argued that they should enable people to exercise their capabilities (Nussbaum, 2006; Rawls, 1971). Juggling these (sometimes competing) demands is challenging enough with idealised equal and independent citizens, but it is more so when attempting to meet the needs of people whose community engagement, well-being and self-determination are compromised by disability or mental health issues.

For most of the twentieth century (perhaps driven by utilitarian considerations) the common arrangement for such people was to institutionalise them. Towards the end of the century an advocacy movement occurred and raised concerns relating to the treatment of residents and their quality of life (Gee & McGarty, 2013). The concerns included specific instances of abuse and neglect and general issues of rights, finances and satisfying life experiences. A process of de-institutionalisation followed. Facilities closed and residents moved to a variety of accommodation. Some lived independently, some with families and some in various forms of supported community housing (Bostock, Gleeson, McPherson, & Pang, 2001; Health & Community Services, 1993; Picton, Cooper, & Owen, 1997).

It is worth asking whether the change has been for the better. The question can be put using ethical frameworks. Applying a consequentialist approach, has the welfare of the clients improved? How is their health and their access to health services? Do they experience satisfactory lives? Addressing the issue of autonomy, one might ask if they make decisions about their own lives, manage their own finances and choose leisure and employment options. From a communitarian perspective, do they engage with others? Do they have friends, visit family and participate in social groups?

These ethical questions can be translated, for empirical purposes, into the related paradigm 'Quality of Life'. In this study, the situation of a selection of de-institutionalised people was investigated using this tool, and it was hoped a comparison with living in institutions would be made. The study comprised of a selection of people who were living in Supported Residential Services in the State of Victoria, Australia and these people were interviewed using the 'Lehman Quality of Life Questionnaire' (Lehman, Kernan, & Postrado, 1995). The findings indicate that while closing institutions may have benefited some of their residents, it is doubtful that it resulted in an improvement for others, such as those now in Supported Residential Services. But to be confident that a change is effective, in terms of practical ethics or quality of life, policy makers need to record key measures before the change, which regrettably was not done.

THE SETTING

A number of Quality of Life models have been developed with a focus on the disability sector (Kober & Eggleton, 2006; Murphy, Herrman, Hawthorne, Pinzone, & Evert, 2000; Schalock & Keith, 1993). Such models have been developed recognising the difficulty many of these people may have in identifying their goals and wishes, and communicating their feelings and concerns. However, the only model that appeared to be a study of the Quality of Life of people with a variety of disabilities in an institutional setting was the 'Lehman Quality of Life Questionnaire'. First used in the 1980s, it developed over the years to be utilised in measuring the quality of life for people with a mental illness and intellectual disability in a variety of settings. These settings included hospitals, private board and care homes and community settings. This questionnaire was thus selected as the one that would be used to investigate contemporary Supported Residential Services in Victoria, Australia.

The study defined an institution as a large congregated residential setting
of more than 20 beds (Australian Institute of Health and Welfare, 2005;
Stancliffe, 2002; Young, Sigafoos, Suttie, Ashman, & Grevell, 1998) typically 'characterized by their segregation from the community, the age of
the buildings, the large population of residents, structured routines, and
congregate living arrangements' (New South Wales Community Services
Commission, 1997, p. 3).

In contrast, Supported Residential Services are a form of communal
accommodation defined as 'premises where accommodation and personal
support are privately provided or offered to residents for a fee or reward'
(*Supported Residential Services (Private Proprietors) Act 2010 (Vic)*,
Section 5). In the United States, a similar model providing support for people with mental illness is known as 'board and care homes' (Hawes et al.,
1995). Supported Residential Services were originally established to house
older persons who needed minimal support – a form of accommodation
for aged care with low support needs (Sach et al., 1987). The majority of
beds in pension-level Supported Residential Services are now taken by people with disabilities (96%), primarily mild intellectual disability, acquired
brain injury, mental illness or multiple disabilities (Bigby & Fyffe, 2006;
Bostock et al., 2001; Greenhalgh et al., 2004; Office of the Public Advocate,
2009; Van Dyke, 2009; Warner, 1989).

A number of studies have examined the transition into community living
settings (Bigby, Frederico, & Cooper, 2007; Dunt & Cummins, 1990; Picton
et al. 1997; Picton, Cooper, Owen, & Chanty, 1997). These studies brought
forth consistent evidence that when individuals with disabilities moved into a
community setting, their lives improved in a number of areas. Such improvements were identified in skill development, opportunities and choice, family
contact, adaptive behaviour, communication and general health. Such findings were consistent with the evidence that was coming forth from international studies (Emerson, 2004; Emerson & Hatton, 1996; Larson, Lakin, &
Charlie, 1991). Studies into the transition of people with an intellectual
disability into community settings established clear evidence that their lives
improved with such a move (Young et al., 1998). Evidence included improvement in areas such as adaptive skills, general health, communication, socially
acceptable behaviour and skill development (Bigby et al., 2007; Dunt &
Cummins, 1990; Picton et al. 1997). In contrast, evidence for the transition of
people with mental illness from an institutional setting into the community
showed few changes in the quality of their life (Horan, Muller, Winocur, &
Barling, 2001; Shadish, Lurigio, & Lewis, 1989).

Although these studies showed benefits of de-institutionalisation generally, the current study was prompted by doubts that were raised about the adequacy of the Supported Residential Services scheme specifically and whether it provided an improvement to residents' previous institutional arrangements. A number of inquests have noted that the clients being referred to these services now have needs far more complex than when the services were first established, especially in the below-pension services (Green, 2001; Van Dyke, 2009). These complexities included multiple disabilities, brain injury or alcohol and drug abuse (Office of the Public Advocate, 2009; University of Wollongong, 2011). The referrals for below-pension services nearly all come from mental health and disability support services. Despite their additional and more complex needs, only a minimal number have additional support from other disability or mental health services. Many residents have no other social activities outside the Supported Residential Service, and approximately 50% have less than one visit per month by family members (Van Dyke, 2009). The Supported Residential Services are required by regulation to have just one staff person on duty at any one time who is trained, to just Certificate 3 (Personal Care Assistant), and the staff ratio required is 1:30 (Department of Human Services, 2001).

METHODOLOGY

There are currently approximately 60 Supported Residential Services facilities providing pension-level services. The current study restricted the pool to those that were mid-size and in a metropolitan area, and contacted 16 of the facilities. Eight proprietors provided permission for their residents to be contacted to participate in the study.

While 32 people initially signed up to take part in the questionnaire, only 27 of those actually participated in the questionnaire. One person declined taking part on the day, while two people had moved out of their accommodation between the time of their initial meeting and the appointment for the interview. Two further residents were absent at the time of their appointment and were unable to be contacted. Of all those who took part in this study, only one person identified as having their own phone and contact number.

The fact that several people who offered to take part in this study moved out of their accommodation in just a few weeks between appointments shows a factor that could influence results. There is a substantial group that move between Supported Residential Services regularly, and are never in a stable accommodation setting (Office of the Public Advocate, 2009). This part of the population did not appear to take part in the study, even though some initially wished to. The bulk of people taking part in this study made it clear that they had been living in their current residence for at least three years, and some for up to 20 years.

Most interviews were carried out in a single face-to-face interview session. Client behaviour and non-verbal signals were monitored, and a number of interviewees were offered a break when their concentration appeared to wane, or stress levels increased. All interviewees completed the interview.

The vulnerability and susceptibility of the participants presented ethical issues in the conduct of this research. All of the people in this group had a form of disability, primary mental health issue, acquired brain injury or an intellectual disability, and, as was discovered during the study, were also segregated from the community. Safeguards needed to be established to ensure participants were not manipulated or influenced to take part in the study, or in the responses they gave. Hence they were provided sufficient information on avenues to pursue if they felt intimidated. Participants received regular reassurances that they were able to withdraw from the study at any time, and staff within the facilities were not informed of who was participating. Participants' stress and anxiety levels were monitored during the interviews. Adaptations to the interview were made as necessary, including brief breaks when required and ending the interview when required or requested by participants. Participants were able to have some input into where they wished to be interviewed (on or off-site) to ensure they felt secure, private and relaxed. A list of counselling services was provided. All participants expressed confidence that there would not be repercussions from the staff within the Supported Residential Service they lived in. Ethical approval and oversight was provided by Flinders University.

THE QUESTIONNAIRE

The Lehman Quality of Life Questionnaire has been developed to ensure consistency, and minimise interviewer influence on the participant's response (Lehman, 1988). It is also focused on a person's current perceptions on the criteria, due to the likelihood that they may have some memory shortfalls. Questions are brief and tangible, and all answers are given a numerical value. This is then calculated against all eight criteria at the end of the questionnaire, giving a numerical value to each that allows for comparisons.

The questionnaire addresses both objective and subjective criteria. As other studies have found, there may often be a great variance between the objective evidence of what is actually occurring in an individual's life and the subjective evidence of how that person actually feels about their life (Barlow & Kirby, 1991; Horan et al., 2001). This Quality of Life tool is thus able to give a more balanced view of an individual's quality of life.

PARTICIPANTS

The demographic characteristics of the participants can be seen in Table 1.

FINDINGS – OBJECTIVE MEASURES

The objective data for Lehman's questionnaire (Table 2) was gathered in several different forms. This included establishing a numerical value between 1 and 5 for the criteria of family contact, social relations and health, based on the responses to questions from participants. A rating of 1 was the lowest possible, and 5 the maximum. For example, if someone did not see their family at all, their answer was rated 1; if they saw them on a daily basis it was rated 5. Leisure was given a rating of between 0 and 1; if an individual received 1 for this criterion it would indicate they took part in several activities. The remaining criterion were measured by the factual data given of a participant's spending money, and the percentage of participants who had been involved in specific occurrences in the previous year.

Table 1. Sample Characteristics.

N	27
% of residents women	33
Age (mean years)	51
Education (mean years)	10
% of residents Caucasian	78
% of residents never married	59
% of residents to visit hospital in last year	41

Table 2.   Objective Measures.

Objective measure of family contact	2.44
Objective measure of social relations	1.90
Objective measure of leisure	.375
Objective measure of health	3.30
$ monthly spending in 2013[a]	A$86
Residents currently employed	3% (See below in Analysis)
Residents arrested in last year	0%
Residents robbed in last year	22%
Residents assaulted in last year	3%

Note: [a]Monetary figures multiplied by 1.71 as per US inflation calculator (www.usinflationcal-culator.com) and divided by 1.05 as per exchange rate on 13 April 2013 (www.xe.com/currencyconverter).

FINDINGS – SUBJECTIVE DATA

The second portion of Lehman's Quality of Life Questionnaire requested clients to give feedback on their personal feelings about various aspects of their life. Participants were given a visual scale to assist their rating of all these issues in their life, with clients asked to give a rating from 1 (Terrible) through to 7 (Delighted) on how they felt about issues raised in the questionnaire.

As other studies have found on a regular basis, subjective measures of how people with disabilities feel about their residences and life situation are not always fully reflective of objective measures of quality of life factors (Barlow & Kirby, 1991; Horan et al., 2001; Lehman, Slaughter, & Myers, 1991). All these studies have found that residents show higher levels of satisfaction with their quality of life than would be expected with the poor results from objective measures – the current study's results echoed this. Participants were 'mostly dissatisfied' with finances but were 'mixed' on all other measures. The disparity between the objective measures and the subjective measures was intriguing, though not unusual. It can be argued that the level of satisfaction of their 'adaptive preferences' expressed by the participants does not mean that their lives were satisfactory by other measures (Begon, 2015).

ANALYSIS

Reviewing the objective measures (see Table 2), the low scores are a matter of concern. Measures of family contact suggest that participants had low levels of interaction with their family. Considering the average age of participants, this may have had a notable impact on their quality of life. With 70% of participants having no children, as the participants aged, they would have become reliant on older siblings with their own families and limitations, and parents for contact, making it more difficult. Significantly, many who took part in the questionnaire had no phone contact with their family at all (44%). Anecdotal evidence during discussions also suggested access to a phone in a private setting was very difficult, as per previous studies (Doyle, Hume, McAvaney, Rogers, & Stephenson, 2003; Green, 2001; Office of the Public Advocate, 2009), and this was likely to discourage regular contact. Strikingly, only one participant had their own phone.

Social relations measured were lower than family contacts, with a measure of 1.90. In the current study only 22% of participants identified as using a computer to communicate. Presumably, this would play a big role in negating access to the community in these days of social networking. Only a third of participants identified as using the telephone at all to contact friends. In terms of social relationships, many participants (60%) suggested they were involved socially with other people. However, only 40% identified this as involving someone off the Supported Residential Services site, suggesting for many their social involvement is non-existent or completely limited to fellow tenants in their residence. These findings were also reflective of the most recent study on Victorian Supported Residential Services, completed by the Office of the Public Advocate (Office of the Public Advocate, 2009).

The measures of leisure activities were not high. Victorian Supported Residential Services facilities have limited space and minimal common areas. Leisure activities were limited to watching television in most facilities, while only one had a pool table. Most organised regular trips into the community, though these trips appeared to be having little impact in broadening an individual's social networks. Many people appeared indifferent to being involved in such activities.

Health measures were good. Almost all participants advised that they had regular access to a General Practitioner. Many people felt confident that they could access other therapists such as a psychologist as required.

Finances available to individuals were low – monthly spending money available for participants averaged out to be only $86. It is notable that only two individuals could identify how much money they received for their pensions, and only five managed their own money. Most participants identified State Trustees as their financial administrators. When individuals were asked if they were able to cover their daily costs, they identified satisfaction with the cost of most things, with food and accommodation already covered. Health costs were not an issue for most participants under Medicare, but social activities and transport were two issues that were notably restricted for individuals. Generally social activities needed to be activities that would be of no cost due to their minimal spending money.

In regard to finance and poverty, the most noteworthy factor here appeared to be the fact that only one participant identified himself as employed. Despite this, he said his salary was $6 per day, which suggests that he was actually engaged in voluntary work or in a supported employment organisation. This is reflective of recent research showing the low level of employment opportunities for people with intellectual disability and mental illness in Australia (Harvey, Modini, Christensen, & Glozier, 2013; Stancliffe, 2002). Lack of employment, even in the form of supported employment, exacerbates the issues of poverty and lack of social interaction that have appeared in the findings of this study. Notably, all 27 participants, at some time, had some involvement in the Australian workforce, but at the time of the study had none. While in some cases this may have been due to the onset of their illness, in many cases it was clear that they had had their disability all of their life.

While any level of robbery or assault is deplorable, only a small number of participants had been victims. No participants had been arrested, or spent any time in jail in the past year. This may well have been due to the practices mentioned by a number of proprietors, who said that it had become necessary that they 'become more selective' of incoming tenants. This was something they felt was necessary to protect their residents and the stability of their facilities. The statistics showing low levels of assault reflected this to be a good outcome for those within the facility, as it was in contrast to the high levels of violence in similar facilities outlined in recent New South Wales reports (New South Wales Ombudsman, 2010, 2011) and media articles (Carlisle, 2012; Tomazin, 2012).

The subjective results (Table 3) were more positive than the objective results. In the family category, participants' feelings about their relationships were higher than might be expected in light of objective indicators that large numbers of participants having contact with their family only once or twice per year, and some having no phone calls at all.

Many clients were very happy about the regularity and consistency of their access to medical support. All participants and proprietors advised that a General Practitioner would visit their facility at least once per week, making medical access easy for all residents. Despite participants having no

Table 3. Subjective Measures.

Residents' feelings about...	
Family	4.23
Health	4.36
Home	4.75
Leisure	4.31
Social Relations	4.31
Safety	4.60
Finances	3.83
Global QOL	4.57

Notes: Ratings scale for subjective measures: 1 = Terrible; 2 = Unhappy; 3 = Mostly dissatisfied; 4 = Mixed; 5 = Mostly satisfied; 6 = Pleased; 7 = Delighted.

choice in who provided their medical care, none indicated negative feelings about this factor.

Participants returned high ratings for their perception of leisure, social relations and safety. The issue of finances was the lowest of all ratings, with most people relatively dissatisfied with the money they had available to them. This was despite the fact most participants did not have any real knowledge of how much the current rate of pension was, and were not able to give reliable answers to many questions around finances.

COMPARISONS WITH INSTITUTIONALISED LIVING

The everyday lives of residents with disabilities or mental health issues in Supported Residential Services appear to be very poor by ordinary community standards. It is a common situation for a resident to have no phone, no friends outside the residence, little or no family contact, no disposable money and no job. This should surely be a matter of concern for policy makers and service providers.

However, in terms of the change in policy from institutionalised living to living in supported residential accommodation, it is worth asking whether the residents are any better off now, or are their lives actually very similar? Are Supported Residential Services an improvement on institutions, as intended, or practically indistinguishable from them?

This question cannot be answered satisfactorily because of the lack of comparable data about residents' Quality of Life in their preceding institutions.

Given that the implementation of Quality of Life measures began to grow at the same time that institutional settings began to decline, evidence about the Quality of Life of people with disabilities living in such settings is not easy to find. When studies into the transition of people from institutions into community settings first began, the outcomes were often measured by monitoring factors such as adaptive behaviour, activity levels and involvement in the community at large (Emerson, 1985; Felce, 1988). Later studies into the transition from institutional to community living began to use Quality of Life as a measure of the outcomes of these changes. More emphasis was placed on what the benefits were in the minds of the individuals concerned (Dagnan, Ruddick, & Jones, 1998; Picton et al. 1997).

Larson et al. (1991) pointed out that most research into institutionalisation and de-institutionalisation used retrospective data – taking information from people looking back at their life in an institution after they had moved on from the institution. Few studies actually took a Quality of Life measure prior to vacating a facility. Upon conducting a literature, no studies of the Quality of Life prior to de-institutionalisation in Victoria could be found, a point which will be raised again in the conclusion.

However, there is data about other institutions. It is possible to compare the findings of the current study with other studies that have employed Lehman's Quality of Life instrument (Lehman et al., 1991). Table 4 shows data from three studies. The first column is the State Psychiatric Hospital of New York, the second is a large 200-bed 'Private Proprietary Home for Adults' in New York (PPHA in column three) and the third is a study of 'board and care homes' in Los Angeles. While the latter two reflected a model of care that was comparable to the Supported Residential Services facilities of Victoria today, all three are 'institutions' in the sense of being large facilities according to our introductory definition.

Life is safer for residents of Victorian Supported Residential Services than for inmates of American institutions. However, on other measures, the Quality of Life for Victorian residents is lower than for the American residents.

It appears that residents of Victorian Supported Residential Services facilities have less contact with their families than residents of large American institutions did twenty years ago. The extent of their social relationships were even less. Their leisure activities were fewer and their employment prospects were non-existent.

Table 4. Objective Measures.

Objective Measures	SRS 2013	State Hospital	PPHA	Board and Care
Objective measure of family contact	2.44	2.84	2.66	2.73
Objective measure of social relations	1.90	3.11	3.06	2.96
Objective measure of leisure	.375	.48	.47	.4
Objective measure of health	3.30	2.45	2.82	2.59
$ monthly spending in 1991	N/A	US$41	US$82	US$68
$ monthly spending in 2013[a]	A$86	A$65.69	A$132.44	A$109.49
Residents currently employed	3%	23%	14%	18%
Residents arrested in last year	0%	15%	6%	10%
Residents robbed in last year	22%	34%	23%	24%
Residents assaulted in last year	3%	28%	4%	18%

[a]Monetary figures multiplied by 1.71 as per US inflation calculator (www.usinflationcalculator.com) and divided by 1.05 as per exchange rate on 13 April 2013. (www.xe.com/currencyconverter).

According to this data, people with disabilities or mental health issues who have been de-institutionalised may not find their Quality of Life 'in the community' to be any better than in the institutions they used to live in — or at least, the Quality of Life of people in current Victorian Supported Residential Services is no better than people in American institutions of the past. Logically, if the Australian institutions they used to live in were much worse than the American counterparts, then it is possible their lives now are better than previously, but this reasoning is convoluted and of little comfort.

THE CAPABILITIES APPROACH

As indicated previously, quality of life measurement is commensurate with the ethical paradigms of welfare, autonomy and communitarianism. Putting to one side the difficulties of empirical comparisons, an ethical analysis can be applied. Nussbaum (2006) offers a Capabilities approach in *Frontiers of Justice — Disability, Nationality, Species Membership*. Since the first frontier is Disability, the Capabilities approach is very relevant. Nussbaum proposes that a just society should be positive, affirmative and explicit concerning the respect for persons. Each person has a unique life, intentions and purposes. These are not just characteristics that people *have,* but what people *do.* People are capable of expressing themselves, forming relationships with others and engaging with their physical and social environments. Respecting persons, their rights and freedoms, requires, in practice, making sure that they can flourish as human beings (Jewell, 2010).

Nussbaum proposes the following.

Capabilities

1. *Life*. Being able to live to the end of a human life of normal length; not dying prematurely, or before one's life is so reduced as to be not worth living.
2. *Bodily Health*. Being able to have good health, including reproductive health; to be adequately nourished; to have adequate shelter.
3. *Bodily Integrity*. Being able to move freely from place to place; to be secure against violent assault, including sexual assault and domestic violence; having opportunities for sexual satisfaction and for choice in matters of reproduction.
4. *Senses, Imagination, and Thought*. Being able to use the senses, to imagine, think, and reason — and to do these things in a "truly human" way, a way informed and cultivated by an adequate education, including, but by no means limited to, literacy and basic mathematical and scientific training. Being able to use imagination and thought in connection with experiencing and producing works and events of one's own choice, religious, literary, musical and so forth. Being able to use one's mind in ways protected by guarantees of freedom of expression with respect to both political and artistic speech and freedom of religious exercise. Being able to have pleasurable experiences and to avoid nonbeneficial pain.
5. *Emotions*. Being able to have attachments to things and persons outside ourselves; to love those who love and care for us; to grieve at their absence; in general to love and to grieve, to experience longing, gratitude, and justified anger. Not having one's emotional developing blighted by fear or anxiety. (Supporting this capability means supporting forms of human association that can be shown to be crucial in their development.)
6. *Practical reason*. Being able to form a conception of the good and to engage in critical reflection about the planning of one's own life. (This entails protection for liberty of conscience and religious observance.)

7. *Affiliation.*
   A. Being able to live with and towards others, to recognise and show concern for other human beings, to engage in various forms of social interaction; to be able to imagine the situation of another. (Protecting this capability means protecting institutions that constitute and nourish such forms of affiliation, and also protecting the freedom of assembly and political speech.)
   B. Having the social bases of self-respect and non-humiliation; being able to be treated as a dignified being whose worth is equal to that of others. This entails provisions of non-discrimination on the basis of race, sex, sexual orientation, ethnicity, caste, religion, national origin.
8. *Other Species.* Being able to live with concern for and in relation to animals, plants, and the world of nature.
9. *Play.* Being able to laugh, to play, to enjoy recreational activities.
10. *Control over one's environment.*
   A. *Political.* Being able to participate effectively in political choices that govern one's life; having the rights of political participation, protections of free speech and association.
   B. *Material.* Being able to hold property (both land and movable goods), and having property rights on an equal basis with others; having the right to seek employment on an equal basis with others; having the freedom from unwarranted search and seizure. In work, being able to work as a human being, exercising practical reason and entering into meaningful relationships of mutual recognition with other workers. (Nussbaum, 2006, pp. 77–78)

Applying these capabilities to the residents, it appears that the first and second are met. Residents have access to good health services and we have no evidence of reduced longevity. The third is mostly met. They are not subject to assault. With regard to the remainder of the third capability, though, there appears to be no opportunities for sexual satisfaction. The passive nature of the residents' lives, as opposed to flourishing, is striking with regard to all the rest of the capabilities from fourth to tenth. They do not produce works that are 'religious, literary, musical and so forth' or engage much, if at all, in education or pleasurable experiences (Capability 4). They have little practical engagement with things or people outside themselves (Capabilities 5, 7 and 8). They do not appear to 'engage in critical reflection about the planning of one's own life' (Capability 6), though on the other hand they did not express dissatisfaction with their lives as they were.

They do not take part in 'play' to any appreciable amount (Capability 9). They have little control over their environment (Capability 10). There was no indication that they were deprived of their ordinary citizens' political rights, but within their immediate environment they do not control, for example, the times or contents of their meals. They do not 'hold property' or work.

It should be noted that there are no regulations *prohibiting* the residents from exercising these capabilities. Instead, the overwhelming feature of their lives is passivity, rather than a fulfilment of ordinary human capabilities. In this, their lives do not differ significantly from life in an institution.

CONCLUSION

This study set out to investigate whether the change of social services policy for people with disability or mental health issues from institutional accommodation to community living with Supported Residential Services had resulted in improvements to their lives.

It was found that in contemporary Australia, it is a common situation for a resident of a Supported Residential Service to have no phone, no friends outside the residence, little or no family contact, no disposable money and no job.

If society expects social arrangements, government services and public health policy to aim at providing good outcomes, then our expectations have an ethical dimension (Jewell, 2010). Society hope for good consequences for recipients, as well as valuing their autonomy and their opportunities for engaging with the community.

If policy makers are to take consequentialism seriously, then they need to ask whether a change in policy might be expected to produce better consequences. If those consequences are the sorts of outcomes that can be measured practically, then, it can be argued, they should be measured before effecting a policy change and again afterwards, to see if things are better than before (Davidson, 2005).

The current study reflected on whether the participants' situation was satisfactory or unsatisfactory using a Quality of Life paradigm and ethical paradigms of welfare, autonomy, communitarianism and the capabilities approach. It does not appear that the policy change of de-institutionalisation has been effective in terms of those paradigms for residents of Supported Residential Services.

REFERENCES

Australian Institute of Health and Welfare. (2005). Some trends in the use of accommodation support services for people with intellectual disabilities in Australia. *Journal of Intellectual & Developmental Disability, 30*(2), 120–124.

Barlow, J., & Kirby, N. (1991). Residential satisfaction of persons with an intellectual disability living in an institution or in the community. *Australia and New Zealand Journal of Developmental Disabilities, 17*(1), 7–23.

Begon, J. (2015). What are adaptive preferences? Exclusion and disability in the capability approach. *Journal of Applied Philosophy, 32*(3), 241–257.

Bentham, J. (1965 [1873]). An introduction to the principles of morals and legislation. In O. Johnson (Ed.), Ethics: Selection from classical and contemporary writers. New York, NY: Holt, Rinehart and Winston.

Bigby, C., Frederico, M., & Cooper, B. (2007). *Settled in the community: An evaluation of five years of community living for residents relocated from Kew Residential Services, 1999–2005*. Melbourne: Department of Human Services.

Bigby, C., & Fyffe, C. (2006). Tensions between institutional closure and deinstitutionalisation: What can be learned from Victoria's institutional redevelopment? *Disability and Society, 21*(6), 567–581.

Bostock, L., Gleeson, B., McPherson, A., & Pang, L. (2001). *Deinstitutionalisation and housing futures: Final report*. Sydney: Australian Housing and Urban Research Institute.

Carlisle, W. (2012). Boarding house of horrors [Radio broadcast]. *ABC Radio National*, June 24. Australia. Retrieved from http://www.abc.net.au/radionational/programs/backgroundbriefing/2012-06-24/4082060

Dagnan, D., Ruddick, L., & Jones, J. (1998). A longitudinal study of the quality of life of older people with intellectual disability after leaving hospital. *Journal of Intellectual Disability Research, 42*(2), 112–121.

Davidson, E. (2005). *Evaluation methodology basics: The nuts and bolts of sound evaluation*. Thousand Oaks, CA: Sage.

Department of Human Services. (2001). *Supported residential services: The department of human services' response to advice from associate professor green*. Melbourne: Department of Human Services.

Doyle, M., Hume, A., McAvaney, J., Rogers, N., & Stephenson, T. (2003). *A place to call home – supported residential facilities: The sector, its clientele and its future*. Adelaide: Department of Human Services.

Dunt, D., & Cummins, R. (1990). The deinstitutionalisation of St. Nicholas hospital: I. Adaptive behaviour and physical health. *Australia and New Zealand Journal of Developmental Disabilities, 16*(1), 5–18.

Emerson, E. (1985). Evaluating the impact of deinstitutionalization on the lives of mentally retarded people. *American Journal of Mental Deficiency, 90*(3), 277–288.

Emerson, E. (2004). Deinstitutionalisation in England. *Journal of Intellectual and Developmental Disability, 29*(1), 79–84.

Emerson, E., & Hatton, C. (1996). Deinstitutionalisation in the UK and Ireland: Outcomes for service users. *Journal of Intellectual and Developmental Disability, 21*, 17–37.

Felce, D. (1988). Evaluating the extent of community integration following the provision of staffed residential alternatives to institutional care. *The Irish Journal of Psychology, 9*(2), 346–360.

Gee, A., & McGarty, C. (2013). Developing cooperative communities to reduce stigma about mental disorders. *Analyses of Social Issues and Public Policy, 13*(1), 137–164.

Green, D. (2001). *Advice to the department of human services on supported residential services.* Melbourne: Department of Human Services.

Greenhalgh, E., Miller, A., Minnery, J., Gurran, N., Jacobs, K., & Phibbs, P. (2004). Boarding houses and supply – Side intervention. *Final Report Series of the Australian Housing and Urban Research Institute, 54,* 1–67.

Harvey, S., Modini, M., Christensen, H., & Glozier, N. (2013). Severe mental illness and work: What can we do to maximize the employment opportunities for individuals with psychosis? *Australian and New Zealand Journal of Psychiatry, 47*(5), 421–424.

Hawes, C., Wildfire, J., Mor, V., Wilcox, V., Spore, D., Iannacchione, V., & Phillips, C. (1995). *A description of board and care facilities, operators, and residents.* Research Triangle Park, NC: US Department of Health & Human Services, Brown University.

Health & Community Services. (1993). *New directions: The changing face of disability services.* Melbourne: Victorian Government Printer.

Horan, M., Muller, J., Winocur, S., & Barling, N. (2001). Quality of life in boarding houses and hostels: A residents' perspective. *Community Mental Health Journal, 37*(4), 323–334.

Hume, D. (1978 [1888]). *A treatise of human nature.* New York, NY: Oxford University Press.

Jewell, P. (2010). *Disability ethics: A framework for practitioners, professionals and policy makers.* Altona, Melbourne: Common Ground Publishing.

Kant, I. (1981 [1797]). *Grounding for the metaphysics of morals* (J. Ellington Trans.). New York, NY: Hackett Publishing Company.

Kober, R., & Eggleton, I. (2006). Using quality of life to assess performance in the disability services sector. *Applied Research in Quality of Life, 1*(1), 63–77.

Larson, S., Lakin, K., & Charlie, K. (1991). Parent attitudes about residential placement before and after deinstitutionalization: A research synthesis. *Journal of the Association for Persons with Severe Handicaps, 16*(1), 25–38.

Lehman, A. (1988). A quality of life interview for the chronically mentally ill. *Evaluation and Program Planning, 11*(1), 51–62.

Lehman, A., Kernan, E., & Postrado, L. (1995). *Toolkit for evaluating quality of life for persons with severe mental illness.* Cambridge, MA: Human Services Research Institute.

Lehman, A., Slaughter, J., & Myers, C. (1991). Quality of life in alternative residential settings. *Psychiatric Quarterly, 62*(1), 35–49.

Mill, J. (1984 [1861]). In H. Acton (Ed.), *Utilitarianism, on liberty and considerations on representative government.* Darlington: J M Dent & Sons.

Murphy, B., Herrman, H., Hawthorne, G., Pinzone, T., & Evert, H. (2000). *Australian WHOQoL instruments: User's manual and interpretation guide.* Melbourne: Australian WHOQoL Field Study Centre.

New South Wales Community Services Commission. (1997). *Performance audit report: Large residential centres for people with a disability in New South Wales.* Sydney: Audit Office of New South Wales.

New South Wales Ombudsman. (2010). *People with disabilities and the closure of residential centres.* Sydney: New South Wales Ombudsman.

New South Wales Ombudsman. (2011). *More than board and lodging: The need for boarding house reform.* Sydney: New South Wales Ombudsman.

Nussbaum, M. (2006). *Frontiers of Justice — Disability, nationality, species membership.* Cambridge, MA: The Belknap Press of Harvard University Press.

Office of the Public Advocate. (2009). *Status report on supported residential services (SRSs) — Sept 2009.* Melbourne: Office of the Public Advocate.

Picton, C., Cooper, B., & Owen, L. (1997). *Evaluation of the relocation of the Aradale and Mayday Hills clients project.* Melbourne: Human Resource Centre, La Trobe University.

Picton, C., Cooper, B., Owen, L., & Chanty, R. (1997). *Evaluation of the relocation of Caloola clients project: A three year follow-up of former Caloola training centre clients.* Melbourne: Human Resource Centre, La Trobe University.

Rawls, J. (1971). *A theory of justice.* Cambridge, MA: Harvard University Press.

Rousseau, J. (1983). *The social contract and discourses.* London: Dent.

Sach & Associates. (1987). *Viability of special accommodation: A report to the ministerial advisory committee of special accommodation houses.* Melbourne: Ministerial Review Committee of Special Accommodation Houses.

Schalock, R., & Keith, K. (1993). *Quality of life questionnaire manual.* Worthington, OH: IDS Publishing Corporation.

Shadish, W., Lurigio, A., & Lewis, D. (1989). After deinstitutionalization: The present and future of mental health long-term care policy. *Journal of Social Issues, 45*(3), 1–15.

Stancliffe, R. (2002). Provision of residential services for people with intellectual disability in Australia: An international comparison. *Journal of Intellectual & Developmental Disability, 27*(2), 117–124.

Tomazin, F. (2012). Violent deaths and soaring abuse in residential homes. *The Age,* October 28. Retrieved from http://www.theage.com.au/victoria/violent-deaths-and-soaring-abuse-in-residential-homes-20121027-28cmh.html

University of Wollongong. (2011). *Needs of residents in unlicensed boarding houses.* Retrieved from http://www.pwd.org.au/documents/project/UnlicBoarding110223.pdf

Van Dyke, N. (2009). *2008 Supported residential services census — summary report: Residents.* Melbourne: Social Research Centre.

Warner, R. (1989). Deinstitutionalization: How did we get where we are? *Journal of Social Issues, 45*(3), 17–30.

Young, L., Sigafoos, J., Suttie, J., Ashman, A., & Grevell, P. (1998). Deinstitutionalisation of persons with intellectual disabilities: A review of Australian studies. *Journal of Intellectual & Developmental Disability, 23*(2), 155–170.

RISKY BUSINESS – THE ETHICS OF JUDGING INDIVIDUALS BASED ON GROUP STATISTICS

Vanessa Scholes

ABSTRACT

In this chapter, I analyse the ethics of organisations assessing applicants based on group risk statistics; for example, parole boards consider information predicting recidivism risk, and employers want to minimise the risk of selecting lower-productivity employees. The organisational rejection of applicants from risky groups is explored as a form of discrimination to help identify the distinct ethical implications for applicant autonomy from the use of group risk statistics. Contra arguments from Schoeman (1987) and Schauer (2003), I argue that there is a substantive difference between assessing applicants directly through group statistics rather than including 'individualised' evidence. This difference impacts on the agency of applicants in the process. As organisations have reason to statistically assess applicants, some considerations for increasing applicant agency in the process are suggested. These include focusing on the nature of the factors used to assess applicants (static or

Contemporary Issues in Applied and Professional Ethics
Research in Ethical Issues in Organizations, Volume 15, 169–188
Copyright © 2016 by Emerald Group Publishing Limited
ISSN: 1529-2096/doi:10.1108/S1529-209620160000015010

*dynamic), the transparency of the process to applicants, and the use of
statistics specific to individuals.*

Keywords: Applied ethics; decision-making; discrimination;
organisations; risk; statistical discrimination

INTRODUCTION

When people apply to an organisation to access a good or service offered by
the organisation, some person or group has to assess the application and make
a decision on it. Decision-makers can be interested in predicting the risk that
an applicant will impose a significant cost on the organisation or on other
people. For example, parole boards consider information relevant to predicting
the likelihood that a prisoner will re-offend once released. In the commercial
context, insurance companies calculate the risk that an insured will make a
claim, and managers want to ensure they hire a productive and reliable
employee. Even in the education field, institutions are interested in predicting
which applicants for tertiary study are a higher risk for dropping out or failing.

To assess the risks associated with applicants, decision-makers can use
evidence we might think of as 'individualised'. This could include the applicant or their referees attesting to their attributes and personal history,
through character or academic references. Individualised evidence could
also include an applicant's efforts, achievements and competencies; for
example, rehabilitation and anti-violence programs completed by prisoners,
work tests by job applicants, or healthy exercise regimes by insurance applicants. Conversely, decision-makers can identify features correlated with
higher risks of undesirable outcomes across the group of people that have
that feature, and assess applicants based on these risk statistics. The particular features will differ depending on the purposes of the organisation and
the relevant laws, but could include factors such as age, gender, ethnicity,
place of residence, employment status and recreational activities.

Schauer (2003) refers to a practice of assessing applicants solely
according to group risk statistics as using 'naked statistical evidence'.
Organisations will be interested in the consequences of using or not using
naked statistical evidence, for the organisation, the applicant and other
people. The potential consequences will differ depending on the organisational decision-maker's purpose. However, the implications for the agency
of applicants − their autonomy − will be similar whether the applicants
are prisoners being assessed for parole, people applying for insurance or

jobs, applicants to tertiary education programmes, or any situation where organisational decision-makers are assessing applicants using group risk statistics. This chapter focuses on the implications for applicant autonomy from the use of group risk statistics to assess applicants.

The chapter proceeds as follows. The next section outlines the strong motivations for organisations to use 'naked statistical evidence' to assess applicants, and notes the similarity to what we ordinarily think of as discrimination in cases where the assessments of applicants are used to exclude or otherwise disadvantage them. Following this, a brief canvas of philosophical accounts of wrongful discrimination identifies the lack of agency and autonomy for applicants as distinctive ethical concerns in these cases. This is undergirded by the lack of recognition of applicants as individuals when assessing them using group risk statistics. Schoeman (1987) and Schauer (2003), however, contend there is little fundamental difference in this regard between 'naked statistical evidence' and so-called 'individualised' evidence. I address their arguments and reject them. In the final section of the chapter I propose some ways of reconciling organisational use of 'naked statistical evidence' with a desire to recognise and include a greater degree of applicant agency and autonomy in the process.

WHY ASSESS APPLICANTS ON THE BASIS OF GROUP RISK STATISTICS?

Schauer (2003) discusses the use of 'naked statistical evidence' for prisoners applying for parole. This involves first identifying factors statistically correlated with recidivism. For example, age at first conviction is strongly correlated with the likelihood of recidivism (see e.g. Piquero, Jennings, Diamond, & Reingle, 2015; Rice & Harris, 2014). Researchers have also found links between the following factors and re-offending: the number and nature of prior offences; drug use, accommodation and employment in the community; in-prison attitudes and behaviour; regular truancy from school in childhood (Brunton-Smith & Hopkins, 2013, p. 2); and lower anterior cingulate cortex activity in the brain (Aharoni et al., 2013).[1] Using 'naked statistical evidence' would entail a computer program screening prisoners applying for parole on factors such as these. The result would be a recidivism risk score (a prediction of the likelihood that a prisoner applying for parole will re-offend once released), on the basis of which the parole decision is made. This is a more efficient process than bringing in experts who will need to do extensive individual assessments of prisoners to generate a recidivism risk score.

Schauer (2003, p. 96) draws on empirical studies on the use of a set of relevant statistical indicators for parole decisions to argue that the use of naked statistical evidence can have a better predictive success rate than use of expert examination. He suggests the 'naked statistical evidence' can produce more accurate predictions of the recidivism risk for individual prisoners than experts (for example, clinical psychologists) using individualised evidence.[2] Furthermore, says Schauer, even if experts are allowed access to the statistical evidence and can take account of it in their judgements, use of 'naked statistical evidence' still has a better success rate (Schauer, 2003, p. 97). People have biases, have their own agendas and simply make mistakes when assessing information.[3] Overall then, the claim is that the use of group risk statistics is more efficient and can be more accurate in general than using individualised examinations.

The use of statistical evidence on group risk seems benign or even preferable if the purpose is to obtain something applicants would consider a benefit. Consider, for example, if 'naked statistical evidence' were used to classify prisoners' risk of re-offending simply in order to obtain extra resources to support the release of high-risk prisoners. Similarly, a tertiary education institution might want to classify a group of students as being a higher risk for dropping out or failing simply in order to target more resources to them to support their study. It must be acknowledged however, that many uses of statistical evidence on group risk will aim to identify applicants that present a statistically higher risk in order to exclude them from a benefit or opportunity. Mortgage applicants identified as high risk are refused mortgages; insurance applicants identified as high risk are offered worse terms (or refused insurance); and prisoners are not classified as at high risk of re-offending in order to direct extra resources to support their release, but to refuse them parole.

The group risk features used when assessing applicants can include broad social groupings such as age or gender that we often see as a discriminatory basis for decision-making. In the employment context, for example, if you discarded or downgraded an applicant on the basis of statistics relating to age, ethnicity, gender, their family status or the socio-economic status of the neighbourhood where they reside, this is discrimination, and depending on the factor used, it may be illegal. But is it unethical? To see what might be ethically concerning with discrimination based on statistical judgement of applicants, we can turn to philosophical literature on wrongful discrimination.

PHILOSOPHERS ON THE ETHICAL CONCERNS OF DISCRIMINATION

Philosophers have not reached a consensus on how to specify the moral wrong(s) of discrimination. However, I see four main concerns emerging from the normative accounts of discrimination in the philosophical literature. Broadly speaking, these concerns are (1) attitudinal, (2) consequentialist, (3) egalitarian and (4) agential. Using beliefs about features of groups, a discriminatory act might involve differential treatment that:

1. stems from bad attitudes (hostility or superiority) on the part of the decision-maker (Alexander, 1992; Arneson, 2006; Vallentyne, 2006)
2. generates bad (worse) welfare consequences (Lippert-Rasmussen, 2006; Segall, 2012)
3. denies a presumptive right of individuals to equal moral standing (Alexander, 1992; Hellman, 2008). For example, Deborah Hellman thinks discrimination is wrong when it is demeaning, because demeaning a person is a way of denying their moral equality
4. violates or disrespects our interests in autonomy (Eidelson, 2013; Moreau, 2010; Segall, 2012).

1. Excluding applicants on the basis of group statistics does not appear to involve bad attitudes (hostility or superiority) on the part of the decision-maker. For example, say an employer has read some research suggesting that smokers are, on average, less productive employees than non-smokers.[4] If the employer dismisses the applications of smokers simply because of the statistic that the group of people who smoke is less productive than the group of non-smokers, this need not involve the employer having any *personal* prejudice against or distaste for smokers. Had the statistics indicated otherwise, the employer would happily have retained the smokers' applications. Provided that the statistics are not sought out in order to try to penalise a group, excluding individuals on the basis of group statistics will not fall foul of the ethical concern that the decision-maker's action stems from bad attitudes (hostility or superiority).

2. Excluding applicants according to group statistics may not be a problem in terms of bad/worse consequences, if we focus on overall welfare. For example, if it is cost-efficient for employers to identify and exclude statistically riskier applicants, this can be expected to benefit their business. Assuming that the jobs from which the riskier applicants are excluded are still being filled by other applicants who are equally happy to get them,

there could be a net benefit. In other contexts, excluding higher-risk prison-ers from parole can be expected to reduce re-offending, and may be a net benefit to society. Excluding or offering worse terms to higher-risk insur-ance applicants will benefit the rest of the insurance pool as well as the insurance companies, which may again provide a net benefit.

3. Excluding applicants due to statistical calculation of risk does not seem to express that individuals are not of equal moral standing. It does not seem to demean a person in the way other forms of discrimination appear to do. Suppose that a person's application for a credit card is rejected because she moved residence twice or more in the last 12 months, and statistics indicate this residential instability factor as a major credit risk. Compare this with a landlord who was intending to approve a potential tenant but decides to reject her simply on finding out she is Muslim. The latter instance of discrimination seems demeaning in a way the former does not.

4. Benjamin Eidelson (2013) suggests that one moral concern with discri-mination (amongst others) is its failure to treat a person properly as an individual. He says discrimination does this to a person by '... failing to treat him as in part a product of his own past efforts at self-creation, and as an autonomous agent whose future choices are his own to make' (Eidelson, 2013, p. 395). The point that part of who you are is the efforts you have made at creating yourself, and your autonomy over future deci-sions, is central to Moreau's (2010) account of discrimination. Moreau defines wrongful discrimination as differential treatment that impacts on 'deliberative freedoms'; that is, freedoms to access core life opportunities without the concern that certain traits will be counted as costs against one-self. She suggests traits such as gender or skin colour or religious tradition are 'normatively extraneous': we think these should not be evaluated in the distribution of opportunities to access some goods and services. Moreau (2013, p. 136) thinks that who you are is, at least in part, the choices you make. When you face discrimination, these choices are unfairly constrained by other people's assumptions about extraneous traits of yours and by their treatment of you regarding these traits. The concern is for the autonomy of persons as agents.

I think the ideas of Eidelson and Moreau capture the distinctive ethical concerns inherent in the practice of assessing persons based on group risk statistics. The practice takes little account of persons as individuals. Eidelson (2013, p. 355) argues that failing to treat a person properly as an individual is part of the badness of discrimination due to the importance of individuality to our autonomy.[5] If we treat an applicant to an organisation differently just because she belongs to a particular group, we do not make an effort to take account of the ways the person may differ from the group, and we also decide which feature of her (that feature of belonging to that group) will loom large in our assessment. In so doing, we deny her input as an individual agent in the process. This focus on individuals as agents is reinforced in Edmonds' (2006) conceptual analysis of discrimination on statistical correlations. He suggests we think it morally more appropriate to categorise people on the basis of what they have done,[6] and where the doing of a thing is 'directly, causally linked in the appropriate fashion' (Edmonds, 2006, p. 33). Assessments based on risk statistics for groups are liable to fail on both accounts.

DISPUTING THE DISTINCTION BETWEEN USE OF 'INDIVIDUALISED' ASSESSMENT AND USE OF 'NAKED STATISTICAL EVIDENCE'

Schoeman (1987) and Schauer (2003) argue that assessing people on the basis of group risk statistics is not different in kind from what we think of as 'individualised' assessment. Schoeman (1987) asks whether we can say we get information about individuals when all we have to go on is statistical classes. 'Direct' information such as from an eyewitness report seems to apply to an individual in a way that statistical information does not. He suggests that perhaps our dislike of using group statistics when judging an individual is due to a perception that the information used is not really *about* the individual concerned. Schoeman (1987, p. 183) characterises the concern thus:

> [perhaps] 'direct' evidence points to an individuated claim in the sense that it refers explicitly to a specific agent in a specific situation having done a specific thing whereas in the statistical case what the evidence points to is the conjunction of [reference] classes − a generic conclusion.

Suppose that Jane Comb has become comatose through eating poisoned fast food in New Buckshire. Compare an eyewitness report of Jane Comb entering an Organics-to-go cafe on the morning of the day she went into the coma, with a report that says 90% of all fast-food servings in New Buckshire are served in Organics-to-go cafes. The former 'direct' evidence refers to a specific agent in a specific situation having done a specific thing.

The latter 'statistical' evidence suggests that for any generic person ordering at a fast-food outlet in New Buckshire, there's a very high probability
they are ordering at an Organics-to-go cafe. The combination of the reference classes 'person dining out on fast food' and 'New Buckshire fast-food
outlets' is evidence of a high likelihood of eating at an Organics-to-go cafe.
However, it does not seem to apply to Jane in the same way that the eyewitness report seems to.

Schoeman, however, suggests that the judgements we make on the basis
of statistics about groups can be just as much judgements of individual
cases as of groups. He presents the example of hearing a radio report that
70% of the eggs sold at a store where he just bought eggs have been found
to be contaminated with salmonella (Schoeman, 1987, p. 184). Given this,
Schoeman asks, why wouldn't he throw them out, or have them tested, or
return them for a guaranteed safe batch? But in this situation, he says,
'I am making an assessment about ... the eggs that I own, and not just the
class of eggs generally as if this did not relate to my dozen' (Schoeman,
1987, p. 185). So Schoeman argues that statistical judgements can just as
well be about particular or individual things, not only about classes of
things: 'A belief that there is a 70% probability that my dozen eggs is contaminated is a belief about my eggs' (Schoeman, 1987, p. 185).

I believe it is noteworthy that the particulars Schoeman is
discussing — eggs — are not individual agents. We may be quite happy
accepting that Schoeman can and should make such a judgement and take
action to reject his eggs in this way. I suggest it is a different matter, however, if we replace Schoeman's eggs with individual agents, such as people.
Suppose that I am an employer and I hear that two-thirds of rugby-playing
adults suffer from health complications that make them more likely to take
time off work. Suppose too that I have a rugby-playing job applicant, Jeff.
Following Schoeman's example we would continue thus: why wouldn't I
throw out Jeff's application? Or force Jeff to undergo a health-test before I
will even consider his application? Or require Jeff to provide his own clean
bill of health before I consider his job application? My guess is that our
reaction to this scenario differs from that of Schoeman's 'eggs' scenario.
We do not say "but *of course* we should throw out the applications from
the rugby-playing candidates, or make the candidates be tested". Unlike
Schoeman's considerations of his eggs, these actions do not seem uncontro-
versially appropriate. I suggest the reason for this is because we are dealing
with subjects with individual moral worth.

Schoeman himself says that we may have reasons for not wanting to go
from a generic statistical claim, such as the percentage of rugby-playing

adults with health complications, to the individual claim. But he immediately adds that '[t]his ... could not be conceded without recognizing that *even probabilistic claims are about individuals*' (Schoeman, 1987, p. 185). However, this is misleading. The probabilistic claims Schoeman discusses are generated from, and accurate for, a group. The probability is a feature of the group only; it is not a feature of any particular individual. It is not something an individual is or possesses. Probabilistic claims may *extend over* an individual but they are not *about* the individual, qua individual.

We could grant that people do apply statistical claims to individuals, but the fact that people sometimes apply probabilistic claims to individuals does not mean they are picking out a feature of the individual rather than a feature of a group. In assigning a probability to a particular individual, we simply extend the feature of a group over the individual. We, the decision-makers, put it on the individual. Given this, the question of the purpose of decision-makers becomes immediately ethically significant. If the statistical claim represents the interests of the decision-makers, rather than the interests of the individual who is having the claims extended over him or her, the claims are a substantial exercise of power on the part of the decision-maker. If decision-makers choose to assess individual applicants using group probabilities only, the decision-makers will also get to choose the groups under which applicants are subsumed. Individual applicants will have little opportunity to exercise agency in this situation.

Our concerns over the application of group probabilities to applicants could be neutered, however, if what we consider to be individualised assessments *also* turn out to be fundamentally based on assessment of probabilities. This is argued by Schauer (2003, pp. 67–69). To focus on the conceptual issue of applying generalisations to judge individuals, Schauer (2003, pp. 39–41) wants to insulate it from our moral reactions based on our awareness of invidious historical discrimination against groups of people. He proposes an example of councils considering banning dangerous dogs, based on statistical generalisations about dog breeds. I will argue against Schauer. Using an example that involved individual human applicants may favour my case;[7] however, lest it be thought to illegitimately harness moral reactions, I will instead address my argument to Schauer's example. If my argument has some purchase in the context of assessing dogs, it is to be expected that it will apply even more strongly to the case of assessing individual human applicants.

Schauer (2003) asks what a council should make of any statistical evidence that some dog breeds are more dangerous than others. When councils have proposed considering breed statistics, people owning dogs of those breeds have protested, calling this 'canine racism' (Schauer, 2003, p. 56). The protestors have noted that the majority of individual dogs of that breed do not pose a risk to people's safety, and that plenty of other dogs are more dangerous than most individual dogs of this breed (*ibid.*). Instead of banning dogs based on breed, councils could do individualised assessments, testing individual dogs for aggressiveness. Schauer considers (2003, p. 65) whether councils concerned about dog violence should arrange to have individual dogs tested for their aggressive behaviour, and ban all and only dogs who test as vicious, rather than banning dogs based on group risk for the breed.

Testing dogs for aggressiveness also involves assessing individual dogs against a *group*, suggests Schauer (2003, pp. 67–69), namely, the group of dogs that was used as the basis for developing the test. The individual test also compares the dog against generalisations: we generalise from the actions of the group of dogs that was used as the basis for developing the test. It is on the basis of aggregate evidence from past events involving these other dogs that we say that the relevant characteristic of 'failing a test' is 'probabilistically predictive' of engaging in vicious behaviour (Schauer, 2003, p. 68). Basically, Schauer points out that individual testing is based on generalisations from test-performance to real-life behaviour. He declares that 'using membership in the class of pit bulls as a predictor of the likelihood of aggressiveness under real-world conditions is not fundamentally different from using clinical testing of this pit bull as a predictor of the likelihood of aggressiveness' (Schauer, 2003, pp. 66–67).

Schauer (2003, pp. 68–69) would also note that neither of our generalisations will produce error-free predictions. Clearly 'pit bull breed' will be an inaccurate predictor – some pit bulls would be as docile or more so than other dogs. But tests are imperfect too, and so will also inaccurately predict for some cases: some pit bulls who pass the test will still prove too aggressive. Suppose that we have a set of three characteristics – pit bull plus male plus over a year old – that has been shown to correctly predict aggression in 85% of the dogs with those characteristics. Suppose also that we have an aggression test that, if administered to all dogs, correctly predicts aggression in 85% of the dogs that fail that test. Why should an organisation use the results of a test to exclude dogs, rather than using the fact that the dog is a male pit bull over a year old? Schauer (2003, p. 68) concludes that 'What distinguishes the individualised examination from the so-called stereotype or the so-called profile, therefore, is only the fact that the latter is obvious without closer inspection while the former is not...'.

Schauer's analysis thus suggests that with regards to generalising, a council decision-maker using membership in the class 'pit bull' to judge something about a particular pit bull dog does nothing fundamentally different from a council decision-maker who does a clinical test of a particular pit bull dog. However, there's something missing here. Let us imagine a particular pit bull, 'Nobbo'. Suppose that the image in Fig. 1 is Nobbo.

Suppose too that the image in Fig. 2, once reproduced multiple times, represents the class of pit bulls generally.

Finally, suppose that Fig. 3 represents a pit bull test norm.

Schauer's alternatives seem to be presented as: 'Nobbo lumped in with the class of pit bulls' versus 'Nobbo facing individual testing'. This makes it look like we are *considering Nobbo against the pit bull class*, as in Fig. 4 versus *considering Nobbo against a testing norm*, as in Fig. 5.

As Schauer says, if both the class and the test are generalising at base, then we could say our judgement of Nobbo is based on generalisations either way. But this wrong-foots it from the start. If a council considers a ban on dangerous dogs, and uses a classifier of 'pit bull' as indicating a higher risk of dangerousness, *Nobbo* the pit bull is not judged. Fig. 4 misrepresents the situation. Fig. 6 is how Fig. 4 should look.

The crucial point is that beyond being identified as a pit bull, *Nobbo* the pit bull is given *no consideration at all*. Any council policy banning pit bulls

Fig. 1. Nobbo. *Source*: Image credit: CC_BY-SA 2.5, http://criticalmiami.com/images/914.jpg

Fig. 2. Class of Pit Bulls. *Source*: Image credit: CC-BY-SA-3.0, https://commons.
wikimedia.org/wiki/File:Pit_bull_sampler.jpg

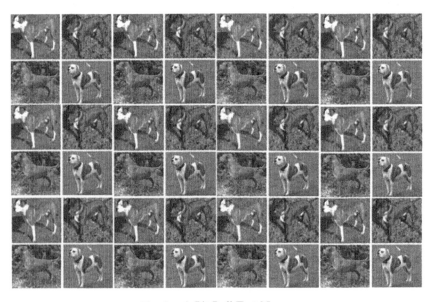

Fig. 3. A Pit Bull Test Norm.

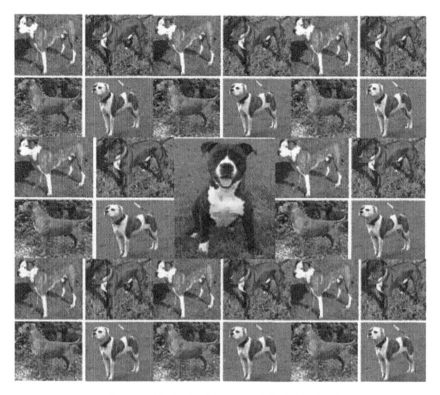

Fig. 4. Considering Nobbo against the Pit Bull Class.

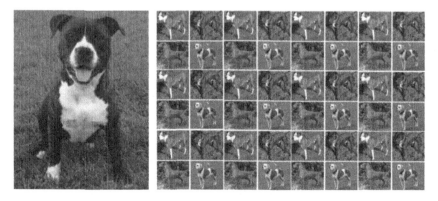

Fig. 5. Considering Nobbo against a Test Norm.

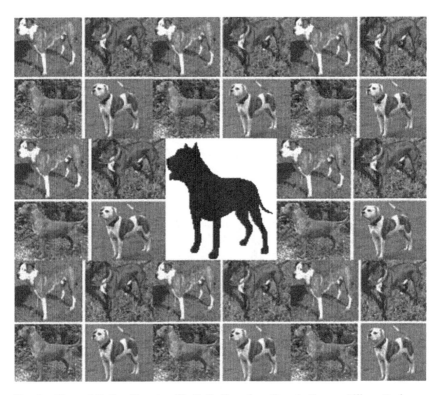

Fig. 6. Council Policy Banning Pit Bulls Based on Breed. *Source*: Silhouette image
public domain: https://openclipart.org/detail/233373/pit-bull-dog-silhouette

based on breed risk statistics would be *applied* to individual pit bulls without being *about* this or that particular pit bull. This harks back to the point
raised in the discussion of Schoeman, that class-based probabilistic claims
extend over (or quantify over) an individual but are not *about* the individual
(qua individual). The application of a test, by contrast, does consider the
particular pit bull that is Nobbo, and *is about* Nobbo. There is thus a fundamental distinction between class-based and test-based assessing, and the
latter is about individuals in a way the former is not. Judging individuals
on the basis of group statistics *is* different from the test-based assessments
we think of as individualised. It manifestly fails to consider persons as
individuals.

RECONCILING USE OF 'NAKED STATISTICAL EVIDENCE' AND A DESIRE TO INCLUDE APPLICANT AGENCY

When a decision-maker fails to consider the people she is dealing with as individuals, she cannot help but make decisions that feature the participation of only herself and the selves of those on behalf of whom she is tasked with making decisions. She and her principals are the only selves in the decision. She/they get to spread their selves over actions that affect others, without those others' selves being able to participate in any way. This denies any possibility of agency in the process by the people being dealt with.[8] On the face of it, this does not seem desirable. Yet organisational decision-makers and the societies in which they reside will not be able to resist the use of 'naked statistical evidence' when assessing applicants. As noted initially, use of such evidence has the potential to make decision-makers' judgements more accurate and more efficient, with benefits both to the organisation and society. The practical ethical question at this point is not whether organisations *should* do this, but rather whether applicants' agency can be included in some way when organisations *do* do this. I believe there are three key possibilities for organisations in this regard.

The Type of Factors Considered in the Statistical Correlations

There are two main questions here. First, do the factors examined for statistical correlations reflect the individual choices and efforts by applicants? For example, for applicants to tertiary study, factors to assess their risk could include evidence of prior courses they have undertaken and a study timetable for their courses that they have completed. These factors reflect personal choices and efforts of individual applicants. Assessing their risk based purely on risk statistics for factors such as ethnicity, or the status of the educational institution they attended, however, reflect features over which individual applicants have little or no power.

The second question on the type of factors to be considered concerns the nature of the factors over time. Are the risk factors *static* or *dynamic*? Static risk factors are historical factors that do not change (or do not change much) (Witt, Dattilio, & Bradford, 2011 p. 111). General examples are gender, ethnicity, factors from childhood and work history. Dynamic risk factors are factors that are in flux, factors that can change relatively quickly. Examples include present employment situation, health status and current courses of study.[9] Ethically speaking, what is distinctively salient here is that static risk factors are not usually easily amenable to change. So if someone is assessed on static risk factors and classed as high risk, then assessed a year later on the same static factors, they will still be classed as high risk, regardless of any otherwise risk-reducing efforts they have made throughout the year.[10] Static factors tend to be quicker and cheaper to assess, dynamic factors can be more expensive. But assessing only or primarily static factors ignores the agency of the individual applicant.

The Transparency of the Process for Applicants

Again, there are two main questions here. The first is about transparency regarding the risk assessments that are attached to specific individuals. Can applicants access any risk assessments the organisation makes about them? The second is whether applicants or others get to know in advance any group risk factors that will be included in their assessment. For example, do prisoners have access from the start of their internment to the factors on which their parole applications will be assessed? Both questions are particularly important where risk assessments are based more on dynamic risk factors over which an applicant has some control. In these cases an applicant might be able to exercise their agency by doing things in advance to improve risk assessments in their favour.

Use of Statistics Specific to Individuals

Schauer depicts decision-makers as having a choice between two methods that produce three options for assessing a person's risk, namely, (1) expert examination, (2) evidence from group risk statistics ('naked statistical evidence') or (3) expert examination where the experts have access to the group risk statistics. However, there is another method, namely, to include individual behavioural analytics. This involves using a collection of (reasonably recent) behavioural data across time *from the same individual*. This could be done by any organisation that captures data on individual behaviour that can be correlated with outcomes for that individual. We could see this, for example, in higher education institutions offering online learning that track learners' behaviours (see, e.g., Wagner & Hartman, 2013).

In the parole context, if behavioural information on individual prisoners is regularly captured and fed into a database, then a computer-facilitated analysis of the data around their good/bad behaviour incidents could identify any patterns of factors that correlate with good/bad behaviour for them as individuals. This could show, for example, that taking medication X seems to make a difference to Joe's behaviour, but not to Sam's behaviour; or that choosing to work in the prison library correlates with improved behaviour for Sam whereas choosing to work in the kitchen correlates with improved behaviour for Daniel. If this behavioural information were made available to the relevant individuals, this gives them more chance to exercise their agency over some factors that affect their risk assessment.

We now have three approaches to assessing individuals to predict their future performance: individualised assessment by experts; statistical assessment using probabilistic claims derived from *extending other people's behaviour* over an individual; and statistical assessment based on individual analytics, using probabilistic claims derived from extending *the individual's past behaviour* over the individual. This last is a use of evidence that is both statistical and specific to the individual (see Colyvan, Regan, & Ferson, 2001, p. 175). My suggestion is that the more individual analytics can be included in the statistical assessment of applicants, the more the process recognises and includes opportunity for individual agency on the part of applicants.

CONCLUSION

Organisational use of group risk statistics to assess applicants can only be expected to increase with the generation of knowledge of such statistical correlations, and the interest in mining 'big data' to derive such correlations suggests this will proceed apace. This chapter has examined the implications for applicant autonomy from the use of statistical evidence on group risk to assess applicants. A key concern was identified regarding the lack of recognition of applicants as individuals. After defending this concern against challenges offered by Schoeman (1987) and Schauer (2003), I make recommendations for reconciling organisational use of group risk statistics with a desire to recognise and include a greater degree of applicant agency and autonomy in the application process. These involve the type of factors considered in the statistical correlations; the transparency of the process for applicants; and the use of statistics specific to individuals.

NOTES

1. Lower anterior cingulate cortex (ACC) activity is associated with chronic drug use (marijuana) (Gruber & Yurgelun-Todd, 2005), but Aharoni et al. (2013) control for lifetime prevalence of alcohol or drug abuse or dependence and find that lower ACC activity has independent predictive validity for re-offending.

2. The claim that automated actuarial recidivism risk prediction instruments outperform human assessments does not rest undisputed; see, e.g. Starr (2013). However, evidence is emerging in other areas of automated risk prediction instruments that outperform experienced human assessors; see, e.g. Dare, Vaithianathan, and De Haan (2014) on automated prediction of child maltreatment risk, and Jia (2014) on automated prediction of student risk of failing courses and dropping out of study.

3. Dare et al. (2014, p. 90) are similarly disparaging of the accuracy of the experts they consider (social workers) at predicting risk of child abuse using Actuarial Risk Assessment tools.

4. See e.g. Chadwick (2006) and Lecker (2009).

5. I should note that Eidelson suggests this as a partial and prima facie wrong-making aspect of a discriminatory action; other aspects of discriminatory actions such as producing good consequences could override the wrongness.

6. Or sometimes failed to do.

7. My thanks to an anonymous reviewer for pointing this out, and the accompanying comments that prompted my explanation in this paragraph.

8. This also means the decision cannot but unilaterally represent the decision-maker's interests. As briefly noted previously, if decision-making situations are set up to unilaterally represent the interests of the decision-maker, this is a substantial exercise of power.

9. Age is generally considered a static factor. Whether neurological activity, such as lower anterior cingulate cortex activity, counts as static or dynamic depends on whether it is stable through time. Aharoni and colleagues suggest it can be a dynamic factor, if it can be targeted for treatment interventions, and they see evidence in favour of this (Aharoni et al., 2013, p. 2).

10. Suppose that we have two prisoners, Ana and Maurice. They are both up for parole at the start of the year, and both have their applications declined on static risk factors that class them as high risk. Throughout the ensuing year, Ana constantly picks fights with fellow inmates and with prison guards, refuses to take part in a rehabilitation programme and attempts to smuggle her prescribed medication out of the prison for illegal sale on the streets. Maurice, by contrast, has worked hard to be a model prisoner, and completes not only a rehabilitation programme but also a certificate in plumbing that will let him access a plumbing apprenticeship on release. The next year when both are up for parole, if they were assessed only on

static risk factors, it is likely they would both have similar scores and both be declined as high risk.

ACKNOWLEDGEMENTS

The author would like to thank Dr Ramon Das, an anonymous reviewer for the journal and Andrew McCaw for helpful comment and proofing work on this chapter. The author would also like to thank the audience at the 2015 Australian Association of Professional and Applied Ethics conference for helpful feedback, particularly Associate Professor Tim Dare.

REFERENCES

Aharoni, E., Vincent, G. M., Harenski, C. L., Calhoun, V. D., Sinnott-Armstrong, W., Gazzaniga, M. S., & Kiehl, K. A. (2013). Neuroprediction of future rearrest. *Proceedings of the National Academy of Sciences of the USA*, PNAS April 9, *110*(15), 6223–6228.

Alexander, L. (1992). What makes wrongful discrimination wrong? Biases, preferences, stereotypes and proxies. *University of Pennsylvania Law Review*, *141*(1), 149–219.

Arneson, R. J. (2006). What is wrongful discrimination? *San Diego Law Review*, *43*, 775–808.

Brunton-Smith, I., & Hopkins, K. (2013). *The factors associated with proven re-offending following release from prison: Findings from waves 1 to 3 of SPCR*. Ministry of Justice Analytical Series. London: Ministry of Justice. Retrieved from https://www.gov.uk/government/uploads/system/uploads/attachment_data/file/261620/re-offending-release-waves-1-3-spcr-findings.pdf

Chadwick, K. (2006). Is leisure-time smoking a valid employment consideration? *Albany Law Review*, *70*, 117–141.

Colyvan, M., Regan, H., & Ferson, S. (2001). Is it a crime to belong to a reference class? *Journal of Political Philosophy*, *9*(2), 168–181.

Dare, T., Vaithianathan, R., & De Haan, I. (2014). Addressing child maltreatment in New Zealand: Is poverty reduction enough? *Educational Philosophy and Theory: Incorporating ACCESS*, *46*(9), 989–994.

Edmonds, D. (2006). *Caste wars: A philosophy of discrimination*. London: Routledge.

Eidelson, B. (2013). Treating people as individuals. In D. Hellman & S. Moreau (Eds.), *The philosophical foundations of discrimination law* (pp. 354–395). Oxford: Oxford University Press.

Gruber, S. A., & Yurgelun-Todd, D. A. (2005). Neuroimaging of marijuana smokers during inhibitory processing: A pilot investigation. *Brain Research Cognitive Brain Research*, *23*(1), 107–118.

Hellman, D. (2008). *When is discrimination wrong?* Cambridge, MA: Harvard University Press.

Jia, P. (2014). *Using predictive risk modeling to identify students at high risk of paper non-completion and programme non-retention at university.* MBus thesis, Auckland University of Technology.

Lecker, M. (2009). The smoking penalty: Distributive justice or smokism? *Journal of Business Ethics, 84,* 47–64.

Lippert-Rasmussen, K. (2006). Private discrimination: A prioritarian, desert-accommodating account. *San Diego Law Review, 43,* 817–856.

Moreau, S. (2010). Discrimination as negligence. *Canadian Journal of Philosophy, 40*(Suppl. 1), 123–149.

Moreau, S. (2013). In defense of a liberty-based account of discrimination. In D. Hellman & S. Moreau (Eds.), *The philosophical foundations of discrimination law.* Oxford: Oxford University Press.

Piquero, A. R., Jennings, W. G., Diamond, B., & Reingle, J. M. (2015). A systematic review of age, sex, ethnicity, and race as predictors of violent recidivism. *International Journal of Offender Therapy and Comparative Criminology, 59*(1), 5–26.

Rice, M. E., & Harris, G. T. (2014). What does it mean when age is related to recidivism among sex offenders? *Law and Human Behavior, 38*(2), 151–161.

Schauer, F. (2003). *Profiles, probabilities and stereotypes.* Cambridge, MA: Harvard University Press.

Schoeman, F. (1987). Statistical vs direct evidence. *Nous, 21*(2), 179–198.

Segall, S. (2012). What's so bad about discrimination? *Utilitas, 24*(01), 82–100.

Starr, S. B. (2013). *Evidence-based sentencing and the scientific rationalization of discrimination.* Law & Economics Research Paper Series, Paper No. 13-014.

Vallentyne, P. (2006). Left libertarianism and private discrimination. *San Diego Law Review, 43,* 981–994.

Wagner, E., & Hartman, J. (2013). *Welcome to the era of big data and predictive analytics in higher education.* SHEEO (State Higher Education Executive Officers Association) Higher Education Policy Conference 2013. Retrieved from http://www.sheeo.org/sites/default/files/0808-1430-plen.pdf

Witt, P. H., Dattilio, F. M., & Bradford, J. M. W. (2011). Sex offender evaluations. In E. Drogin, F. M. Dattilio, R. L. Sadoff, & T. G. Gutheil (Eds.), *Handbook of forensic assessment: Psychological and psychiatric perspectives.* Hoboken, NJ: Wiley. doi:10.1002/9781118093399

ABOUT THE AUTHORS

Hugh Breakey is Research Fellow at Griffith University's *Institute for Ethics, Governance and Law*, Australia. Currently Chief Investigator in two federally funded projects and research fellow on a third, Hugh's work spans the philosophical sub-disciplines of political theory, normative ethics, applied philosophy and legal theory. The author of *Intellectual Liberty: Natural Rights and Intellectual Property* (Ashgate), Hugh's work explores ethical issues emerging in myriad practical fields, including peacekeeping, safety industries, institutional governance and personal integrity, climate change, sustainable tourism, professionalism, education, private property and intellectual property, medicine, and international law and human rights. As well as writing for newspapers, online encyclopedias, academic-journalistic outlets, NGO websites and high-impact policy guides, Hugh has published in an extensive array of international journals, including *The Philosophical Quarterly, The Modern Law Review* and *Political Studies*. Since 2013, Hugh has been honored to serve as President of the Australian Association for Professional and Applied Ethics.

Tim Dare and Marco Grix conduct their research and teaching at Philosophy at the University of Auckland's School of Humanities. Tim is an Associate Professor and one-time lawyer. He has written on the philosophy of law and legal and medical ethics. His current research focuses on the significance of social roles and the use of predictive analytics in child protection. He sits on a number of local and national research and clinical ethics committees. Marco is a doctoral student who strayed from management and marketing to pursue his PhD in the area of ethics and political philosophy. His current research revolves primarily around the ethics and politics of consumption, with a particular focus on human needs and human flourishing.

Ian H. Gibson holds degrees in Arts, Law and Education from Monash University, a Masters in Professional Ethics from UNSW and a Doctorate of Organisation Dynamics from Swinburne University. He practises as a lawyer in the Victorian Public Service. In addition, he is Secretary of the Australian Association of Professional and Applied Ethics and Secretary of

Amnesty International Australia, and holds roles in the governance of the Anglican Diocese of Melbourne and the Anglican Church of Australia.

Paul Jewell, Ruth Crocker and Matthew Dent conduct research within the social paradigm of disability, in the department of Disability and Community Inclusion, School of Health Sciences, Flinders University. The role of the Disability and Community Inclusion Department is to educate human service professionals to facilitate, advocate and support the quality of life, community inclusion and self-determination of all people living with disabilities and their families. The authors combine their expertise derived from their various academic and professional expertise and interests. Paul Jewell is a Philosopher and the author of *Disability Ethics* (Common Ground Publishing 2010). Ruth Crocker specialises in Rehabilitation Counselling and Mathew Dent is a Disability Advocate, currently working with Advocacy Tasmania.

Stephen Kemp, B.A., M.A. is completing a PhD in the School of Historical and Philosophical Inquiry at the University of Queensland. His thesis, which he commenced in 2010, is concerned with the ethical issues surrounding the commodification of childcare.

Frederick Kroon is Professor of Philosophy at the University of Auckland. His main research areas are formal and philosophical logic, philosophy of language, and metaphysics, and he has authored papers in these and other areas for a range of journals, including *The Philosophical Review*, *The Journal of Philosophy*, *Ethics*, and *Noûs*. He is on the editorial board of the *Australasian Journal of Philosophy* and is a subject editor for 20th Century Philosophy for the *Stanford Encyclopedia of Philosophy*.

Stephan Millett is Professor in the School of Occupational Therapy and Social Work at Curtin University. He was formerly Chair of the Curtin University Human Research Ethics Committee and Director of the Centre for Applied Ethics and Philosophy. His interests include research ethics, philosophy in schools and health ethics. He is the author of *Aristotle's Powers and Responsibility for Nature* (Peter Lang, 2011).

Nicholas Munn is Senior Lecturer in Philosophy at the University of Waikato, where he has worked since 2012. His research interests are primarily in democratic theory and applied ethics, with a focus on political exclusion and the means through which we overcome it.

Giuseppe Naimo is Senior Lecturer and Undergraduate Coordinator for the School of Philosophy and Theology, University of Notre Dame Australia teaching in Philosophy and Ethics. Current areas of research are Metaphysics and Ethics. More broadly interested in Process philosophy, Philosophy of science (biology and physics) and Cosmology. Executive Committee member of the AAPAE and long-time supporter of the Association of Philosophy in Schools (APIS).

Vanessa Scholes is Senior Lecturer in the School of Business and Enterprise at Open Polytechnic/Kuratini Tuwhera. She teaches degree courses online in applied ethics and in learning. Her research interests in applied ethics include discrimination, business ethics and experimental philosophy. Her professional interests in higher education include online teaching and critical thinking. She is currently working on a PhD thesis on the ethics of organizational decision-makers using statistical data to risk-screen applicants, including job applicants and applicants to higher education. She has published papers in *Educational Philosophy and Theory*, and *Rationality, Markets and Morals*, and a book chapter in *Ethics and Public Policy: Contemporary Issues* (VUW Press, 2011). She has a forthcoming paper in *Educational Technology Research and Design*.

Ruth Walker is Senior Lecturer in Philosophy at the University of Waikato, New Zealand. She is currently doing research on surrogacy, developing a professional model to replace the current altruistic/commercial dichotomy. The research, jointly carried out with Liezl van Zyl, has generated numerous publications. A book for Palgrave Macmillan will be published in 2017. Other research interests include research ethics, professional ethics and business ethics. Dr Walker served a number of years as Chair of the Faculty of Arts and Social Sciences Human Research Ethics Committee and Deputy Chair of the University of Waikato's Human Research Ethics Committee. She retains a particular interest in the ethics of social science research.

Liezl van Zyl is Senior Lecturer in Philosophy at the University of Waikato, New Zealand. She completed a DPhil in Philosophy at the University of Stellenbosch, South Africa. She has a particular interest in virtue ethics and applied ethics, and is the author of *Death and Compassion: A Virtue-Ethical Approach to Euthanasia* (2000). Together with Ruth Walker, she is currently doing research on surrogate motherhood. Their aim is to develop a professional model for surrogacy as an alternative to both the altruistic and commercial model. She is also writing a book to be entitled, *Virtue Ethics: A Contemporary Introduction* (Routledge).